Lights Over Carolina

Reflections of a Southern Table

The Junior League of Anderson County

The Junior League is an organization of women committed to promoting voluntarism, developing the potential of women, and improving communities through the effective action and leadership of trained volunteers. Its purpose is exclusively educational and charitable.

Money raised by the sale of *"Lights Over Carolina"* furthers the purpose and projects of the Junior League of Anderson County.

For additional copies, use the order forms at the back of this book or
send a check for $22.95 plus $4.50 shipping and handling
(South Carolina residents add $1.15 sales tax) to:

Lights Over Carolina
The Junior League of Anderson County
P.O. Box 931
Anderson, SC 29622

Phone (864) 231-0470

First Printing   April 2002   7,500 copies

WIMMER
C O O K B O O K S
ConsolidatedGraphics
1-800-548-2537

Table of Contents

Highlights

"One cannot think well, love well, sleep well, if one has not dined well."

~ *Virginia Woolf*

Southern Lights

"Laughter is the brightest, in the place where the food is."

~ *Irish Proverb*

Rise and Shine

"All happiness depends on a leisurely breakfast."

~ *John Gunther*

Sparkling Delights

"Lettuce is like conversation: it must be fresh and crisp
and so sparkling that you scarcely notice the bitter in it."

~ *Charles Dudley Warren*

Soulful Sandwiches and Soups

"A man may be a pessimistic determinist before lunch
and an optimistic believer in the will's freedom after it."

~ *Aldous Huxley*

Sidelights

"To the best of our knowledge, our Sun is the only star proven to grow vegetables."

~ *Philip Sherrer*

Electric City Entrées

"Tomatoes and oregano make it Italian; wine and tarragon make it French; sour cream makes it Russian; lemon and cinnamon make it Greek; soy sauce makes it Chinese; garlic makes it good."

~ *Alice May Brock*

Fireflies and Mudpies

"Cooking is at once child's play and adult joy. And cooking done with care is an act of love."

~ *Craig Claiborne*

Sweet Reflections

"All I really need is love, but a little chocolate now and then doesn't hurt."

~ *Lucy Van Pelt in "Peanuts" by Charles M. Shultz*

Lights Over Carolina Foreword

Dear Friendly Reader:

I am William Church Whitner, a native son of Anderson County. My parents, Major Benjamin Franklin Whitner and Anna Church Whitner, made their home in Anderson and I was born here September 22, 1864. I'd like to tell you a little bit about how I had a small part in putting **Lights Over Carolina.**

Growing up, I enjoyed watching my father work for the betterment of the state as he served in the South Carolina state legislature, and vowed that I would do my part also to make a difference. I once thought I would do that as a lawyer, but changed my mind and became an engineer, graduating from the University of South Carolina with a degree in Civil Engineering in 1866.

For several years, I worked with railroad systems across the southeast. But then came that once-in-a-lifetime opportunity that I could not resist. Anderson called me home. The city was attempting to construct a system of waterworks and an electric light plant — and they wanted me to do it. I teamed with Mr. John T. Roddey, a former partner who had helped to raise needed capital when I had worked for the railroad.

With the necessary funding secured, we began work, and in 1895, the city of Anderson was lighted with 750 incandescent lamps. This electricity was generated using steam power. We realized, however, that steam wasn't a very efficient way to generate electricity. Since the stockholders expected profits, I began to research less expensive methods of producing electricity.

After studying these various methods and researching other experiments being conducted in Europe, I became convinced that it would be possible to utilize some of the fine waterpower from the waterfalls in the vicinity of Anderson. Always ready for a challenge, I started work.

I traveled to New York to meet with Nicolas Tesla, a Serbian immigrant who perfected the alternating current motor, and studied his machinery. Convinced I was on the right track, I made an announcement that shocked the community: I would attempt to build a plant to generate electric current using water power. My proposal was not considered very practical. I endured ridicule and had a lot of trouble raising capital. But I persevered and eventually the money came through.

With $25,000, some of which was from Anderson investors, and a lease on part of McFall's Mill at High Shoals on the Rocky River, I started planning for my grand experiment. When the machinery finally arrived and was eventually installed, I knew it was almost time to test my theory. On the morning of May 1, 1895, our designated test date, the switches were flipped. For the first time in the South, electricity was transmitted from the point of generation over wires to a distant point of consumption. (Over six miles of wire from point to point, to be exact.) We used a 5,000-volt generator, the first in the world to go into operation, to produce 200 electrical horsepower, and we did it without step-up transformers. Local skeptics, as well as those more distant, were stunned. Our achievement was recognized in newspaper headlines throughout the South. We had succeeded in putting up the very first water-powered electric *Lights Over Carolina*. What a wonderful day that was!

In Charleston, *The News and Courier* provided extensive coverage of the plant's construction, and bestowed on Anderson the moniker "the Electric City." Our success and our new "nickname" was reported in the *Anderson Intelligencer's* June 19, 1895 issue.

After such success, stockholders realized that more power could be made at a larger plant, so I designed a more substantial hydro-electric plant that was constructed at Portman Shoals on the Seneca River. This plant began operation on November 1, 1897.

I left Anderson for other challenges in other cities. I have often thought that I would have been far better off had I stayed in Anderson. I never made another development that gave me such pleasure as the first ones I made there in Anderson.

I could never have predicted all of this could have happened from following my convictions. I don't think anyone could have. But, it's so typical of the people and leaders of Anderson and Anderson County. The combined efforts of the city and county, along with other public-private partnerships, helped this area win the coveted All-America City Award in 2000. Although Anderson is still known today as the Electric City, I know deep within my soul that the people of this area truly represent the best and brightest *"Lights Over Carolina"* and it is to them that this book is dedicated.

With warmest regards and respect,

William Church Whitner

Disclaimer: Much of the information in this "letter" was gleaned from Beth Ann Klosky's instrumental work on Whitner and his contribution to the Electric City, *Six Miles That Changed the Course of the South*. Several of Whitner's letters were quoted in that book, and parts of those letters were used in this introduction.

Cookbook Chair and Advisor
Alicia Mansuetti

Cookbook Editor
Libby Holliday

Recipe and Testing

Chairperson
Martie Manning

Co-Chairs
Linda Loparo
Meridith Moorhead

Recipe and Testing Committee

Trina Alexander
Dale Baughman
Andrea Craft
Mary Ann Groves

Karen Hagner
Dana Hill
Tamara Lindley
Anita May

Suzanne Rogers
Tina Seawright
Katey Yeats

Sidebar
Libby Holliday
Alicia Mansuetti
Paula Reel
Sarah Ricketson
Rette Stokes

Art and Design
Alexandria Stathakis

Marketing and Distribution
Dana Hill
Jackie Walsh

Cover Artist
Scott Foster

The cookbook committee greatly appreciates the work of Dale Baughman and Tina Seawright who piloted our whole cookbook project in 1999.

We would also like to gratefully acknowledge Kathy Roser and Patti Brosche of Geranium II for their creative input.

Special thanks are extended to the Anderson County Museum for providing the historical information used throughout the book.

Menus

Appetizers Before the Camellia Ball

Cranberry Margaritas, p. 41

Artichokes in Blue Cheese and Butter Sauce, p. 15

Asparagus Rolls, p. 19

Stuffed Cherry Tomatoes, p. 19

Bayside Shrimp Tarts, p. 21

Junior League Cheese Ball with Assorted Crackers, p. 26

A Little Something Sweet, p. 25

Valentine's Day Candlelight Dinner for Two

Spinach Salad with Hot Citrus Dressing, p. 76

Grilled Veal Chops with Mustard-Herb Butter, p. 147

Roasted Potatoes, p. 123

Steamed Broccoli with Lemon Butter Sauce, p. 108

Spinach and Cheese Bread, p. 70

Nouveau Napoleons, p. 207

Good Night Kiss, p. 42

Snowed In

J.R.'s Salsa with Tortilla Chips, p. 27

Apple Spinach Salad, p. 78

Favorite Chili Beans, p. 105

Sour Cream Corn Sticks, p. 71

Cream Cheese Pound Cake with Chocolate Glaze, p. 202

The Boss is Coming to Dinner

Hearts of Palm and Artichoke Salad
with Creamy Herb Dressing, p. 74

Capital Chicken, p. 158

St. Paul Rice, p. 130

Green Beans with Toasted Pecan Dressing, p. 109
or Cabbage Casserole, p. 113

Bourbon Glazed Carrots, p. 113

Cheddar Dinner Scones, p. 54

Sour Cream Lemon Pie, p. 216

Breakfast at the Mountain Cabin

Freshly Squeezed Orange Juice

Coffee

Rainbow Fruit Salad, p. 79

Denver Omelet Scrambler, p. 63

Good Morning Grits, p. 61

Farmhouse Sweet Rolls, p. 51

Gourmet Supper Club

Almond Ginger Tea, p. 43

Dinner Party Tomato Bouillon, p. 104

Strawberry-Mango Mesclun Salad, p. 73

Cheese-Stuffed Chicken in Phyllo, p. 159

Sweet 'n Sour Green Beans, p. 109

Almond Cheese Cauliflower, p. 114

Baked Sweet Red and Yellow Pepper Wedges, p. 123

New World Tiramisu, p. 203

Freedom Weekend Picnic Lunch

Fresh Vegetables with Versatile Veggie Dip, p. 33

Lemon Drumsticks, p. 164

Picnic Wild Rice Salad, p. 92

Marinated Mushrooms, p. 28

Raspberry Green Beans, p. 109

Caramel Cookie Bars, p. 219

Raspberry Walnut Bars, p. 222

Graduation Brunch

Summertime Slush, p. 40

Carolina Shrimp and Grits, p. 62

Tomato Cheese Pudding, p. 61

Parmesan Bacon Bread, p. 67

Strawberry-Orange Muffins with
Strawberry Butter, p. 56

Children's Picnic at the Park

Lemonade For Sale!, p. 184

Dog Gone Good, p. 187

Chunky Cinnamon Applesauce, p. 188

Carrot and Celery Sticks

Frosted Brownie Pizza, p. 191

Labor Day Backyard Barbecue Bash

Strawberry Watermelon Lemonade, p. 43

Boiled Peanuts, p. 37

Grilled Ribs with Cowboy Grilling Sauce, p. 141

Bruschetta, p. 18

Cashew Vegetable Slaw, p. 82

Cajun Spiced Corn on the Cob, p. 117

Crowd-Pleasing Baked Bean Medley, p. 110

Peanut Butter Ice Cream, p. 208
or Banana Split Ice Cream, p. 209

Clemson-Carolina Tailgate Party

Fire Nuts, p. 36

Green Onion Dip with Pita Chips, p. 31

Gourmet Philly Steak Sandwiches, p. 93

Southern Fried Kickin' Chickin', p. 165

Potato Salad with a Heart, p. 89

Marinated Vegetable Medley, p. 87

Tiger Tailgate Cookies, p. 230

Surprise Oatmeal Raisin Cookies, p. 227

Debutante Luncheon

Sparkling Hibiscus Tea, p. 43

Onion Soup Gratinée, p. 100

The Queen's Chicken Salad in Pineapple Boats, p. 84

Roasted Asparagus, p. 108

Buttery-Rich Crescent Rolls, p. 67

Merlot Sorbet, p. 208

Home for the Holidays

Old English Wassail, p. 38

Traditional "Southern Sweet Tea", p. 42

Frosted Cranberry Salad, p. 77

Roasted Turkey with Fresh Sage Stuffing, p. 168

Basic Turkey Gravy, p. 168

Damn Good Ham, p. 157

Apricot Casserole, p. 157

Green Beans with Pine Nuts and Goat Cheese, p. 108

Company Corn, p. 116

Orange Sweet Potato Cups, p. 125

Favorite Yeast Rolls, p. 66

Aunt Ruth's Coconut Cake, p. 200

Southern Christmas Fruitcake Pie, p. 217

Appetizers and Beverages

Southern Lights

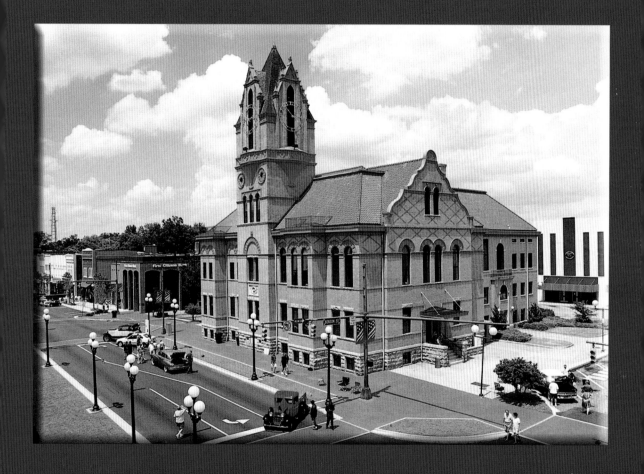

Appetizers and Beverages

On the front:

June 17, 2000 – Taken at 1st Annual Main Street Car Show
at historic Anderson County Courthouse

Photograph by *Tom Gibson*

Artichokes in Blue Cheese and Butter Sauce

Forget that artichoke dip you've been making for years!

4	ounces blue cheese crumbles
½	cup butter
¼	cup heavy cream

1	(14 to 15-ounce) can artichoke hearts, drained and coarsely chopped
	Freshly ground black pepper to taste

- Slowly melt blue cheese and butter in the top of a double boiler. Whip in cream. Add artichokes and pepper to taste. Cover and heat slowly. Serve hot in chafing dish with Melba rounds.

Makes 4 to 6 servings.

Off the Chart Blue Cheese Mushrooms

A wonderfully intense combination of flavors.

3	pounds large mushrooms (about 40)
1	cup chopped green onions
1	cup (2 sticks) butter, divided
7	ounces blue cheese, crumbled

¼	teaspoon salt
¼	teaspoon pepper
½-¾	cup breadcrumbs
2-3	teaspoons hot pepper sauce

- Remove stems from mushrooms and set caps aside.

- Finely mince stems with food processor or knife.

- Sauté minced stems and green onions in 6 tablespoons of the butter. Add blue cheese and stir to melt over medium heat. Add salt and pepper. Add breadcrumbs, mixing well, until consistency is appropriate for stuffing. Stir in hot pepper sauce to taste and let stuffing mixture cool.

- Sauté mushroom caps in remaining butter. Cool, and stuff.

- Heat stuffed mushrooms at 425° for 5 to 10 minutes, or until hot.

These may be made ahead of time and cooked just before serving.

Makes 36 to 40.

Eating is not merely a material pleasure. Eating well gives a spectacular joy to life and contributes immensely to good will and happy companionship. It is of great importance to the morale.

~ Elsa Schiaparelli

Stuffed Mushrooms
with Sun~Dried Tomatoes

A very rich and elegant appetizer.

24 mushrooms (about 2½ pounds), the stems removed and finely chopped, reserving 1 cup, and the caps left whole

12 ounces sun-dried tomatoes packed in oil, drained, reserving 4 tablespoons of the oil, and the tomatoes minced

⅓ cup finely chopped shallot

1 teaspoon finely chopped garlic

Pinch of crumbled dried thyme

2 tablespoons heavy cream

Freshly grated Parmesan cheese

- Brush the mushroom caps with some of the reserved tomato oil and arrange them, stemmed sides down, on the rack of a broiler pan. Broil the mushroom caps under a preheated broiler about 6 inches from the heat for 2 minutes, or until they are barely softened. Arrange them, stemmed sides up, in one layer on a baking sheet and set aside.

- In a large skillet cook shallot and garlic in remaining reserved oil over moderately low heat, stirring occasionally, or until they are softened. Stir in reserved mushroom stems, tomatoes, and thyme. Add salt and pepper to taste, and cook the mixture, stirring occasionally, for 5 to 10 minutes, or until the liquid has evaporated and the mixture is thick. Stir in the cream and again, salt and pepper to taste.

- Divide the mixture among the mushroom caps and sprinkle them with the Parmesan cheese.

- Bake the stuffed mushrooms on the middle rack of a preheated 350° oven for 12 to 18 minutes, or until the filling is completely heated.

Makes 24.

Bacon Mushroom Poppers

This appetizer is such a crowd pleaser that you
may want to double the recipe. We bet you'll still run out!

8	ounces fresh mushrooms, cleaned	¾-1	teaspoon very finely chopped onion
1	(3-ounce) package cream cheese, slightly softened	6	slices bacon, cooked and crumbled

- Remove stems from mushrooms and set aside.

- Combine cream cheese and onion; form into small balls, and roll in crumbled bacon, stuffing one into each mushroom cap.

- Place mushrooms onto a microwave-safe plate and cook on medium high heat for 1½ to 2½ minutes, or until mushrooms and filling are hot. Serve immediately.

Makes 6 to 8 servings.

Broiled Shrimp 'n Bacon

14	unpeeled jumbo fresh shrimp (approximately 1 pound)	¼	cup butter or margarine, melted
2	ounces Monterey Jack cheese, cut into 14 (1½-inch) strips	1	tablespoon grated Parmesan cheese
7	bacon slices, cut in half lengthwise	1	clove garlic, crushed
		1	teaspoon lemon juice

- Peel shrimp, leaving tails on, and devein if desired. Butterfly shrimp by making a deep slit down back from large end to tail, cutting to, but not through, inside curve of shrimp.

- Place a cheese strip inside each slit and wrap sides of shrimp around cheese. Wrap each shrimp in a bacon slice and secure with two wooden picks.

- Stir together butter and remaining 3 ingredients, and brush on each shrimp. Arrange shrimp on a baking sheet.

- Broil 5½ inches from heat for 4 minutes on each side, or until bacon is crisp.

Makes 14.

Make your holiday buffet or appetizer table look more festive by using red, green, yellow or orange bell peppers as containers for serving. Remove the tops of the peppers and scoop out the seeds. Rinse the peppers with water and fill them with savory dips, sauces or relishes.

Buena Vista Park was a beautiful recreation spot for residents of Anderson County. The owners of one of the street car lines created the park in 1905 on East River Street, near the edge of the city limits, in the hopes that it would draw streetcar riders on the weekends when ridership was traditionally low. The original name was Hollywood, which was changed after a month. Features of the park included an alligator viewing pond, a dance hall pavilion, a tethered hot air balloon ride, and a swimming pool. As popular as the park proved to be, it didn't raise the streetcar ridership as desired because citizens realized that they could walk to the park and save the nickel fare, and in 1915 the park was closed. Buena Vista Drive still exists today as a reminder of the grand landmark that used to entertain Anderson County residents.

Bruschetta

A wonderful appetizer for company, or a perfect compliment to grilled ribs and corn, or a fresh green salad.

½ cup extra virgin olive oil	1-1½ tablespoons balsamic vinegar
2 large garlic cloves, minced	½ teaspoon salt
4-5 medium fresh tomatoes (approximately 1 pound), seeded and chopped	½ teaspoon ground black pepper
½ cup red or sweet onion, chopped	8 slices crusty Italian bread, ½ inch thick
⅓ cup fresh basil, coarsely chopped	1 cup grated mozzarella cheese Parmesan or feta cheese (optional)

- In a small bowl combine oil and garlic, and let stand for 15 minutes.

- In a medium bowl combine tomatoes, onion, basil, balsamic vinegar, salt, pepper, and 2 tablespoons of the garlic mixture. Stir well to blend and let stand for 20 minutes.

- Brush both sides of bread slices with garlic and oil mixture. Place on baking sheet.

- Broil 5 inches from the heat, turning slices until each side is lightly toasted. (The bread will brown very quickly, so watch carefully to prevent scorching.)

- Spoon tomato mixture onto each bread slice and top with mozzarella cheese, and Parmesan or feta cheese if desired.

- Return baking sheets to oven and broil until cheese is melted and tomato mixture is warmed.

Makes 8 large or 24 appetizer servings.

Two baguette loaves sliced ½ inch thick may be substituted for Italian bread.

Asparagus Rolls

These appetizers are guaranteed
to be the first to disappear at any party.

1   loaf white or whole wheat bread
1   (8-ounce) package cream
    cheese, softened
3   tablespoons prepared
    horseradish
1   (14-ounce) can asparagus
    spears, drained
    Melted butter
    Paprika

• Remove crusts from bread. Flatten bread slices with a rolling pin.

• In a medium mixing bowl, combine cream cheese and horseradish;
  mix well. Thinly spread cream cheese mixture on one side of each
  bread slice. Place 1 asparagus spear on cheese side of each slice
  of bread; roll bread tightly around asparagus.

• Cut each asparagus roll into thirds; place pieces on lightly
  greased baking sheet. Lightly brush each piece with melted
  butter; sprinkle with paprika. Bake at 350° for 15 to 20 minutes
  or until golden. Serve warm.

Makes about 60.

Sausage and Cheese Wraps

The men won't stay away from these!

1   pound hot sausage
1   cup grated sharp Cheddar
    cheese
2   frozen pie shell pastries, thawed
2   tablespoons Dijon mustard,
    divided

• Cook sausage until brown and crumbly. Drain on paper towels.

• Add cheese to drained sausage.

• Place pie shells on a flat surface and spread each with 1 tablespoon
  mustard. Spread half of sausage mixture over one of the pastries.

• Begin with one edge and wrap pastry into a spiral. Place on
  greased baking sheet. Repeat with remaining pastry.

• Bake at 350° for 30 to 35 minutes or until golden brown. Cut into
  slices. Serve hot.

Makes 12 to 15.

Stuffed Cherry Tomatoes

These are wonderful to
mix on a pretty platter with
other appetizers.

2 dozen cherry tomatoes
1 (8-ounce) package
cream cheese, softened
1½-2 tablespoons
prepared horseradish
¼ cup bacon bits
Garnish: small dill sprigs
and green onion curls

• Cut top off each cherry tomato;
scoop out pulp. (Reserve pulp, if
desired, for another use.) Invert
tomatoes on paper towels to drain.

• Combine cream cheese,
horseradish, and bacon bits in
small bowl. Beat at medium speed
of an electric mixer until light
and fluffy.

• Spoon or pipe cream cheese
mixture into tomato shells.
Garnish, if desired. Serve chilled
or at room temperature.

Makes 2 dozen.

Hot & Tasty Crab Dip

Serve warm, in a chafing dish, with Melba rounds, crackers, or tart shells.

3	tablespoons margarine	¼	cup chopped pimento
2	small onions, chopped	2	tablespoons parsley, chopped
¼	cup celery, finely chopped	2	(6½-ounce) cans crabmeat, drained
3	tablespoons all-purpose flour	1	tablespoon Worcestershire sauce
½	teaspoon paprika		
1	teaspoon dry mustard	¾	cup almonds, chopped
1	teaspoon salt	2	tablespoons chili sauce
½	teaspoon ground black pepper		Hot pepper sauce to taste
1½	cups milk		

• **Melt margarine in medium skillet. Add onions and celery, and cook until soft.**

• **Add flour, paprika, mustard, salt, and pepper, stirring until smooth.**

• **Add milk slowly, stirring until smooth. Stir in remaining ingredients. (If sauce is too thick, add more milk.)**

Makes approximately 6 cups.

Bayside Shrimp Tarts

These delicious treats are definitely worth the effort.

½ cup butter, softened	⅔ cup finely chopped green onions
½ (8-ounce) package cream cheese, softened	½ cup finely chopped fresh parsley
1½ cups all-purpose flour	⅔ cup mayonnaise
¼ cup grated Asiago cheese	2 tablespoons capers
¼ teaspoon salt	1 teaspoon lemon juice
2 pounds unpeeled large fresh shrimp	½ teaspoon salt
	¼ teaspoon ground red pepper
	1 clove garlic, minced

- Prepare tart shells by combining butter and cream cheese, stirring until blended.

- Add flour, cheese, and salt, blending well. Cover and chill dough 1 hour.

- Divide dough into 3 parts. Shape each portion into 12 balls. Press dough onto bottom and up sides of lightly greased 1¾-inch miniature muffin pans.

- Bake at 350° for 15 to 17 minutes, or until golden. Cool and remove from pans.

- Prepare shrimp filling by bringing 6 cups of water to a boil. Add shrimp and cook 3 to 5 minutes, or until shrimp turn pink. Drain well and rinse with cold water. Cover and refrigerate.

- After chilling, peel, devein, and coarsely chop shrimp.

- Combine shrimp, green onions, and next 7 ingredients in a large bowl. Spoon mixture into baked tart shells.

Makes 36.

Andersonians frequently say "Cut off the light" when they want a light turned off.

Bacon Roll Ups

A delicious appetizer to serve with a glass of wine.

1	(8-ounce) package cream cheese, softened	½	teaspoon garlic powder
¼	cup mayonnaise	1	loaf white bread with crusts removed
1	tablespoon chives	1	pound bacon, slices cut in half

- Mix cream cheese, mayonnaise, chives, and garlic powder.

- Spread mixture on trimmed loaf bread.

- Starting on one edge of each bread slice, roll each one and slice twice across roll to make 3 canapés. Wrap bacon slice around each bread roll.

- Broil on high 6 inches from heat for 3 to 5 minutes on each side or until bacon is crisp. Serve immediately.

Makes about 75.

Any pasteurized cheese spread can be substituted for the cream cheese. Also, either 3 olives or 3 pearl onions may be placed in the center of each bread slice before rolling and cutting.

Portobello Pizzettas

Different and delicious.

½	(10-ounce) package frozen chopped spinach, thawed	¼	teaspoon coarsely ground black pepper
1½	cups shredded mozzarella cheese	12	portobello mushrooms (3 to 4 inches in diameter), cleaned, with stems removed
½	cup coarsely chopped pepperoni	2	tablespoons margarine, melted
1	teaspoon dried basil, crushed		Fresh basil sprigs (optional)

- Press liquid out of spinach; finely chop.

- In a mixing bowl, combine spinach, cheese, pepperoni, basil, and pepper.

- Place mushrooms on a lightly greased baking sheet, open side up; brush with melted margarine. Spoon 2 tablespoons spinach mixture into each mushroom.

- Bake at 350° for 12 minutes or until heated through. Garnish with fresh basil, if desired.

Makes 12 servings.

Sausage Ryes

Great for casual entertaining.

1	pound hot sausage	1	(8-ounce) can mushrooms, drained
1	pound ground chuck		
1	pound processed cheese loaf	2	loaves party bread (1 each rye and pumpernickel)
½	teaspoon garlic salt		
1	tablespoon Worcestershire sauce		

- **Brown sausage and ground chuck. Drain.**

- **Add cheese to meat mixture and cook until melted. Add garlic salt, Worcestershire, and mushrooms. Spread on party rounds.**

- **Broil until hot and bubbly. Serve immediately.**

Makes approximately 40.

These appetizers may be made ahead and frozen. After spreading with meat mixture, place on trays and put in freezer until party rounds are frozen. Remove from trays and place in gallon size freezer bags. When needed, place frozen rounds on baking sheet and broil until hot and bubbly.

Tailgate Party Spread

A must for the Clemson-Carolina game!

6	slices bacon, fried crisp and crumbled	1	cup mayonnaise
1	cup grated sharp Cheddar cheese	¼	cup finely chopped onion
			Dash garlic powder
1	cup Parmesan cheese		Small bag slivered almonds, lightly toasted

- **Mix bacon and all other ingredients.**

- **Spread on crackers, party bread rounds, or toast points.**

Makes approximately 3 cups.

Anderson County, as well as the city of Anderson, bears the name of Robert Anderson, a Revolutionary War hero. A native of Virginia, Robert Anderson moved to South Carolina to assist his good friend Andrew Pickens as they surveyed the recently-ceded Cherokee lands for the state of SC. They joined the SC forces fighting off the British where they received great accolades and acclaim. After the war, Anderson settled on property on the Seneca River and lived there until his death in 1813. His kind and gentle manner endeared him to many, and his dedication to the state of South Carolina and its residents was rewarded in 1826 when the Pendleton District was divided, and one of the resulting counties was given his name.

Optional sauces for dipping:

Orange-Horseradish "Fire" Sauce

½ cup horseradish
⅓ cup orange marmalade
3 dashes hot pepper sauce

• Combine ingredients in small bowl and stir until well mixed. Chill until serving.

Makes approximately ¾ cup.

"Plum Spicy" Sauce

½ cup plum sauce
⅓ cup pineapple juice
1½ teaspoons hot Chinese mustard
1½ teaspoons cornstarch

• Combine ingredients in blender. Pulse blend until well mixed. Chill until serving.

Makes approximately ¾ cup.

Sesame Chicken Strips with Dipping Sauce

The sesame seeds and coconut make a wonderful variation of traditional chicken strips.

½ cup shredded, sweetened coconut	1½ pounds chicken breasts, cut into strips
2 tablespoons sesame seeds	2 egg whites
½ cup unseasoned dry breadcrumbs	2 teaspoons sesame oil
	Non-stick cooking spray

• Place coconut and sesame seeds in a dry skillet over medium heat. Cook until golden brown, stirring frequently. Transfer toasted mixture into a dish. Add breadcrumbs.

• Place chicken strips in a large bowl. In a small bowl, lightly beat egg whites and oil, and then pour over chicken.

• Roll chicken strips in dry mixture, one at a time, and place on baking sheet that has been sprayed with cooking spray. Continue until all pieces are covered.

• Bake at 425° for 10 minutes. Remove from oven and turn pieces over. Spray the other side with cooking spray and return to the oven and bake for 5 minutes. Serve with honey mustard, oriental duck, or plum sauce.

Makes 16 to 20 appetizers.

A Little Something Sweet

This refreshing dip is simple to prepare, and offers a surprise
for the palate in the midst of a table full of appetizers.

1	(8-ounce) package cream cheese, softened	2	teaspoons grated orange peel, divided
1	cup powdered sugar	1/4	teaspoon orange extract
1	tablespoon frozen orange juice concentrate, undiluted		Gingersnap cookies, for dipping

• **In a mixing bowl, combine cream cheese, sugar, juice concentrate, 1 teaspoon orange peel, and extract; beat on medium speed of electric mixer until well blended and fluffy. Spoon into serving dish. Sprinkle remaining orange peel over dip. Serve with gingersnaps as dippers.**

Makes about 1½ cups.

Artichoke Cheesecake

1	(3-ounce) jar marinated artichoke hearts	1½	teaspoons chopped fresh oregano
3	(8-ounce) packages cream cheese, softened	3	large eggs
1¼	cups (5 ounces) feta cheese, crumbled	1/4	cup chopped green onions
2	cloves garlic, minced	1	teaspoon chopped pimento
			Garnish: sliced pimentos and fresh basil leaves

• **Drain artichokes, reserving 2 tablespoons of the marinade; chop artichokes.**

• **Combine cream cheese, feta cheese, garlic, and oregano in a large bowl; beat on medium speed of electric mixer until smooth. Beat in eggs just until well mixed. Stir in artichokes, green onions, pimento, and reserved marinade.**

• **Spoon mixture into a greased 9-inch springform pan; cover loosely with foil. Bake at 325° for 35 to 40 minutes or until the edge is firm but the center is still slightly soft when pan is shaken. Cool on a wire rack. Chill, covered, for to 24 hours.**

• **Place on a serving plate and remove the side of the pan. Garnish with pimentos and basil. Serve slightly chilled or at room temperature.**

Makes 16 servings.

Notes

Lynchburg Blue Cheese Sauce

This versatile dip is great with wings, celery, carrots, or crackers.

1 cup mayonnaise

½ cup sour cream

1 cup (4 ounces) crumbled blue cheese

¼ teaspoon garlic powder

1 teaspoon Worcestershire sauce

1 tablespoon hot pepper sauce

2 tablespoons Jack Daniels whiskey

- Combine all ingredients, blend well, and chill.

Makes approximately 2½ cups.

Tex-Mex Black Bean Dip

You may use low-fat cheese without sacrificing taste in this hearty dip.

1 (15-ounce) can black beans, drained	½ teaspoon ground cumin
1 teaspoon vegetable oil	½ teaspoon chili powder
½ cup chopped onion	¼ cup (1 ounce) shredded Monterey Jack cheese
2 cloves garlic, minced	¼ cup chopped fresh cilantro
½ cup diced tomato	1 tablespoon fresh lime juice
⅓ cup mild picante sauce	

- **Place beans in bowl; partially mash until chunky. Set aside.**

- **Heat oil in a medium nonstick skillet over medium heat. Add onion and garlic; sauté 4 minutes or until tender.**

- **Add beans, tomato, and next 3 ingredients; cook 5 minutes or until thickened, stirring constantly.**

- **Remove from heat; add cheese and remaining ingredients, stirring until cheese melts. Serve warm or at room temperature with tortilla chips.**

Makes 1⅔ cups.

Junior League Cheese Ball

1 (8-ounce) package cream cheese, slightly softened	1½ teaspoons Worcestershire sauce
2 tablespoons grated onion	1 cup grated extra sharp Cheddar cheese
1 teaspoon prepared yellow or brown mustard	1 cup chopped pecans
	½ cup dried parsley

- **In a mixing bowl, combine first 5 ingredients. Mix well by hand; roll into ball.**

- **Pour chopped nuts into bowl; roll again.**

- **Add parsley; roll again. Serve with crackers.**

Makes 18 to 24 servings.

For hot seafood variation, omit nuts and add 1 cup of chopped boiled shrimp or crabmeat. Bake in oven proof serving bowl at 350° for 20 to 25 minutes; serve hot.

J.R.'s Salsa

This salsa will last for several weeks in the refrigerator.

1	large onion, coarsely chopped (2 cups)	1	(28-ounce) can whole tomatoes, drained, reserving juice
3	large cloves garlic	1	(6-ounce) can tomato paste
1	large fresh green Anaheim chili pepper	2	ounces white wine vinegar
3	small fresh yellow chili peppers	1	teaspoon ground cumin
1	fresh jalapeño chili pepper (or more)	2	tablespoons fresh oregano leaves
½	cup fresh cilantro leaves	1	teaspoon salt
		1	teaspoon ground black pepper
			Juice of 1 lime

- Combine onion, garlic, and chilies in food processor. Process with metal blade until chopped medium-fine.

- Add cilantro leaves, tomatoes, tomato paste, vinegar cumin, oregano, salt, pepper, and lime juice. Blend again but do not overblend. Salsa should be chunky. (If mixture is too thick, thin out by adding juice reserved from tomatoes.)

- Chill thoroughly and serve with tortilla chips.

Makes approximately 4 cups.

Fiesta Corn Salsa

Because of the chunky consistency of this salsa, it also makes a tasty side dish for grilled or blackened chicken or fish.

2	cups canned corn, drained	2	tablespoons chopped fresh parsley or cilantro
¼	cup each red pepper, green pepper, and yellow pepper, cut into strips	2	tablespoons lemon juice
⅛	cup red onion, cut into small slices or rings	2	tablespoons lime juice
1	tablespoon chopped chives	½	jalapeño pepper, finely chopped
		1	teaspoon sugar
			Salt and pepper to taste

- Combine all ingredients, cover, and chill.

- Serve with tortilla chips.

Makes approximately 3 cups.

When making salsa, if a milder version is preferred, remove seeds from chilies. For hotter salsa, add more jalapeño and leave seeds in chilies.

When cutting or seeding hot peppers, use rubber or plastic gloves to protect your hands. Avoid touching your face.

Great Guacamole

Easy to make and delicious with tortilla chips, or along with your favorite Mexican dish.

1 small tomato, finely chopped

1 small jalapeño pepper, seeded and finely chopped

1 green onion with top, finely chopped

1 small clove garlic, minced

1 teaspoon lemon juice

¼ teaspoon salt

1 medium avocado

- In a medium mixing bowl, combine tomato, jalapeño, green onion, garlic, lemon juice, and salt; mix well.

- Peel and seed avocado; cut into ½-inch cubes. Stir avocado cubes into tomato mixture; serve immediately.

Makes about 1½ cups.

Mango Salsa

Serve this salsa with blue corn tortilla chips. It is also delicious served atop grilled oysters, salmon fillets, or chicken breasts.

4 ripe mangoes, peeled, pitted and diced	1/4 cup chopped fresh cilantro
1-2 jalapeño peppers, seeded and minced	1/4 cup olive oil
1/2 small red bell pepper, finely chopped	1 clove garlic, minced
1 shallot, finely diced	2 tablespoons fresh lime juice
	Salt and freshly ground black pepper to taste

- **In a medium mixing bowl, combine all ingredients; gently mix. Cover and refrigerate overnight to let flavors blend.**

Makes about 2 cups.

Marinated Mushrooms

2/3 cup tarragon vinegar	Dash of hot pepper sauce
1/2 cup vegetable oil	1 pound fresh mushrooms
2 tablespoons water	1 medium onion, sliced in thin rings
1 tablespoon sugar	Finely diced sweet red pepper
1 1/2 teaspoons salt	
1 clove garlic, minced	

- **In a glass bowl, combine first 7 ingredients.**

- **Add mushrooms and onion. Toss to coat.**

- **Cover and refrigerate overnight.**

- **Sprinkle with red pepper prior to serving.**

Makes 4 cups.

Granny Smith Apple Salsa

4	Granny Smith apples, peeled, cored, and cut into chunks	½	teaspoon cinnamon
½	green bell pepper, chopped	2	jalapeño peppers, seeded and minced
1½	cups purple onion, finely chopped	2-3	tablespoons fresh lime juice
1	teaspoon cumin	½	teaspoon salt
		½	teaspoon ground black pepper

- **Combine all ingredients and cover.**

- **Chill at least 3 hours.**

- **Serve as an accompaniment to pork or poultry.**

Makes 4 cups.

Candied Holiday Pickles

2	gallons fresh cucumbers, peeled and sliced lengthwise, with large seeds removed	1	ounce red food coloring
		1	tablespoon alum
		1	tablespoon salt
2	cups pickling lime	10	cups sugar
8½	quarts water	4	cinnamon sticks
3	cups apple cider vinegar, divided	1	(8 to 10-ounce) bag cinnamon red hot candies

- **Place cucumbers in a large pan. Mix lime and water together and pour over cucumbers. Let soak for 24 hours.**

- **Drain and wash in cool water.**

- **Put cucumbers in cool water and soak for 3 hours. Drain.**

- **Mix 1 cup of vinegar, red color, and alum, adding enough water for mixture to cover cucumbers. Heat thoroughly on stove and drain.**

- **Mix 2 cups vinegar, salt, sugar, cinnamon sticks, and candies and bring to a boil. Pour mixture over cucumbers and let stand overnight.**

- **For the next 2 mornings drain liquid, heat thoroughly, and pour back over cucumbers.**

- **On the third morning heat syrup and cucumbers to a boil. While very hot, place cucumber sticks in jars. Fill jars with hot syrup and seal.**

Makes 6 to 8 quarts, or 12 to 14 pints.

Perfect Party Shrimp

1	cup white wine or tarragon vinegar		1	cup thinly sliced Vidalia or red onion
½	cup water		2	lemons, scrubbed, thinly sliced, and seeded
¼	cup coriander seeds		1	(3 or 3½-ounce) jar capers, drained
1	tablespoon mustard seeds			
1	tablespoon fennel seeds		6	garlic cloves, peeled and cut in half
1	teaspoon allspice berries			
4	(¼-inch-thick) slices fresh ginger		2	bay leaves
1	tablespoon salt		2	dried red chilies
1	cup olive oil		2½	pounds medium shrimp

- Combine vinegar, water, coriander, mustard, fennel, allspice, and ginger in a small stainless steel saucepan. Bring to boil; reduce heat and simmer for 10 minutes. Add salt; cool.

- Strain vinegar mixture through sieve into bowl and discard spices.

- Stir in oil, onion, lemons, capers, garlic, bay leaves, and chilies.

- Bring 4 quarts of water to a boil in Dutch oven. Add shrimp and cook 2 to 3 minutes until opaque throughout. Drain and cool.

- Peel and devein shrimp. Add shrimp to marinade and toss to combine.

- Spoon shrimp and marinade into large resealable plastic bag. Seal and refrigerate overnight.

- To serve, drain; remove bay leaves and arrange on platter.

Makes 24 to 30.

"The Dagwood Canapé"

Entertaining for the busy hostess at its best!
Let you guests "build" their own appetizers with a
selection of goodies to tempt the taste buds.

3	tablespoons sliced green onions	1	(4-ounce) piece smoked salmon or trout, cut ½ to 1 inch thick
1½	teaspoons finely shredded lemon peel	24	olives (medley of black, green, Greek, etc.)
4	teaspoons fresh lemon juice	6	hard-cooked eggs, cut into ½-inch slices
4	teaspoons olive oil	2	roasted sweet red peppers, coarsely chopped
4	teaspoons capers		Crackers, pita chips, or toasted party rounds
1½	teaspoons anchovy paste (optional)		
2	cloves garlic, minced		
¼	teaspoon freshly ground black pepper		

• **In a small serving bowl stir together green onion, lemon peel, lemon juice, olive oil, capers, anchovy paste, garlic, and ground pepper.**

• **To assemble, place salmon or trout on a serving plate. Surround plate with small bowls of olives, egg slices, red peppers and capers mixture.**

• **Serve with crackers, pita chips, or toasted party rounds.**

Makes 12 servings.

Olive Nut Spread

Very different and tasty.

1	(8-ounce) package cream cheese, softened		Dash of ground black pepper
½	cup mayonnaise	1	cup chopped green olives
2	tablespoons liquid from jar of green olives	½	cup chopped pecans, lightly toasted

• **Combine cream cheese and mayonnaise in a medium bowl until smooth and creamy. Stir in olive liquid and pepper. Fold in olives and pecans. Cover and refrigerate until ready to serve. Serve with assorted crackers.**

Makes 2 cups.

Green Onion Dip

**This thick dip is also
a wonderful party sandwich
spread, especially on
pumpernickel bread.**

*1 (8-ounce) carton small-curd
regular or low-fat cottage cheese*

*2 tablespoons chopped
green onions with tops*

2 tablespoons chopped fresh parsley

1 medium shallot, chopped

1 clove garlic, chopped

*2 teaspoons white wine
or white vinegar*

¼ cup olive oil

½ teaspoon salt, or to taste

• In a blender or food processor, combine cottage cheese and next 5 ingredients. Process until smooth. With machine running, slowly add oil. Add salt to taste. Serve with pita chips or crackers.

Makes about 1½ cups.

Here are our 2 favorite variations of the always popular pita chips. Serve with dips or enjoy as a side with pasta.

Pita Chips

1 pita bread package
1 tablespoon olive oil
1 garlic clove, minced
1-2 tablespoons butter, melted

• Cut pita into sections or "chips".

• Combine olive oil, garlic and butter. Brush on pita sections.

• Bake in a preheated 350° oven on a baking sheet or stone for 10 minutes.

Parmesan Pita Crisps

3 pita bread rounds
6 tablespoons unsalted butter, melted
3 ounces (¾ cup) freshly grated Parmesan cheese
⅓ cup chopped fresh parsley

• Cut around edges of the 3 pita rounds, making 6 round halves. Place bread, smooth side down, on baking sheet. Brush each piece liberally with melted butter. Cut each round into 8 wedges. Sprinkle Parmesan cheese on top of each wedge and top with parsley. Broil in preheated oven until hot, golden brown, and bubbly.

Layered Mediterranean Dip

2	(15-ounce) cans black beans, drained	1	tablespoon olive oil
1	medium tomato, diced	½	tablespoon vinegar
1	medium cucumber, peeled and diced	¼	teaspoon garlic salt
2	green onions, diced	¼	teaspoon oregano
⅓	cup sliced black olives	1	(5-ounce) package of tomato-basil feta cheese
			Pita chips

• **Mash black beans to a smooth consistency and place in the bottom of a shallow dish.**

• **Mix tomato, cucumber, onion, olives, oil, vinegar, and seasonings together. Spoon mixture evenly over black beans.**

• **Top with a layer of feta cheese.**

• **Serve with pita chips.**

Makes 8 to 10 servings.

Presto Pesto!

Serve with pita or bagel chips.

2	cups fresh basil	1	cup grated Parmesan cheese
4	cloves garlic	¼	cup grated Romano cheese
1	cup pine nuts		Large pinch each of salt and pepper
1	cup olive oil		

• **In blender combine basil, garlic, and pine nuts. Process until finely chopped. Transfer to bowl and slowly drizzle in olive oil, stirring to blend.**

• **Add Parmesan and Romano cheeses, and salt and pepper.**

• **Serve at room temperature.**

Makes 1½ to 2 cups.

Summertime Tomato Lime Dip

**This dip is so yummy you'll find
yourself using it as a salad dressing, too.**

1	(16-ounce) container sour cream	2	tablespoons chopped fresh dill weed
1	cup fresh peeled, seeded, and diced tomatoes	12	drops liquid red pepper seasoning
½	cup chopped green onions with tops	1½	teaspoons grated lime rind
		¼	teaspoon salt
		¼	teaspoon ground white pepper

• **Mix together sour cream, tomato, green onion, dill, red pepper seasoning, lime rind, salt and pepper in a large bowl. Cover and refrigerate for about 30 minutes to allow flavors to blend. Serve with fresh celery sticks, broccoli florets, and other fresh vegetables. May also serve with pita chips.**

Makes 2⅔ cups.

Shrimp Butter

**Serve this rich and delicious spread
with Melba rounds or crackers.**

½	cup mayonnaise	¼	teaspoon ground black pepper
1	cup butter	1	clove garlic, crushed
1	(8-ounce) package cream cheese, slightly softened	1	tablespoon minced onion
2	shakes Worcestershire sauce	2	hard-cooked eggs, chopped
¼	teaspoon salt	½	pound shrimp, cooked and chopped

• **Combine mayonnaise and next 7 ingredients. Beat on medium speed of electric mixer until creamy. Stir in eggs and shrimp. Chill until serving.**

Makes 12 servings.

Versatile Veggie Dip

2 cups mayonnaise
1 tablespoon curry powder
1 teaspoon lemon juice
1 teaspoon Worcestershire sauce
1 teaspoon steak sauce
*1 teaspoon ground white
or black pepper*
½ teaspoon celery salt
Dash hot pepper sauce
Raw vegetables, for dipping

• In a small mixing bowl, combine mayonnaise and next 7 ingredients; mix well. Serve chilled with fresh vegetables as dippers.

Makes about 2 cups.

Creole Hummus

You'll be tempted to double-dip!

1	(19-ounce) can garbanzo beans	2-3	tablespoons fresh lemon juice
⅓	cup olive oil	1-2	garlic cloves
⅓	cup tahini	¾	teaspoon Cajun or Creole seasoning
⅓	cup water	½-¾	teaspoon ground cumin

- Purée all ingredients in a food processor until smooth.

- Serve with pita or bagel chips.

Makes approximately 2 cups.

Blue Cheese Walnut Bites

These are so simple, but oh so good!

1½	cups all-purpose flour	¼	cup butter
2-3	tablespoons cracked black pepper	1	cup chopped walnuts
8	ounces blue cheese	3	egg yolks, slightly beaten

- In a medium mixing bowl combine flour and pepper. Using a pastry blender cut in cheese and butter until mixture resembles coarse crumbs.

- Add walnuts and egg yolks. Stir until combined.

- Form the mixture into a ball and knead until well blended. Divide dough in half. Shape each half into a log about 9 inches long. Wrap logs in plastic wrap and chill at least 2 hours.

- Cut each log into ¼-inch-thick slices. Place slices 1 inch apart on an ungreased baking sheet.

- Bake for 9 to 12 minutes at 425° or until bottoms and edges are golden brown. Transfer to a wire rack. Serve warm or at room temperature.

Makes approximately 6 dozen.

These wafers may be stored, tightly covered, in the refrigerator up to 1 week.

Apricot Cheddar Thumbprints

1	cup extra sharp grated Cheddar cheese	½	teaspoon cayenne or red pepper
½	cup butter, softened	½	jar (approximately 6 ounces) apricot preserves or spreadable fruit
1	cup all-purpose flour		
¼	teaspoon salt		

- **Cream cheese and butter together.**

- **Combine flour, salt and pepper. Add to creamed mixture.**

- **Roll dough into 1-inch balls and place on ungreased baking sheets.**

- **Using thumb, make a small indention in each ball. Spoon approximately ½ teaspoon apricot preserves into each thumbprint.**

- **Bake in preheated oven at 375° for 11 to 13 minutes.**

Makes 3 dozen.

Spicy Mixed Nuts

Be warned! These are addictive!

½	cup (1 stick) butter	2	cups cashews
2	teaspoons salt	2	cups pecan halves
2	teaspoons chili powder	2	cups peanuts
2	teaspoons cayenne pepper	2	cups walnut halves
1	teaspoon cumin		

- **In a large skillet, melt butter. Add salt, chili powder, cayenne, and cumin.**

- **Add the nuts and toss to coat.**

- **Spread the nuts out on a baking sheet and bake at 350° until lightly browned, about 10 minutes.**

Makes 8 cups.

These nuts can be prepared ahead and stored in an airtight container or kept in the freezer.

I'll have a "coke"

This is no mere brand preference. It refers to any soft drink - unless you specifically want a "Pepsi Cola." Then you must ask for it by name.

Notes

Fire Nuts

The intense combination of white, red, and
black peppers enkindles these buttery toasted almonds.

2	(6-ounce) cans whole natural almonds	1	teaspoon salt
3	tablespoons butter or margarine	1	teaspoon chili powder
		½	teaspoon garlic powder
3	tablespoons white wine Worcestershire sauce	⅛	teaspoon ground white pepper
		⅛	teaspoon ground red pepper
		⅛	teaspoon ground black pepper

- Place whole almonds in a medium bowl, and set aside.

- Melt butter in a small saucepan over medium heat. Add Worcestershire sauce and remaining 6 ingredients, stirring well to combine. Cook 1 minute, stirring occasionally.

- Pour butter mixture over almonds, stirring gently to coat. Let almond mixture stand at room temperature 30 minutes.

- Place almond mixture in a single layer in an ungreased 15 x 10 x 1-inch jelly-roll pan.

- Bake at 300° for 35 minutes, stirring often. Cool.

Makes 2 cups.

You may use regular Worcestershire sauce if you are unable to find the white wine variety, but the nuts will be very dark in color. The lighter white wine Worcestershire sauce yields a prettier color.

Boiled Peanuts

A big bowl or bucket full of these is great
for an outdoor picnic or barbecue.

4	pounds green peanuts, unshelled	6	quarts water
		6-10	tablespoons salt

- Wash peanuts and place in a large pot with water and salt. Cover and bring to a boil. Boil slowly for 1½ to 2 hours. Water should be briny. Add more water and salt while cooking if necessary. Test for doneness after 1½ hours. Peanuts should be soft, but not mushy inside. Rinse in plain unsalted water and drain well.

In our area, green peanuts are available during the summer months. Boiled peanuts may be frozen in heavy-duty zip-top plastic bags after cooling. To serve, simply reheat to a boil, and drain.

Black Pepper Goat Cheese Log

2	tablespoons cracked black pepper	Toasted baguette slices
1	(11-ounce) goat cheese log	Garnish: fresh rosemary sprigs (optional)
2	tablespoons extra virgin olive oil	

- Sprinkle pepper on a square of wax paper. Roll goat cheese log over pepper to coat and place on serving dish.

- Drizzle log with olive oil.

- Serve with toasted baguette slices. Garnish, if desired.

Makes 6 to 8 servings.

Boiled peanuts are a Southern staple. Salty and somewhat mushy, they're often served warm at a roadside stand or from Mom's well-used pressure cooker.

Old English Wassail

1	gallon apple cider	6	lemons, cut in half
1	quart sherry wine	4	whole cinnamon sticks
1	pint applejack brandy	6	whole cloves
6	apples, cut in half		

- Mix all ingredients in a large pot. Simmer slowly for 4 to 6 hours. Serve warm.

Makes about 5½ quarts.

Mulled Raspberry Tea

A delightful way to warm the senses and the soul.

1	cup frozen loose-pack raspberries, slightly thawed	3	whole allspice
2	cups brewed orange pekoe tea	¼-½	cup sugar (to taste)
2	cups cranberry-raspberry juice	1	lemon, thinly sliced
1	cup prepared lemonade		Fresh or frozen raspberries (optional)
¼	cup water		

- Mash raspberries in a 2 or 3 quart saucepan.

- Stir tea, juice, lemonade, water, and allspice into the raspberries.

- Bring to a boil and reduce heat. Simmer uncovered for 10 minutes.

- Strain and discard fruit pulp and spices.

- Ladle into heat proof glass mugs or cups. Sweeten with sugar, if desired. Serve with lemon slices and additional raspberries, if desired.

Makes 6 servings.

Mocha Punch

So good you will invite guests over just so you can make it!

4	cups hot coffee	1	quart vanilla ice cream
½	cup sugar	1	cup whipping cream, whipped
¼	teaspoon almond extract		Ground nutmeg
1	quart chocolate ice cream		

• Combine coffee and sugar; stir until sugar dissolves. Chill. Add almond extract; stir well.

• Scoop chocolate and vanilla ice cream into coffee mixture; stir well. Fold in whipped cream.

• Pour beverage into serving glasses and sprinkle with nutmeg.

Makes 3 quarts.

Punch for a Bunch!

This sparkling punch is perfect for a summer party.

1	(12-ounce) can frozen limeade, divided	1	(12-ounce) can frozen lemonade
6	cups water, divided	1	(10-ounce) package frozen sweetened strawberries
1	(12-ounce) can frozen orange juice	1	(2-liter) bottle ginger ale, chilled

• Combine 6 ounces of the frozen limeade and 1½ cups water and freeze into ice cubes.

• Thaw remainder of limeade, orange juice, and lemonade; mix with 4½ cups water. Transfer to punch bowl or chill until serving time.

• Thaw strawberries for 10 minutes before serving. Right before serving add strawberries, ginger ale, and limeade ice cubes to juice mixture.

Makes 24 to 40 servings.

Tango Mango Coladas

Make your taste buds dance!

½ cup unsweetened pineapple juice

1 cup sliced ripe mango

2 tablespoons fresh lime juice

⅓ cup (3 ounces) cream of coconut

⅓ cup (3 ounces) light rum

1 cup crushed ice

• Place all ingredients in a blender and blend until smooth and thick. Pour into tall glasses and serve.

Makes 4 (6-ounce) servings.

Summertime Slush

Excellent and refreshing!

3	cups water		1	(6-ounce) can frozen lemonade concentrate, undiluted
1	cup sugar		2	tablespoons lemon juice
2	medium-size ripe bananas, sliced		2	cups vodka or light rum (optional)
2	(12-ounce) cans pineapple juice, divided			Ginger ale or carbonated lemon-lime beverage
1	(6-ounce) can frozen orange juice concentrate, undiluted			Orange and lemon slices, frozen in water in molds

• Combine water and sugar in a saucepan over medium-high heat; stir until sugar dissolves. Bring to a boil; reduce heat, and simmer for 3 minutes. Let cool. Pour into one-gallon container.

• Place bananas and 1 can pineapple juice in blender. Process until smooth. Stir banana mixture into cooled sugar syrup. Add remaining can of pineapple juice, orange juice, lemonade, lemon juice, and vodka; stir well to blend. Cover mixture and store in freezer. To serve, combine equal amounts of slush and ginger ale in punch bowl. If desired, float unmolded frozen fruit in bowl.

Makes about 1 gallon.

Tequila Banana Blizzards

Relax by the pool with a good book and one of these creamy treats.

3	ounces tequila		½	cup half-and-half
¼	cup (2 ounces) crème de banana		1	large ripe banana
			4	scoops vanilla ice cream

• Place all ingredients in blender and mix just until blended. Serve immediately.

Makes 4 servings.

Cranberry Margaritas

A festive twist on a southern favorite.

1	cup cranberry juice	¾	cup tequila
½	(scant) cup sugar	½	cup triple sec
1½	cups fresh or frozen cranberries	3	cups cracked ice
			Cranberry juice
¾	cup lime juice		Sugar

- Using half of the ingredients at a time, combine cranberry juice, sugar, cranberries, lime juice, tequila, triple sec, and ice in a blender. Blend until slushy. Repeat process with remaining half of ingredients.

- To serve, dip rims of glasses in cranberry juice or water, and then into sugar to coat. Pour juice mixture into prepared glasses.

Makes 4 to 6 servings.

Mango-Ritas

For a fun touch, use colored sugar crystals instead of plain course sugar.

1	(26-ounce) jar mangoes with juice, undrained, reserving 3 tablespoons juice	4	ounces Triple Sec or Cointreau
		2	ounces Grand Marnier
8	ounces gold tequila		Crushed ice
1	(6-ounce) can frozen limeade concentrate		Coarse sugar

- In a blender, combine mangoes and juice, and next 4 ingredients. Mix well. Pour half of the liquid in a pitcher and set aside.

- Dip rims of margarita glasses in reserved juice and then in sugar.

- Add crushed ice to liquid mixture in blender, blending until slushy. Pour into prepared margarita glasses and serve. Repeat with remaining half of liquid mixture.

Makes 6 servings.

Rid a thermos or thermal coffee carafe of smells and stains by filling it with boiling water and adding a denture-cleaning tablet. Let soak all day, then rinse.

Our tasters liked all of these different Carolina cool teas so much that we had to include them all! They are sure to become summertime favorites.

Berry Breeze Tea

1 cup boiling water

6 (regular size) blackberry tea bags, or any berry-flavored tea

½ cup pineapple juice

1 (8-ounce) can crushed pineapple, drained

¼ cup sugar

18 ice cubes

• Pour boiling water over tea bags; cover and steep until tea is cool.

• Remove tea bags from water, squeezing gently. Discard bags. Cover and chill tea.

• Process chilled tea, pineapple juice, pineapple, and sugar in blender until smooth. With blender on high, add ice cubes, one at a time, processing until smooth and frothy. Serve immediately.

Makes 2 quarts.

Good Night Kiss

A night cap for a special evening.

2	ounces orange-flavored vodka	1	tablespoon powdered sugar
¾	ounce amaretto		Chocolate hard shell
1	ounce white chocolate liqueur	1	chocolate candy kiss
1	tablespoon cocoa powder		

• Fill shaker with cubed ice. Add vodka, amaretto, and white chocolate liqueur. Shake to mix well.

• In a small container, combine cocoa powder and powdered sugar. Stir, or cover and shake gently to mix. Pour into shallow bowl, just large enough to dip glass rim.

• Dip rim of a chilled martini glass into the chocolate shell. Dip into cocoa and powdered sugar. Place candy kiss in glass. Strain the vodka mixture into prepared glass.

Makes 1 serving.

Traditional "Southern Sweet Tea"

A tall glass of iced "sweet tea" is the ultimate way of saying "Welcome to the South!"

6	cups water	1-1½ cups sugar	
4	family-size tea bags		

• Bring 6 cups water to a boil in a saucepan; add tea bags. Boil 1 minute and remove from heat. Cover and steep for 10 minutes. Remove tea bags, squeezing gently.

• Add sugar, stirring until dissolved. Pour into a 1-gallon pitcher, and add enough water to fill pitcher. Serve over ice.

Makes 1 gallon.

Junior League Iced Tea

Add a thin lemon slice to each glass for a cooling refreshment.

5	family-size tea bags	1	(6-ounce) can frozen lemonade, undiluted
3	cups boiling water		
1	cup sugar	2½	cups pineapple juice
2	quarts cold water		Lemon slices

- Place tea bags in a large pitcher or gallon jug; add boiling water. Set aside and let steep for 15 minutes.

- Remove tea bags and add sugar, stirring until dissolved. Stir in cold water, lemonade, and pineapple juice. Cover and freeze, stirring occasionally, until almost frozen. Serve slushy.

Makes about 1 gallon.

Strawberry Watermelon Lemonade

1	(6-pound) watermelon, seeded and cut into chunks	1	(12-ounce) can frozen lemonade, thawed
2	pints strawberries, hulled	¾	cup fresh lemon juice
½	cup sugar		Garnish: fresh lemon slices

- Purée watermelon by batches in food processor until smooth; strain through a sieve into large bowl or 2-quart pitcher.

- Process strawberries with sugar until smooth.

- Add strawberry purée, lemonade concentrate, and lemon juice to watermelon juice. Refrigerate until serving. Serve over ice and garnish with lemon slices.

Makes 8 servings.

Sparkling Hibiscus Tea

4 cups boiling water

8 (regular size) hibiscus or Red Zinger tea bags

1 cup sugar or honey

1 (25.4-ounce) bottle sparkling cider, chilled

2-3 fresh lemons

• Pour boiling water over tea bags in large container and let steep for 10 minutes; remove tea bags. Stir in sugar or honey while tea is hot.

• Refrigerate until ready to serve. Right before serving, add sparkling cider. Serve over ice in tall glasses and garnish with lemon slices.

Serves 6.

Almond Ginger Tea

1 cup boiling water

5 (regular size) orange pekoe tea bags

1 cup sugar

4 cups water

½ cup fresh lemon juice

1 teaspoon vanilla extract

1 teaspoon almond extract

1 quart ginger ale, chilled

• Pour boiling water over tea bags; cover and steep for 5 minutes. Remove tea bags, squeezing gently. Stir in sugar and next 4 ingredients; chill.

• Just before serving, stir in ginger ale. Serve over ice.

Makes 3 quarts.

Old-Fashioned Lemonade

**Frost tall glasses in the freezer to serve
this all-time favorite extra cold!**

4	cups cold water	1	cup fresh lemon juice
¾	cup sugar	1	lemon, sliced into thin rounds

- Bring water to a boil in a medium saucepan. Add sugar, stirring to dissolve. Let cool.

- Pour sugar water mixture and lemon juice into large pitcher, blending well. Serve over ice and garnish with lemon slices.

Makes 6 servings.

Breakfast, Brunch and Breads
Rise and Shine

Breakfast, Brunch and Breads

On the front:
Light of Day
Photograph by *Kathleen McAlhaney*

Blueberry Cream French Toast Casserole

1	loaf Texas toast or egg bread, cut into cubes		Cinnamon
1	(8-ounce) package cream cheese, slightly softened	8	large eggs
1½	cups fresh blueberries, tossed lightly with flour	1½	cups milk
		¾	cup maple syrup
		6	tablespoons butter, melted

- Coat a 13 x 9-inch baking dish with nonstick cooking spray. Layer one half of bread cubes. Cut cream cheese into cubes and scatter over bread. Layer blueberries over cream cheese. Cover blueberries with remaining bread.

- Sprinkle generously with cinnamon.

- Mix remaining ingredients and pour over bread; press bread with spatula to help soak up mixture. Cover and refrigerate overnight.

- Bake at 350° for 45 to 50 minutes.

Makes 8 servings.

Hearty Whole Wheat Pancakes

1	cup whole wheat flour	1	large egg, slightly beaten
½	teaspoon baking soda	1	cup buttermilk
1	teaspoon baking powder	1	tablespoon butter, melted
1¾	teaspoons sugar	¼	cup pecan pieces
⅛	teaspoon salt		

- Sift together flour, soda, baking powder, sugar, and salt.

- Stir together egg, buttermilk, and melted butter.

- Blend flour mixture into egg mixture and stir in pecan pieces.

- Using ¼-cup measuring cup, pour batter onto griddle. Turn when pancakes start to bubble, and remove from griddle when edges start to brown.

Makes 8 to 10 pancakes.

Crème Brûlée French Toast

The perfect beginning for a nice, quiet weekend after a hectic week.

½   cup unsalted butter
1   cup firmly packed light brown
      sugar
2   tablespoons light corn syrup
6   (1-inch) slices country-style
      bread

5   large eggs
1½ cups half-and-half
1   teaspoon vanilla extract
1   teaspoon Grand Marnier or
      other orange-flavored liqueur
¼   teaspoon salt

- Remove crusts from bread, if desired, and set aside.

- Melt butter in a heavy saucepan over medium heat. Add brown sugar and corn syrup, stirring until well blended. Pour into a 13 x 9-inch baking dish. Place bread slices over sugar mixture in a single layer.

- In a mixing bowl, combine eggs, half-and-half, vanilla, liqueur, and salt. Whisk until well blended. Pour over bread. Cover and refrigerate 8 hours or overnight.

- Uncover French toast and let stand to room temperature. Bake at 350° for 30 to 40 minutes or until golden brown.

Makes 6 servings.

Sweet Potato Waffles

*This golden potato, appreciated by Southerners,
makes a wonderfully different breakfast entrée.*

2	cups all-purpose flour	1½	cups milk
1	tablespoon baking powder	¼	cup vegetable oil
1	tablespoon sugar	¾	cup cooked, mashed sweet
1	teaspoon salt		potato (about 1 medium)
¼	teaspoon ground cinnamon	¼	cup chopped walnuts
3	eggs, separated, at room temperature		

- Combine first 5 ingredients; set aside.

- Beat egg yolks in a medium bowl; add milk and oil, mixing well. Stir in sweet potato.

- Add sweet potato mixture to flour mixture, stirring briskly until blended.

- Beat egg whites at high speed of electric mixer until stiff peaks form; fold into batter.

- Pour about ¼ of batter onto a preheated, lightly oiled waffle iron. Sprinkle 1 tablespoon walnuts evenly over batter. Cook about 5 minutes or until done. Repeat procedure with remaining batter and walnuts.

Makes 4 (8-inch) waffles.

The first air fatality in South Carolina occurred when Mrs. Maude Broadwick fell out of a tethered hot air balloon in which she was riding in Buena Vista Park. It was never determined if her fall was caused by her husband or if it was accidental.

Orange-Glazed Coffee Cake

This light and refreshing cake doubles
the flavor and fragrance of fresh orange.

Cake

1	package active dry yeast	½	cup ricotta cheese
¼	cup warm water	1	tablespoon grated orange zest
½	cup warm milk	½	teaspoon salt
½	cup fresh orange juice	1	large egg, lightly beaten
½	cup sugar	3½-4 cups all-purpose flour	

Glaze

1   large egg, lightly beaten

Icing

1	cup powdered sugar	1½-2 tablespoons fresh orange juice	

- In a large bowl, dissolve yeast in warm water. Let stand until foamy, 5 to 10 minutes.

- Stir warm milk, orange juice, sugar, ricotta cheese, orange zest, salt, and egg into yeast mixture.

- Using heavy-duty electric mixer fitted with paddle attachment and set on low speed, beat 2 cups flour into yeast mixture until a wet dough forms. Beat in remaining flour, ½ cup at a time, until a stiff dough forms.

- Turn dough out onto a lightly floured surface and knead until smooth and elastic, 5 to 10 minutes, adding more flour as needed to prevent sticking.

- Place dough in a large greased bowl, turning to coat. Cover loosely with a damp cloth and let rise in a warm place until doubled, about 1½ hours.

- Grease a 10-inch springform pan; set aside.

- Punch down dough. Turn out onto a lightly floured surface and knead for 1 to 2 minutes.

- Divide dough into 3 equal pieces. Roll each piece into a 20-inch-long rope. Braid the ropes together.

- Coil braided dough in prepared pan; tuck ends under. Cover loosely with a damp cloth and let rise in a warm place until almost doubled, 30 minutes.

Orange-Glazed Coffee Cake, continued

- Brush dough with egg glaze.

- Bake at 425° until top of cake is golden brown, 25 to 30 minutes. Turn cake out onto wire rack to cool slightly.

- To prepare icing, in a small bowl, stir together powdered sugar and orange juice until smooth. Spread icing over warm cake. Serve warm.

  Makes 12 servings.

Raspberry Cream Cheese Coffee Cake

3	ounces cream cheese	½	cup raspberry preserves
¼	cup margarine	1	cup sifted powdered sugar
2	cups biscuit baking mix	½	teaspoon vanilla extract
⅓	cup milk	2	tablespoons (or less) milk

- Cut cream cheese and margarine into baking mix in bowl. Add ⅓ cup milk; mix well. Roll or pat into 12 x 8-inch rectangle on waxed paper. Invert onto greased baking sheet; remove waxed paper.

- Spread preserves down the center of dough.

- Make 2½-inch cuts at 1-inch intervals on long sides. Fold strips over filling, alternating sides.

- Bake at 425° for 12 to 15 minutes or until golden brown.

- Combine powdered sugar, vanilla, and milk, adding the milk a little at a time and mixing until smooth. Drizzle over coffee cake.

  Makes 6 to 8 servings.

Rhubarb Coffee Cake

Cake

½	cup margarine		½	teaspoon salt
1¼	cups sugar		1	cup buttermilk
1	egg		1	teaspoon vanilla extract
2	cups all-purpose flour		3	cups fresh or frozen chopped rhubarb
1	teaspoon baking powder			

Topping

1	teaspoon cinnamon		2	tablespoons margarine
½	cup sugar		½	cup chopped pecans

- Cream together margarine and sugar until creamy. Beat in egg.

- Combine flour, baking powder, and salt. Add to creamed mixture, alternating with buttermilk. Fold in vanilla and rhubarb.

- Pour mixture into greased 13 x 9-inch baking pan.

- In a small bowl, combine topping ingredients and sprinkle over batter.

- Bake at 350° for 40 minutes. Serve warm.

Makes 12 to 16 servings.

Farmhouse Sweet Rolls

Sweet Rolls

1	cup sour cream, heated	2	packages active dry yeast
½	butter or margarine, melted	½	cup warm water
½	cup sugar	2	eggs, beaten
1	teaspoon salt	4	cups all-purpose flour

Filling

16	ounces cream cheese, softened	2	teaspoons vanilla extract
¾	cup sugar	½	teaspoon salt
1	egg		

Glaze

2	cups powdered sugar, sifted	2	teaspoons vanilla extract
¼	cup milk		

- Combine sour cream, melted butter, ½ cup sugar, and 1 teaspoon salt in a medium bowl and mix well. Let cool to lukewarm.

- Dissolve yeast in warm water in large bowl. Stir in sour cream mixture. Stir in eggs. Add flour gradually, mixing well after each addition until a soft dough forms. Cover tightly and chill overnight.

- For the filling, combine cream cheese, ¾ cup sugar, 1 egg, 2 teaspoons vanilla, and ½ teaspoon salt in a food processor or mixer bowl. Process until blended and smooth.

- Divide dough into 4 equal portions; knead each portion on a lightly floured surface 4 to 5 times. Roll each portion into a 12 x 8-inch rectangle.

- Spread ¼ of the filling on each rectangle, leaving a ½-inch margin on each side. Roll up, jelly roll style, beginning at long side. Pinch edges and ends to seal. Cut each roll into 1½-inch slices. Place cut side down 2 inches apart on greased baking sheets. Let rise, covered, in a warm place for 1½ hours or until doubled in bulk.

- Bake at 375° for 12 minutes or until golden brown.

- To prepare glaze, mix powdered sugar, milk, and 2 teaspoons vanilla in bowl; drizzle over each roll.

Makes 2½ dozen.

Persimmons are a common fruit in Anderson County. We all know that nothing is more bitter and mouth-puckering than a green (unripe) persimmon, so we wait until after the first frost before we eat them. Something about the cold causes them to ripen.

Heavenly Sweet Potato Biscuits

These are even more delicious when served with pineapple preserves!

2	cups self-rising flour	1	cup cooked, mashed sweet potato
¼	cup sugar		
¼	teaspoon ground cinnamon	⅓	cup milk
3	tablespoons shortening	1	tablespoon butter or margarine, melted
2	tablespoons butter, softened		

- **Combine first 3 ingredients; cut in shortening and butter with pastry blender until mixture resembles coarse meal.**

- **Add potato and milk, stirring until dry ingredients are moistened and mixing until smooth.**

- **Drop by tablespoonful onto greased baking sheet.**

- **Bake at 425° for 10 to 12 minutes. Remove from oven and brush with melted butter.**

Makes 2 dozen.

Batter may be stored up to one week, tightly covered, in refrigerator.

Chocolate Banana Muffins

An excellent after-school snack.

2	very ripe bananas	½	cup cocoa powder, sifted
1	teaspoon vanilla	¾	cup sugar
2	eggs	1½	teaspoons baking powder
¾	cup non-fat buttermilk	¼	teaspoon baking soda
1	cup all-purpose flour		Pinch of salt

- **Purée bananas and vanilla in food processor. Transfer to a mixing bowl and whisk in eggs and buttermilk just until combined. Set aside.**

- **In large bowl, whisk dry ingredients together. Stir in banana mixture and spoon into greased muffin tins. (Paper liners are not recommended for this recipe because they tend to stick.)**

- **Bake at 350° for about 35 minutes or until a wooden pick inserted in center of muffin comes out clean. Remove from pan immediately.**

Makes 1 dozen.

Divine Scones

This wonderful recipe lets you create your favorite
scone to enjoy with a morning cup of coffee.

2	cups sifted all-purpose flour
½	teaspoon salt
1	tablespoon baking powder
4	tablespoons sugar, divided
5	tablespoons plus 1 teaspoon unsalted butter, at room temperature
1	large egg, beaten
½	cup plus 2 tablespoons heavy whipping cream

¾ cup of any of the following: dried currants, dried cranberries, dried cherries, chopped dried apricots, dried strawberries, dried blueberries, seedless raisins, semi-sweet chocolate pieces, chopped pecans, or chopped walnuts

- Combine flour, salt, baking powder, and 2 tablespoons sugar in a large mixing bowl. Cut in butter with a pastry blender until mixture resembles small pebbles. Mix in egg and ½ cup cream. Stir in any ¾-cup combination of the optional ingredients.

- Turn dough out onto lightly floured surface and knead gently. Pat into a 9-inch circle, ½ inch thick, and place on a baking sheet. Using floured knife, cut dough, pie-style, into 12 wedges. (Do not separate wedges.) Brush tops with remaining 2 tablespoons cream and sprinkle with remaining 2 tablespoons sugar. Bake at 400° for 15 minutes or until light brown.

Makes 1 dozen.

½-1 teaspoon ground cinnamon or nutmeg, or ½-¾ teaspoon maple extract may be used in place of, or in combination with, the listed optional ingredients. Also, in lieu of brushing tops with cream and sprinkling with sugar, a simple icing may be prepared by mixing ½ cup powdered sugar and 2-3 teaspoons milk, and drizzled over warm scones.

Market Street received its name from the meat market that was held at that corner of Main Street during the 1890's.

Cheddar Dinner Scones

2	cups all-purpose flour
2	tablespoons sugar
1	tablespoon baking powder
½	teaspoon salt
6	tablespoons cold margarine or butter (¾ stick), cut into small pieces

1	large egg
¾	cup milk
1	cup (4 ounces) shredded extra sharp Cheddar cheese

- In a large bowl, measure flour, sugar, baking powder, and salt. With fingertips, blend margarine or butter into mixture until it resembles fine crumbs.

- In a small bowl, lightly beat egg and milk. Stir egg mixture and cheese into flour mixture just until ingredients are blended.

- Turn dough out onto lightly floured surface. (Dough will be sticky.) Divide dough in half. With lightly floured hands, pat each half into a 5-inch round, about 1 inch high. Place rounds about 3 inches apart on a large greased baking sheet.

- With floured knife, cut each round into 6 wedges. (Do not separate wedges.)

- Bake at 425° for 20 to 25 minutes until golden. Serve scones warm, or remove to wire rack to cool completely. Reheat if desired.

Makes 1 dozen.

A nice complement to these scones is a garlic butter glaze, made by melting 4 tablespoons butter and mixing with ¼ teaspoon garlic salt. Drizzle glaze over hot scones.

Berry Streusel Muffins

¼	cup pecan halves	¼	teaspoon baking soda
¼	cup firmly packed brown sugar	¼	teaspoon salt
1	tablespoon all-purpose flour	2	teaspoons grated fresh lemon rind
2	tablespoons butter or margarine	1½	cups fresh or frozen blueberries, strawberries, raspberries, or cranberries
½	cup uncooked regular oats		
2	cups all-purpose flour	1	large egg, lightly beaten
½	cup sugar	¾	cup buttermilk
2	teaspoons baking powder	¼	cup vegetable oil

• Process pecans in a food processor 2 or 3 times until chopped. Add brown sugar and 1 tablespoon flour. Process 5 seconds. Add butter; pulse 5 times or until mixture is crumbly. Stir in oats and set aside.

• Combine 2 cups flour and next 5 ingredients in a large bowl; add berries, tossing gently. Make a well in the center of mixture.

• Combine egg, buttermilk, and oil; add flour mixture, stirring just until moistened. Spoon batter into greased muffin pans, filling ⅔ full; sprinkle with oat mixture.

• Bake at 400° for 15 to 20 minutes or until golden. Remove from pans immediately and transfer to wire racks to cool.

Makes 1 dozen.

Add old-fashioned sparkle to your holiday decorations using Granny's secret: Brush pieces of fruit with egg white and roll them in fine sugar. Displayed with candles, sugared fruit will make a lovely centerpiece for a special holiday celebration.

Sweet Butters

Sweet butters are delicious to serve with your favorite muffins, scones, or waffles, and they make a lovely gift to go along with a loaf of homemade bread. They may be stored, tightly covered, in the refrigerator, up to 3 weeks.

Beat 1 cup (2 sticks) of softened butter along with one of the following:

• Almond Butter - 1 teaspoon pure almond extract, and 2 tablespoons finely chopped almonds.

• Raspberry Butter - 1 cup raspberries, crushed, and 2 tablespoons sugar. (May also use ½ cup raspberry or strawberry jam.)

• Orange Butter - 2 tablespoons orange juice and 2 teaspoons grated orange peel.

• Cinnamon Butter - 2 tablespoons brown sugar and 2 teaspoons cinnamon.

• Honey Pecan Butter - 4 tablespoons honey. Stir in ⅔ cup pecans that have been toasted in a shallow pan for 6 to 8 minutes and then finely chopped.

Makes 1 cup.

Strawberry-Orange Muffins

Serve with orange or strawberry butter and strawberry jam.

1¼	cups halved ripe strawberries	1¼	cups sugar
3	tablespoons butter or margarine, melted	1	teaspoon baking powder
2	teaspoons grated orange rind	½	teaspoon salt
2	large eggs		Non-stick cooking spray
1½	cups all-purpose flour	2	teaspoons sugar

• Combine first 4 ingredients in a blender, and process just until blended.

• In a large bowl, combine flour, sugar, baking powder, and salt. Add strawberry mixture to flour mixture, stirring just until moist.

• Coat 12 muffin cups with cooking spray and spoon in batter. Sprinkle muffins with 2 teaspoons sugar.

• Bake at 400° for 20 minutes or until muffins spring back when touched lightly in the center. Remove from pan immediately and serve.

Makes 1 dozen.

Coconut Apple Muffins

After an autumn drive to the mountains, save a few apples to make these hearty muffins.

1	cup all-purpose flour	¼	cup vegetable oil
1	teaspoon baking soda	2	cups peeled, cored, and chopped Granny Smith, or other tart apples
1	teaspoon ground cinnamon		
1	teaspoon ground nutmeg	1	cup pecans or walnuts, chopped
½	teaspoon salt		
1	large egg	½	cup shredded coconut
¾	cup sugar		

• Combine flour and next 4 ingredients in a large bowl.

• In another bowl, combine egg, sugar, and oil; add to dry ingredients, stirring just until moistened. Fold in apples, nuts, and coconut. Spoon batter into a greased muffin pan, filling to three fourths full. Bake at 350° for 30 minutes. Cool in pan for 5 to 10 minutes before turning out.

Makes 1 dozen.

Zucchini Pineapple Bread

A wonderful way to welcome a new neighbor.

3	cups all-purpose flour	3	eggs, beaten
¾	teaspoon salt	1	cup vegetable oil
1	teaspoon baking soda	2	cups coarsely shredded zucchini
2	cups sugar	1	(8-ounce) can crushed pineapple, drained
1	teaspoon ground cinnamon		
1	teaspoon ground nutmeg	2	teaspoons vanilla extract
1	cup chopped pecans or walnuts		

- Combine first 6 ingredients; stir in pecans.

- Combine remaining ingredients; add to flour mixture, stirring just until dry ingredients are moistened.

- Spoon batter into 2 greased and floured 8½ x 4½ x 3-inch loaf pans.

- Bake at 350° for 1 hour and 10 minutes or until a wooden pick inserted in center comes out clean. Cool in pans 10 minutes; remove from pans and let cool on wire racks.

Makes 2 loaves.

Breakfast Burritos

1	pound ground sausage	8	eggs
1	small green pepper, quartered and sliced	8	flour tortillas
			Condiments: grated Cheddar cheese, salsa, sour cream
1	small onion, quartered		
1	pint fresh mushrooms, sliced		

- In a large skillet, brown sausage; drain and remove sausage to set aside.

- In same skillet, lightly sauté peppers, onions, and mushrooms; remove vegetables and set aside.

- Scramble eggs to desired hardness. Add in sausage, peppers, onions, and mushrooms; stir to mix. Spoon into tortillas and serve with condiments.

Makes 8 servings.

Sausage-Cheddar Muffins

Great for a breakfast on the run!

½   pound ground pork sausage
2   cups all-purpose flour
2   tablespoons sugar
1   tablespoon baking powder
¼   teaspoon salt
1   cup milk

1   large egg, lightly beaten
¼   cup butter or margarine, melted
½   cup (2 ounces) shredded sharp Cheddar cheese
    Non-stick cooking spray

- Brown sausage in a large skillet, stirring until crumbly; drain and set aside.

- Combine flour and next 3 ingredients; make a well in the center of mixture.

- Combine milk, egg, and butter; add to dry mixture, stirring just until moistened. Stir in sausage and cheese.

- Place paper baking cups in muffin pans and coat lightly with cooking spray. Spoon batter into cups, filling ⅔ full.

- Bake at 375° for 20 minutes or until golden. Remove from pans immediately.

Makes 1 dozen.

Crabmeat and Almond Quesadillas

Served with a salad, this is a wonderful for a brunch.

10	ounces lump crabmeat, drained	¼	teaspoon curry powder
½	cup sliced almonds, toasted	1	(2-ounce) jar diced pimento, drained
⅓	cup minced green onions	8	ounces Brie cheese
¼	cup mayonnaise	10	(8-inch) flour tortillas
½	teaspoon hot pepper sauce		Non-stick cooking spray

• In a medium bowl, combine first 7 ingredients; stir well. Spoon and evenly spread over 5 tortillas.

• Remove rind from cheese; cut cheese into thin slices, and arrange slices evenly over crabmeat mixture, and top with remaining tortillas.

• Coat a large nonstick skillet with cooking spray; place over medium-high heat until hot. Add quesadillas, one at a time, and cook 1 to 2 minutes on each side, or until lightly browned and cheese melts. Cut each quesadilla into 4 wedges and serve immediately.

Makes 20 wedges.

South Carolina is home to several colleges and universities with football teams. The two largest are Clemson University and the University of South Carolina. Their annual rivalry is now renewed as the last game of each team's season. The game was traditionally held for many years on "Big Thursday" during the week of the State Fair in Columbia. "Big Thursday" ended in the late 1950s to allow Clemson the chance to host the game on its home field every other year.

Fontienelle Breakfast Casserole

1	large baguette (about ¾ pound)	1	quart milk
½	stick butter, melted	½	teaspoon salt
2	onions, chopped		Ground black pepper
1	tablespoon olive oil	6	cups spinach leaves (about 1 bunch), coarsely chopped
4	eggs	¾	pound Fontienelle cheese (or Edam), grated
1	pound Italian sausage, cooked and drained		

- Diagonally cut baguette crosswise into ¾-inch-thick slices and brush both sides with melted butter. Toast on a baking sheet under broiler 3 inches from heat until golden, about 30 seconds on each side.

- Sauté onions in oil in a 12-inch nonstick skillet over medium-high heat, stirring occasionally until golden.

- Whisk eggs in a large bowl and whisk in milk, salt, and pepper to taste. Add toasted bread and toss gently. Transfer bread as saturated to a shallow 3-quart casserole, slightly overlapping slices. Add any remaining egg mixture.

- Tuck sausage and spinach between slices, reserving a little sausage to sprinkle over top. Sprinkle cheese over casserole, lifting slices with a spatula to allow some to fall between them. Sprinkle reserved sausage over casserole and bake in middle of oven at 350° for 45 minutes to 1 hour, or until puffed and casserole is set in middle and edges are golden.

Makes 6 servings.

Tomato Cheese Pudding

3	cups coarse bread crumbs, freshly made with untoasted bread	1½	cups milk
2	onions, finely chopped	4	eggs, beaten
	Salt and pepper	¼	teaspoon Worcestershire sauce
12	ounces sharp Cheddar cheese, grated and divided	2	teaspoons prepared mustard
		3	tomatoes, sliced
		3	tablespoons butter

- Combine bread crumbs, onions, salt, pepper, and 8 ounces cheese. Spread in bottom of greased 11 x 8½-inch baking dish.

- Combine milk, eggs, Worcestershire, and mustard, mixing well. Pour over breadcrumb mixture.

- Sprinkle remaining 4 ounces cheese on top. Cover with sliced tomatoes. Sprinkle with salt and pepper. Cut butter into small pieces and dot over top.

- Bake at 300° for about 1 hour, until firm.

Makes 6 servings.

Good Morning Grits

4	cups water	½	cup butter or margarine
1	teaspoon salt	1	teaspoon ground black pepper
2	garlic cloves, pressed	1	teaspoon Worcestershire sauce
1	cup uncooked regular grits	¼	teaspoon hot sauce
1	(12-ounce) block sharp Cheddar cheese, grated	3	large eggs, lightly beaten Paprika

- Bring first 3 ingredients to a boil in a large saucepan; gradually stir in grits. Return to a boil; reduce heat, and simmer, stirring occasionally, 15 minutes or until thickened.

- Add cheese and next 4 ingredients, stirring until cheese melts. Remove from heat; let stand 10 minutes.

- Stir in eggs, and pour into a lightly greased 11 x 7-inch baking dish. Sprinkle with paprika.

- Bake at 350° for 1 hour or until set.

Makes 8 to 10 servings.

"In 1897 Anderson, SC reportedly became the first in the nation and possibly the world to transmit high-voltage electricity using alternating current without using step-down transformers." Direct quote from "Electric World", April 1998 Vol. 212 No.4.

Many foreigners to the South often ask, "What are grits?" They are small ground grains of corn. There are really two types of grits – "corn" grits and "hominy" grits. Most Southerners prefer the hominy grits and eat them boiled with water to make a mush with butter and salt. Traditionally grits have been a breakfast food, but now they are often a side dish enhanced with garlic, cheese and various spices.

Carolina Shrimp and Grits

The Southern breakfast at its best!

Grits

2	cups whole milk	¼	teaspoon hot sauce
1	cup water	¾	teaspoon salt
1	cup quick cooking grits	1	cup shredded sharp Cheddar cheese
¾	teaspoon concentrated chopped garlic	4	tablespoons butter

Shrimp

¼	cup cooking sherry	1½	pounds peeled large raw shrimp, soaked for 1 hour in 1½ cups lemon juice
5	tablespoons butter		
2	tablespoons dried parsley		
¾	teaspoon concentrated chopped garlic		

- Bring milk and water to a boil; add grits and simmer for 5 minutes. Mix in garlic, hot sauce, salt, cheese, and butter.

- While grits are simmering, prepare shrimp. In a large skillet, combine and heat cooking sherry, butter, parsley, and garlic.

- Discard lemon juice and add shrimp to skillet. Sauté until shrimp turn pink and opaque. Add all contents of skillet to grits. Serve immediately.

Makes 6 servings.

Denver Omelet Scrambler

1	(20-ounce) package refrigerated hash browns	10	ounces cooked ham, cut into small pieces
1⅓	cups shredded Cheddar cheese, divided	1	cup chopped bell pepper
6	eggs	½	cup chopped onion
¼	cup milk		Sour Cream
			Salsa

- **In a large nonstick skillet, prepare hash browns according to package directions. After turning once, sprinkle ⅔ cup of cheese over potatoes. Transfer to platter.**

- **In a mixing bowl, beat together eggs and milk. Add ham, chopped pepper, onion and remaining ⅔ cup cheese. Transfer to skillet.**

- **Cook over medium heat, stirring occasionally, 5 minutes or until eggs are set but still moist. Spoon egg mixture over center of hash browns. Serve with sour cream and salsa.**

Makes 4 to 6 servings.

Bacon and Egg Quiche

1	(9-inch) pie shell	4	eggs
½	pound bacon	1½	cups half-and-half
½	cup grated Monterey Jack cheese	¼-½	teaspoon salt
½	cup grated Cheddar cheese	¼-½	teaspoon ground black pepper

- **Partially bake pie shell at 400° for 8 to 10 minutes.**

- **Fry bacon until crisp; crumble into bottom of pie shell.**

- **Mix cheeses together and sprinkle over bacon.**

- **In a medium mixing bowl, beat eggs. Add half-and-half, salt, and pepper, beating well. Pour mixture over cheese and bacon.**

- **Bake at 325° for 50 to 60 minutes or until set.**

Makes 6 servings.

Cheese and Tomato Quiche

1	(9-inch) pie shell	1	cup chopped green onion
2	large tomatoes, chopped	3	slices provolone cheese
3	tablespoons flour	2	eggs
	Salt and pepper	1	cup milk
2	teaspoons vegetable oil	1	cup shredded Cheddar cheese
½	cup sliced black olives		

- Bake pie shell at 425° for 8 minutes. Let cool.

- Dip tomatoes in flour, salt, and pepper. Sauté in vegetable oil.

- Layer olives and green onion in bottom of pie shell. Layer provolone cheese. Place sautéed tomatoes over cheese.

- Beat eggs; add milk and Cheddar cheese. Place pie shell on baking sheet and pour egg mixture over tomatoes. (Shell will be very full.)

- Bake at 375° for 45 minutes.

Makes 6 to 8 servings.

Egg and Artichoke Bake

1	bunch green onions	4	eggs, beaten
2	(6½-ounce) jars marinated artichoke hearts, drained	8	ounces medium Cheddar cheese, grated
1	clove garlic, minced	6	saltine crackers, crushed

- Finely mince onions using half of the tops as well.

- Cut artichokes into thirds.

- Combine all ingredients. Pour into 9-inch square baking dish.

- Bake at 350° for 40 minutes.

Makes 4 servings.

This dish may be prepared a day ahead and refrigerated, or frozen. To serve, thaw and reheat 15 to 20 minutes.

Eggs Gone Salsa!

5	eggs	½	teaspoon salt
½	stick butter, melted	1	(8-ounce) package shredded Monterey Jack cheese
¼	cup flour		Sour Cream
½	teaspoon baking powder		Salsa
1	cup lowfat cottage cheese		
1	(4-ounce) can diced chilies, drained		

- Whisk eggs in large bowl. Whisk in butter, flour, baking powder, cottage cheese, chilies, and salt. Fold in Monterey Jack cheese.

- Pour mixture into 13 x 9-inch glass baking dish.

- Bake at 350° for 40 to 45 minutes. Serve with sour cream and salsa.

Makes 6 servings.

Tomato-Pesto Tart

Very easy and good.

½	(15-ounce) package refrigerated pie crusts	¼	cup Parmesan cheese
2	cups shredded mozzarella cheese, divided	2-3	tablespoons basil pesto
5	tomato slices	½	teaspoon pepper
½	cup mayonnaise	2	tablespoons chopped fresh basil
			Salt

- Unfold pie crust onto a lightly greased baking sheet; roll into 12-inch circle. Brush outer 1-inch edge of crust with water. Fold edges up and crimp. Prick bottom with fork.

- Bake crust at 425° for 8 to 10 minutes. Remove from oven and sprinkle with 1 cup mozzarella cheese; let cool 15 minutes.

- Arrange tomato slices over cheese.

- Stir remaining 1 cup mozzarella cheese, mayonnaise, and next 3 ingredients together and spread over tomato slices.

- Bake at 375° for 20 to 25 minutes. Remove from oven and sprinkle with fresh basil, and salt to taste.

Makes 4 servings.

Notes

Favorite Yeast Rolls

These rolls are worth the time and effort to prepare.

¾	cup buttermilk	2	packages active dry yeast
¾	cup oil	1	tablespoon sugar
⅔	cup sugar	¼	cup lukewarm water
1	teaspoon salt	9-10	cups all-purpose flour
1	egg, beaten	½	cup butter, melted
1	teaspoon baking soda		

- Scald buttermilk with oil, ⅔ cup sugar, and salt in saucepan. Pour into large bowl; stir until lukewarm. Stir in egg and baking soda.

- Dissolve yeast and 1 tablespoon sugar in ¼ cup lukewarm water in mug. Place mug in pan of hot water. Let stand until yeast rises to top of mug. Add to buttermilk mixture; mix well.

- Add flour, 1 cup at a time, mixing well after each addition.

- Knead on floured surface for 10 minutes or until smooth and elastic. Place in greased bowl, turning to coat surface. Let rise for 2 hours or until doubled in bulk.

- Knead for several minutes. Shape into small balls; dip balls into melted butter; arrange 3 balls in each greased muffin cup. Let rise for 1½ hours.

- Bake at 350° for 15 minutes or until golden brown.

Makes 2 dozen.

Buttery-Rich Crescent Rolls

1	package active dry yeast	¼	cup butter, softened
¼	cup warm water	1	egg, beaten
¼	cup sugar	¾	cup milk, scalded
1	teaspoon salt	3	cups all-purpose flour

- Dissolve yeast in warm water in a large bowl. Stir in sugar, salt, butter, and egg. Add milk, stirring well. Add flour; stir well. Cover bowl with towel and let rise in a warm place until doubled in bulk.

- Punch dough down and turn out onto lightly floured surface. Divide dough in half; set aside one half. Roll remaining half into a circle about 10 inches in diameter and ¼ inch in thickness. Cut into 8 wedges. Roll each wedge tightly, beginning at wide end. Seal points. Place on greased baking sheet with ending point underneath. Curve into crescent shape. Repeat procedure with remaining dough. Cover roll with towel and let rise until doubled in bulk, about 45 minutes.

- Bake at 400° for 8 to 10 minutes or until lightly browned.

Makes 16.

Parmesan Bacon Bread

3	(10-ounce) cans refrigerated biscuits, quartered	1	onion, finely chopped
1	stick butter, melted	½	pound bacon, fried crisp and crumbled
1	large bell pepper, finely chopped	1	cup Parmesan cheese

- Dip one can quartered biscuits in melted butter and layer in bottom of Bundt pan. Sprinkle half each of pepper, onion, bacon, and Parmesan cheese. Repeat with one more can of can of biscuits, quartered and dipped in butter, and remainder of pepper, onion, bacon, and Parmesan cheese. Top with third can of biscuits, quartered and dipped in butter.

- Bake at 350° for 45 minutes. Invert onto serving platter; serve immediately.

Makes 1 loaf.

Try this spectacular Italian bread dip! Using a spice or coffee grinder, grind together 1 teaspoon of salt along with 1 tablespoon of each of the following: crushed red pepper, crushed black pepper, dried oregano, dried rosemary, dried basil, dried parsley, garlic powder, and minced garlic. To serve, sprinkle 2 teaspoons of herb mixture onto a small plate. Pour a thin layer of olive oil on top, and serve with warm French bread. It is perfect for any occasion and can be doubled or tripled to accommodate a crowd.

Hawaiian Bubble Bread

2	packages dry yeast	5¼	cups bread flour, divided
1	teaspoon sugar	1	teaspoon salt
1	cup warm water		Nonstick cooking spray
1	cup sliced ripe bananas	¼	cup cream of coconut
½	cup pineapple-orange-banana juice concentrate, undiluted	2	tablespoons pineapple-orange-banana juice concentrate, undiluted
¼	cup honey		
2	tablespoons margarine, melted	½	cup sifted powdered sugar
2	drops yellow food coloring (optional)		

- Dissolve yeast and sugar in warm water; let stand 5 minutes.

- Combine banana and next 4 ingredients in a blender; process until smooth and set aside.

- Combine 2 cups flour and salt in large bowl; stir well. Add yeast mixture and banana mixture, stirring until well blended. Add 2¾ cups flour, stirring to form a soft dough.

- Turn dough out onto lightly floured surface; knead until smooth and elastic, about 8 minutes. Add enough of the remaining flour, 1 tablespoon at a time, to prevent dough from sticking to hands.

- Place dough in a large bowl coated with cooking spray, turning to coat top. Cover and let rise in a warm place (85°), free from drafts, 1½ hours or until doubled in bulk. Punch dough down; turn out onto lightly floured surface, and let rest for 5 minutes. Form the dough into 1½-inch balls (about 30 balls) on lightly floured surface. Layer balls in a 10-inch tube pan coated with cooking spray; set aside.

- Combine cream of coconut and 2 tablespoons juice in a bowl; stir well. Pour 3 tablespoons juice mixture over dough, and set remaining juice mixture aside. Cover dough, and let rise 1½ hours or until doubled in bulk.

- Uncover dough, and bake at 350° for 30 minutes or until loaf sounds hollow when tapped. Let cool in pan 20 minutes. Remove from pan; place on wire rack.

- Stir powdered sugar into remaining juice mixture; drizzle over top of warm bread.

  Makes 1 loaf, 26 servings.

Cheddar Onion Twist

2	cups finely chopped onion	2	cups (8 ounces) shredded sharp Cheddar cheese
1	teaspoon dried whole basil		
1	teaspoon dried whole oregano	2	tablespoons sugar
¼	cup unsalted butter, melted	2	teaspoons salt
6	cups bread flour, divided	2	tablespoons bread flour
2	packages active dry yeast	1	egg, lightly beaten
2	cups very warm whole milk	1	teaspoon water

- Sauté onion, basil, and oregano in butter in skillet over medium heat, cooking until onion is tender. Set aside.

- Combine 2 cups flour and yeast, stirring to blend. Add milk, beating on low speed of electric mixer. Beat 2 minutes on medium speed. Add onion mixture, cheese, sugar, and salt. Stir in enough of the remaining 4 cups flour to make a soft dough.

- Sprinkle 2 tablespoons flour over work surface. Turn dough out; knead until smooth and elastic. Place in a greased bowl, turning to grease top. Cover and let rise in a warm place 20 minutes or until doubled.

- Punch dough down; divide in half. Divide each half into 3 equal portions. Roll each portion into a 16-inch rope. Braid 3 ropes together on a greased baking sheet, pinching ends to seal; tuck ends under. Repeat procedure with remaining ropes.

- Cover and let rise in a warm place 20 minutes or until doubled. Combine egg and water; brush over loaves.

- Bake at 350° for 35 minutes or until loaves sound hollow when tapped. Cover with aluminum foil the last 15 minutes of baking to prevent over-browning, if necessary.

Makes 2 loaves.

Be a Spooner

To make sure your bread is tender, measure flour the same way test kitchens do: Use the correct size dry measuring cup, and stir the flour in the container to loosen it before measuring. Spoon flour into cup, and level it with a flat metal spatula.

Spinach and Cheese Bread

A great snack, appetizer, or side item for a main course soup or salad.

1	(10-ounce) package frozen chopped spinach, thawed, squeezed dry
1	large egg, lightly beaten
2	tablespoons milk
1	tablespoon Dijon mustard
1	teaspoon garlic salt
1	cup grated mozzarella cheese (about 3 ounces)
1	cup grated Cheddar cheese (about 3 ounces)
⅓	cup grated Parmesan cheese (about 1 ounce)
¼	cup fresh white breadcrumbs
1	(11-ounce) tube refrigerated crusty French bread dough

- In a medium bowl, mix spinach, beaten egg, milk, mustard, and garlic salt. Mix in mozzarella cheese, Cheddar cheese, Parmesan cheese, and breadcrumbs.

- Unroll dough on lightly floured surface. Roll out dough to 13-inch square. Cut dough in half, forming 2 (13 x 6½-inch) rectangles. Spoon half of filling in narrow strip lengthwise down center of each rectangle, leaving about ½-inch border on short sides. Fold 1 long side of each rectangle over filling; fold over second long side of each rectangle, enclosing filling completely and overlapping first side slightly. Seal seam of each loaf. Seal short ends. Arrange loaves, seam side down, on heavily buttered baking sheet. Using small sharp knife, cut crosswise slits at 1-inch intervals through top of dough.

- Bake at 375° for about 25 minutes or until golden brown. Run metal spatula under loaves to loosen. Transfer to wire rack and cool 15 minutes. Serve warm or at room temperature.

Makes 2 loaves.

Stone-Baked Focaccia Bread

1 (10-ounce) refrigerated pizza
    crust
2 cloves garlic, pressed
1 cup grated Parmesan cheese
2 cups shredded mozzarella
    cheese

2 teaspoons dried oregano
2 teaspoons dried basil
2 teaspoons dried red pepper
    flakes
2 plum tomatoes, thinly sliced

- Spread pizza crust onto baking stone.

- Mix together garlic and next 5 ingredients; spread over pizza crust. Top with tomato slices.

- Bake at 375° for 30 minutes. Remove from oven and cut into desired serving-size pieces. Serve hot.

Makes 6 to 8 servings.

This bread also makes a great appetizer. Just cut into smaller pieces.

Sour Cream Corn Sticks

3 large eggs, lightly beaten
1 cup self-rising cornmeal
1 (8¾-ounce) can cream style corn

1 (8-ounce) carton sour cream
¼ cup vegetable oil

- Heat lightly greased cast iron corn stick pans in a 400° oven for 5 minutes.

- Combine all ingredients, stirring just until cornmeal is moistened.

- Remove pans from oven; spoon batter into hot pans.

- Bake at 400° for 16 to 18 minutes or until golden.

Makes 16 sticks.

Southern corn bread is subdivided into a number of categories: the most commonly served type is the cake or "pone" of corn bread which is baked in a pan, dish, or pie plate and then cut into servings. There is also the fried "batter cake", usually served for breakfast – "country-style"! The more elegant category includes the deep-dish "spoon breads" a long-time favorite of many Southerners. Muffins, sticks, and gems are also part of the corn bread line-up. The combinations of cornmeal and hominy, and cornmeal and flour go on and on!

Mexican Corn Bread Casserole

This is a great do-ahead dish since it freezes well.

2	large onions, chopped	1	(1-pound) package cornmeal muffin mix
6	tablespoons butter	1	cup sour cream
2	eggs	2	cups (8 ounces) shredded sharp Cheddar cheese
2	tablespoons milk		
2	(17-ounce) cans cream style corn		

- Sauté onion in butter and set aside.

- In mixing bowl, blend eggs and milk. Add corn and muffin mix; mix well. Spread corn bread batter into buttered 13 x 9-inch baking dish.

- Spoon sautéed onion (and green chilies and pimento, if desired) over top of batter. Spread sour cream over onions and sprinkle cheese on top.

- Bake at 425° for 35 minutes or until puffed and golden. Let stand 10 minutes before cutting into squares.

Makes 16 servings.

Salads

Sparkling Delights

Salads

On the front:
Poppy Field
Photograph by *Dr. Mark Hopkins*

Salad Athena

2	bunches green leaf lettuce, washed and torn into pieces	⅔	cup pimento-stuffed green olives, sliced
2	sweet red peppers, sliced into strips	⅔	cup pitted black olives, sliced
1	large green bell pepper, sliced into strips	16	ounces feta cheese, crumbled
3	ripe firm tomatoes, sliced and quartered	2	teaspoons dried oregano
		1	teaspoon dried basil
½	cup diced green onions	1	large cucumber, sliced
			Balsamic vinegar
			Olive oil

• **Place lettuce, peppers, tomatoes, onions, olives, and feta cheese in a large salad bowl. Sprinkle oregano and basil on top and toss well. Place cucumber slices on top and serve with balsamic vinegar and olive oil or your favorite dressing.**

Makes 8 to 10 servings.

Strawberry-Mango Mesclun Salad

½	cup sugar	8	ounces strawberries, quartered
¾	cup canola or vegetable oil	1	large mango, peeled, pitted, and cubed
⅓	cup balsamic vinegar	½	cup chopped onion
1	teaspoon salt	1	cup slivered almonds, lightly toasted
8	cups mesclun or gourmet mixed salad greens		
2	cups sweetened dried cranberries		

• **In a cruet or jar, combine sugar, oil, vinegar, and salt. Cover tightly and shake vigorously.**

• **In a large salad bowl, combine greens, cranberries, strawberries, mango, and onion; toss well to mix. To serve, toss with enough dressing to coat; sprinkle with almonds.**

Makes 6 to 8 servings.

Figs are a common food in Anderson County. You can mix stewed figs with strawberry flavored jell-o and make "mock strawberry jam". The seeds from the figs mimic the seeds of the strawberries and it's virtually impossible to tell the difference!

Hearts of Palm and Artichoke Salad with Creamy Herb Dressing

A wonderful play of flavors.

Salad

2	cups romaine lettuce, torn into bite-size pieces	1	(14-ounce) can artichoke hearts, drained and quartered
1	cup iceberg lettuce, torn into bite-size pieces	½	cup grated carrot
1	cup Bibb lettuce, torn into bite-size pieces	2	tablespoons chopped parsley
1	(14-ounce) can hearts of palm, drained and sliced	2	medium tomatoes, diced

Creamy Herb Dressing

6	tablespoons vegetable oil	2	teaspoons Dijon mustard
6	tablespoons tarragon vinegar	½	cup mayonnaise
½	teaspoon ground black pepper	¼	teaspoon dried dill weed
¼	teaspoon garlic salt	1	teaspoon sugar

- **Combine lettuce, hearts of palm, artichokes, carrot, parsley, and tomatoes in a large bowl. Chill until ready to serve.**

- **Combine all dressing ingredients and mix well. Chill. Just before serving add dressing to salad mixture, and toss well.**

Makes 6 servings.

Mesclun Salad with Walnut-Crusted Goat Cheese Rounds

This is salad sophistication!

Dijon Vinaigrette

1½	teaspoons minced shallots	¼	teaspoon sugar
1½	teaspoons Dijon mustard	¼	teaspoon salt
4	teaspoons red wine vinegar	⅛	teaspoon freshly ground black pepper
1	tablespoon chopped mixture of any of the following herbs: chives, oregano, basil, marjoram, and thyme	1	tablespoon olive oil
		1	tablespoon walnut oil

Salad

4	ounces goat cheese	6	cups packed mesclun or gourmet salad greens
1	egg white, lightly beaten		
½	cup finely chopped walnuts, lightly toasted		

- To prepare vinaigrette, combine shallots, Dijon mustard, vinegar, herbs, sugar, salt, and pepper in a small nonmetallic bowl; whisk until well mixed. Gradually whisk in oils. Chill until ready to serve.

- Shape the goat cheese into 4 (1½-inch) rounds. Dip rounds into egg white and then into walnuts, pressing the walnuts gently to coat well. Place on baking sheet. Bake at 425° for 4 to 5 minutes or until just warm.

- Toss the salad greens with the vinaigrette in a large bowl, coating well. Divide greens evenly among 4 salad plates; top each with a round of goat cheese. Serve immediately.

Makes 4 servings.

Life in the Electric City has not been without its hazards. On November 14, 1931, the Anderson Independant noted that "several pedestrians have fallen recently because citizens have either forgotten or were ignoring the law against throwing banana peels on the sidewalks."

Spinach Salad
with Hot Citrus Dressing

A delightful blend of tastes and textures.

Salad

2	pounds fresh spinach, washed and patted dry, with stems removed		3	ounces goat cheese, crumbled
4	oranges, peeled and sectioned		1	cup sweetened dried cranberries
1	large purple onion, thinly sliced and separated into rings		½	cup chopped pecans, toasted

Hot Citrus Dressing

1	(6-ounce) can frozen orange juice concentrate, thawed		1	tablespoon grated orange rind
1	small onion, diced		1	teaspoon dry mustard
⅓	cup red wine vinegar		1	teaspoon hot pepper sauce
1	cup firmly packed light brown sugar		1	cup peanut oil

- **Arrange spinach and next 5 ingredients on salad plates.**

- **In a blender, combine orange juice, onion, and vinegar; process until smooth. Add brown sugar, orange rind, mustard, and hot pepper sauce; process until smooth. Turn blender on high and add oil in a slow, steady stream; process until well blended. Pour mixture into a medium size non-aluminum saucepan and cook over medium heat for 10 minutes. Drizzle hot dressing over salads and serve immediately.**

Makes 8 servings.

For variation, blue cheese may be substituted for goat cheese, and strawberries may be used in place of cranberries.

Frosted Cranberry Salad

A holiday tradition. It's not only delicious, but pretty, too!

1	(15¼-ounce) can crushed pineapple in syrup	1	(8-ounce) frozen nondairy whipped topping, thawed
2	(3-ounce) packages lemon gelatin	1	(8-ounce) package cream cheese, softened
7	ounces ginger ale	½	cup chopped pecans
1	(1-pound) can plain jellied cranberry sauce	1	tablespoon butter

- Drain pineapple and set aside, reserving syrup. Add water to syrup to make 1 cup and pour into saucepan; heat to boiling and dissolve gelatin in hot liquid. Transfer to a large bowl and let cool. Slowly and gently stir in ginger ale. Chill until partially set.

- With a wire whisk, gently blend crushed pineapple and cranberry sauce together. Fold into gelatin. Turn into a 13 x 9-inch dish and chill until firm.

- Blend whipped topping and cream cheese until smooth; spread over gelatin.

- Toast pecans in butter at 325° for 7 to 10 minutes. Sprinkle on top and chill. To serve, cut into squares and place on red leaf lettuce.

Makes 10 to 12 servings.

Homemade Buttermilk

No buttermilk on hand? Just use regular milk, adding one teaspoon of vinegar to each cup of milk. Let mixture stand for at least 30 minutes before serving.

Tropical Mango Temptation

Simply luscious!

6 cups of any of the following sliced fresh fruits: mango, kiwi, pineapple, nectarine, passion fruit, and honeydew

Juice of 2 oranges, strained

1 large ripe mango

Juice of ½ orange

1 tablespoon kirsch (optional)

1 tablespoon lemon juice

1 tablespoon superfine sugar

1 cup whipping cream

• Drizzle sliced fruit with strained orange juice. Cover with plastic wrap and chill until serving.

• Combine mango, orange juice, kirsch, and lemon juice in a blender and process until puréed. Place mixture into bowl and fold in sugar.

• In a bowl, whip cream until soft peaks form. Fold whipped cream into mango purée, using a knife to create a marbled effect. Serve with fruit.

Serves 6.

Apple Spinach Salad

This salad compliments any meal, with ingredients readily found year round.

Salad

2	large bunches spinach, washed and patted dry, with stems removed	4	Granny Smith apples, peeled and cut into chunks
		1	cup cashew halves
		½	cup golden raisins

Dressing

¾	cup sugar	½	teaspoon garlic powder
½	cup apple cider vinegar	½	teaspoon celery salt
½	cup olive oil		

• In a large serving bowl, combine spinach, apples, cashews, and raisins. Set aside.

• In a small bowl, combine sugar and next 4 ingredients. Mix well. To serve, pour half of the dressing over salad and toss. Remaining dressing may be serve on the side.

Makes 8 to 10 servings.

Dressing may be made several hours ahead of time and refrigerated until ready to serve.

Sunny Fruit Fiesta

1   cantaloupe, halved and seeded
½   honeydew melon, halved and
      seeded
¼   cup superfine or granulated
      sugar
¼   cup fresh lime juice
2   tablespoons fresh lemon juice

1   tablespoon orange-flavored
      liqueur (optional)
1½ teaspoons grated lime peel
1   cup sliced fresh strawberries
1   cup black or red seedless
      grapes

- Using a melon baller, scoop flesh from cantaloupe and honeydew into balls; set aside.

- In a large glass or ceramic bowl, combine the sugar, lime juice, lemon juice, orange liqueur, and lime peel. Stir well to dissolve sugar. Add the melon balls, strawberries, and grapes. Toss gently to combine.

- Cover bowl with plastic wrap and refrigerate for at least 1 hour to blend flavors, gently stirring once or twice. Spoon mixture into serving bowls or hollowed-out melon halves. Serve immediately.

Makes 6 servings.

Rainbow Fruit Salad

This refreshing salad can be made with any fresh fruit that is in season. You may vary the amounts of each fruit according to your preference.

4-6 Granny Smith apples
½ pound red seedless grapes
1 pint strawberries
Blueberries
Cantaloupe
Peaches, pineapple, kiwi, etc.
Bananas
Chopped walnuts or sliced almonds, lightly toasted and cooled
1 (8-ounce) carton vanilla yogurt
1 (8-ounce) can crushed pineapple, undrained

- Slice or cut fruit as desired into large bowl.

- Combine yogurt and pineapple; pour over fruit. Mix well and chill. Add bananas and nuts just before serving.

Serves 6 to 8.

Fruit Terrine with Raspberry Sauce

2	cups cold water, divided	2½	cups sliced peaches
1	cup sugar	1	(14-ounce) package frozen unsweetened raspberries, thawed and undrained
2	envelopes unflavored gelatin		
¾	cup raspberry-flavored liqueur		
1	pint fresh raspberries	¾	cup light corn syrup
1	pint fresh blueberries	¼	cup Grand Marnier

- In a medium saucepan, combine 1½ cups water and sugar; cook over medium heat, stirring occasionally, until sugar dissolves.

- Sprinkle gelatin over remaining ½ cup water in a large bowl; stir and let stand 1 minute. Stir in hot sugar mixture until dissolved. Stir in raspberry liqueur.

- Pour a ½-inch-thick layer of gelatin mixture into 8 x 4-inch loaf pan; chill 30 minutes. Layer raspberries, blueberries, and peaches over gelatin, pouring remaining gelatin over each layer of fruit. Gently shake pan, allowing gelatin to flow into crevices. Cover and chill for 8 hours.

- To prepare sauce, process thawed raspberries in a food processor until puréed; strain and discard seeds. Stir in corn syrup and Grand Marnier.

- To serve, unmold gelatin onto serving dish. Slice and serve with raspberry sauce.

Makes 8 servings.

Cranberry Peach Gelatin Salad

The larger-than-usual yield of this salad makes it a great choice for a dinner party or a pot-luck dinner.

1	(6-ounce) package peach gelatin	1	(6-ounce) package cranberry or raspberry gelatin
4	cups water, divided	1	cup cranberry juice
1	cup orange juice	2	large oranges, peeled
2	(15-ounce) cans sliced peaches, drained	2	cups fresh or frozen cranberries
		1	cup sugar

- Place peach gelatin in a bowl. Bring 2 cups water to a boil and pour over gelatin; stir until dissolved. Add orange juice; mix well. Chill until partially set. Fold in peaches and pour into a 3-quart serving bowl. Chill until firm.

- Place cranberry gelatin in another bowl. Bring remaining water to a boil and pour over gelatin; stir until dissolved. Add cranberry juice; mix well.

- In a blender or food processor, combine oranges, cranberries, and sugar; process until the fruit is coarsely chopped. Add to the cranberry gelatin.

- Carefully spoon cranberry gelatin mixture over the peach mixture. Chill until set.

Makes 14 to 18 servings.

Notes

Cashew Vegetable Slaw

Have fun listening while everyone tries to guess the ingredients in this tasty slaw! You may want to have several copies of the recipe on hand, too!

2	cups shredded zucchini
1½	cups shredded cabbage
½	cup shredded carrots
½	cup thinly sliced radishes
¼	cup sliced green onions
¼	cup chopped fresh parsley
⅓	cup vegetable oil
2	tablespoons whipping cream
3	tablespoons apple cider vinegar
1	tablespoon spicy brown mustard
½	teaspoon salt
1	cup coarsely chopped cashew nuts

- Press zucchini between paper towels until barely moist. Combine zucchini and next 5 ingredients in a large bowl; toss well.

- Combine oil and whipping cream in a small bowl. Beat at high speed of electric mixer until blended. Add vinegar, mustard, and salt; beat well. Pour mixture over vegetables; toss gently to coat. Cover and chill. Just before serving, gently stir in cashews.

Makes 16 to 18 servings.

Cranberry-Walnut Cabbage Slaw

**Make this to go along with sandwiches
made from leftover Thanksgiving turkey!**

¼	cup mayonnaise or salad dressing	2	teaspoons balsamic vinegar
1	tablespoon sweet pickle relish	5	cups shredded green cabbage
1	tablespoon honey mustard	⅓	cup chopped walnuts
1	tablespoon honey	¼	cup finely chopped celery
¼	teaspoon ground white or black pepper	¼	cup finely chopped onion
⅛	teaspoon salt	¼	cup finely chopped sweet red pepper
¼	teaspoon celery seed	¼	cup dried cranberries

- In a small bowl, stir together mayonnaise, pickle relish, honey mustard, honey, pepper, salt, celery seed, and balsamic vinegar.

- In a large mixing bowl, combine cabbage, walnuts, celery, onion, red pepper, and cranberries. Add mayonnaise mixture to cabbage mixture and toss to coat. Cover and chill at least 1 hour or up to 6 hours before serving.

Makes 8 to 10 servings.

Tomatoes & Cukes
Fresh from the garden!

2 tablespoons olive or vegetable oil

1 tablespoon red wine or
other vinegar

1 tablespoon minced fresh parsley

¼ teaspoon salt

¼ teaspoon ground black pepper

3 medium tomatoes, sliced

½ large cucumber, sliced

Lettuce leaves

• In a small bowl, whisk together oil, vinegar, parsley, salt, and pepper.

• On serving plates, arrange tomato and cucumber slices over lettuce leaves. Drizzle with vinaigrette and serve immediately.

Makes 4 servings.

Cool Cucumber Salad

**A simple, yet delicious salad combination
for a summer lunch or dinner on the patio.**

Salad

2	large cucumbers, sliced	½	large Vidalia onion, thinly sliced

Dressing

1	(5-ounce) can evaporated milk (not fat-free)	⅓	cup sugar
¼	cup white vinegar		Salt and pepper

- Combine cucumbers and onion slices in a bowl; set aside.

- Combine milk, vinegar, sugar, salt, and pepper in a large jar; cover and shake vigorously.

- Pour dressing over cucumbers and onions, stirring until well blended. Cover and refrigerate at least 3 to 4 hours, stirring occasionally. Serve cold.

Makes 6 servings.

This salad is also just as good the next day.

The Queen's Chicken Salad

**This delightful chicken salad is rumored to have been
served to Queen Elizabeth II during a visit to the United States.
We know she must have loved it as much as we did!**

¾	cup mayonnaise	½	pound seedless sweet green grapes, cut in half
½-¾	teaspoon curry powder		
2	teaspoons fresh lemon juice	1	(8-ounce) can pineapple chunks in syrup, drained
2	teaspoons soy sauce		
2	cups bite-size chunks cooked chicken breast	¼	cup sliced water chestnuts
		½	cup chopped celery
		½	cup slivered almonds, toasted

- In a large mixing bowl, combine mayonnaise, curry powder, lemon juice, and soy sauce. Whisk until well blended. Gently stir in all other ingredients; chill. Serve in hollowed-out pineapple or melon boats or on lettuce.

Makes 4 to 6 servings.

Chinese Asparagus Salad with Orange Sesame Dressing

A very intriguing salad for a special evening.

1	pound fresh asparagus, washed, with tough stems removed	2	tablespoons white wine vinegar
1	(8-ounce) can sliced water chestnuts, drained	1	tablespoon sugar
			Juice of 1 medium orange
2	tablespoons soy sauce	1	(2-ounce) jar diced or sliced pimento, drained
2	tablespoons sesame oil		

- Cut asparagus spears diagonally into 1-inch pieces; drop into boiling, salted water and cook for 2 to 3 minutes or until barely tender. Drain, cover with cold water, and drain again. Add water chestnuts and toss with asparagus.

- In a small bowl, combine soy sauce, sesame oil, vinegar, sugar, and orange juice; whisk to combine. Pour mixture over asparagus and water chestnuts; toss. Serve at room temperature or chilled. Garnish with pimento.

Makes 4 to 6 servings.

Always choose firm, bright green asparagus spears with compact tips. Break off tough stems by allowing to snap off where they will.

Super Salad

Salad

1	head cauliflower, cut into chunks	4	stalks celery, cut into ½-inch slices
1	bunch broccoli, cut into florets	1	(10-ounce) package frozen peas, thawed and uncooked

Dressing

1	pound bacon, fried and crumbled	¼	cup small cubes fresh Parmesan cheese
¼	cup minced onion	2	tablespoons vinegar
1½	cups mayonnaise	¼	teaspoon salt (optional)
¼	cup sugar (may adjust amount to taste preference)		Dash of ground black pepper
			Colby and Cheddar cheeses, cut into small cubes (optional)

- In a large salad bowl, combine vegetables.

- Combine bacon and next 7 ingredients; pour over vegetables. Add cheese cubes and toss to blend. Chill before serving.

Makes 10 servings.

Marinated Vegetable Medley

A great side dish for grilled or barbecued chicken.

Salad

1	(17-ounce) can small green peas, drained	1	(8-ounce) can sliced water chestnuts, drained
1	(17-ounce) can white shoepeg corn, drained	1	(4-ounce) jar sliced mushrooms, drained (optional)
1	(15½-ounce) can French style green beans, drained	½	cup diced celery
1	(2-ounce) jar diced pimento, drained	½	cup chopped Vidalia or red onion
		½	cup chopped green pepper

Dressing

1	cup sugar	½	cup vegetable oil
1	teaspoon salt	¾	cup apple cider vinegar
½	teaspoon ground black pepper		

- **Combine salad vegetables and toss lightly.**

- **In a medium saucepan, combine sugar, salt, pepper, oil, and vinegar; cook over low heat, stirring frequently, and bring to a boil. Remove from heat and cool slightly.**

- **Pour dressing over vegetables and stir gently to blend. Cover and chill for 24 hours before serving.**

Makes 10 to 12 servings.

One of Anderson County's earliest settlements was the town of Centerville. A gun factory there produced weapons that were used by American forces in the War of 1812.

Tangy Vegetable Salad

Serve this at your next barbecue!

Dressing

½	cup mayonnaise	1	tablespoon lemon juice
2	tablespoons chili sauce	1	teaspoon dried dill weed

Salad

2	cups coarsely chopped broccoli	1	(8-ounce) bottle Italian salad dressing
2	cups coarsely chopped cauliflower	2	cups cherry or grape tomatoes, cut in half
2	cups sliced carrots	2	(6-ounce) jars marinated artichoke hearts, drained and quartered
1	cup sliced celery		

- **One day ahead of serving, separately blanch broccoli, cauliflower, and carrots in boiling water; plunge into ice water and drain well. Place vegetables in a bowl; pour salad dressing over vegetables and lightly toss to coat. Cover and refrigerate overnight, lightly stirring occasionally.**

- **Drain vegetables; add tomatoes and artichokes.**

- **To prepare dressing, combine mayonnaise, chili sauce, lemon juice and dill; mix well. Pour over vegetables and toss well to coat.**

Makes 14 to 16 servings.

Perfect French Dressing

**Spoon over fresh greens with
Mandarin orange segments and mild onion slices.**

1	(10¾-ounce) can tomato soup	1	tablespoon Worcestershire sauce
1	cup vegetable oil		
¾	cup sugar	1	teaspoon salt
¾	cup vinegar	10	drops liquid garlic
½	teaspoon ground black pepper	½	cup finely chopped onion
1	teaspoon prepared yellow mustard		

- **Combine all ingredients in blender and process until well blended. Chill up to 2 weeks in the refrigerator.**

Makes about 3 cups.

Seashells & Shrimp Pasta Salad

1	(8-ounce) package seashell pasta	1½-2	tablespoons fresh lemon juice
1½-2	pounds shrimp, peeled, deveined, and cooked	¾	cup mayonnaise
3	stalks celery, chopped	1	tablespoon plus 1 teaspoon Dijon mustard
5-6	hard-boiled eggs	¼-½	teaspoon dill weed
1	small Vidalia or other mild onion, chopped		Morton's Nature's Seasoning
			Salt and cracked pepper
			Paprika for garnish

• Cook pasta according to package instructions; drain, rinse, and chill. Add shrimp, celery, onion, and eggs. Add mayonnaise, starting with ½ cup and adding a little more at a time until salad binds. Add mustard, dill, and other seasonings to taste. Serve on plate with lettuce and tomato. Garnish, if desired, with paprika.

Makes 4 to 6 servings.

Morton's Nature's Seasoning is recommended for this recipe because it has a base of celery seed and parsley instead of the cumin and turmeric base found in other seasoning salt blends.

Potato Salad with a Heart

A tasty twist on an old favorite.

1	(14-ounce) can artichoke hearts, drained and diced	3	tablespoons chopped fresh chervil
1	pound red potatoes, cooked, peeled, and diced	1	tablespoon chopped fresh parsley
1	bunch green onions, chopped	2	tablespoons chopped fresh dill weed
3	stalks celery, chopped		Juice of ½ lemon
3	cloves garlic, minced		Salt
1	cup mayonnaise		Freshly ground black pepper
2	teaspoons Dijon mustard		
1	tablespoon sugar		

• Combine artichoke hearts and potatoes; set aside.

• Combine chopped onions and next 9 ingredients in a large bowl, blending well. Add potato mixture and stir gently. Season with salt and pepper. Cover and refrigerate for several hours before serving.

Makes 4 to 6 servings.

Try these variations on the Seashells & Shrimp Pasta Salad:

• *Use 2 (6-ounce) cans of tuna, packed in water and drained or 1½ pounds cooked diced chicken breast and toasted sliced almonds in place of shrimp.*

• *Leave out pasta and double the amount of shrimp.*

• *Add chopped Granny Smith apples or grapes to any variation.*

• *For a slightly richer taste, reduce mayonnaise to ½ cup and add ¼ cup sour cream.*

Raspberry Vinaigrette Dressing

Serve on a bed of spinach, with Mandarin oranges, raspberries or halved strawberries, and toasted pecan halves.

⅓ cup oil

2 tablespoons raspberry or strawberry wine vinegar

1½ teaspoon sugar

¼ teaspoon salt

Pinch of ground black pepper

- Whisk all ingredients together and serve.

Makes 4 servings.

Asian Salad Supreme

Add cooked shrimp for a main course luncheon.

Lime Vinaigrette

¼	cup lime juice	2	tablespoons dark brown sugar
3	tablespoons canola oil	1	tablespoon grated orange zest
1	tablespoon sesame oil	1	tablespoon minced garlic
3	tablespoons light soy sauce	½	teaspoon cayenne pepper

Salad

8	ounces snow peas, trimmed	2	cups shredded carrots
1	(8-ounce) package dried Chinese noodles	¼	cup thinly sliced sweet onion

- To prepare vinaigrette, combine lime juice and next 7 ingredients in a bowl and mix well.

- To prepare salad, blanch snow peas until they are crisp-tender and bright green. Rinse under cold water and drain.

- Cook noodles according to package directions. Rinse in cold water and drain.

- Combine snow peas, noodles, carrots, and onion in a bowl. Add vinaigrette, tossing gently to mix well. Serve chilled.

Makes 4 to 6 servings.

The Ultimate 1000 Island Dressing

1	cup mayonnaise	2	tablespoons chopped pimento-stuffed green olives
¼	cup ketchup		
1	tablespoon grated onion	2	tablespoons sweet pickle relish
2	tablespoons chopped green pepper	1	hard-boiled egg
2	tablespoons chopped celery		Dash of hot pepper sauce

- Combine all ingredients in a blender and pulse-blend 3 to 5 seconds at a time until dressing is thick, but not quite smooth. Refrigerate up to 1 week.

Makes about 2 cups.

Garden Potato Salad

Ingredients fresh from the garden make this potato salad one that you'll make all summer!

¼	cup vegetable oil
2	cloves garlic, halved
30-40	new potatoes, skins on, cut into ½ to ¾-inch cubes
½	cup tarragon vinegar
2	teaspoons salt
2	teaspoons sugar

3-4	tablespoons chopped fresh dill weed
⅔-1	cup mayonnaise
2	bunches green onions, chopped
	Garnish: chopped fresh dill and sliced radishes

- **Combine oil and garlic in a small bowl; set aside.**

- **Boil potatoes in salted water until just tender; drain. Transfer to a large bowl.**

- **Remove garlic from oil and discard. Whisk vinegar, salt, sugar, and dill into oil. Pour dressing over warm potatoes, tossing to coat. Cover with plastic wrap and marinate at least 4 hours, or overnight, in refrigerator.**

- **Drain excess liquid from potatoes. Toss marinated potatoes with mayonnaise and green onions. Garnish with fresh dill and sliced radishes. Serve immediately.**

Makes 10 to 12 servings.

Japanese Ginger Dressing

Transform any salad into an oriental delight!

¼	cup minced onion
1	tablespoon minced celery
1	tablespoon minced gingerroot
1½	teaspoons tomato paste
1	tablespoon soy sauce
2	tablespoons water

2	tablespoons rice wine vinegar
¼	cup peanut oil
1	teaspoon lemon juice
1½	teaspoons sugar
¼	teaspoon salt
¼	teaspoon ground black pepper

- **Combine all ingredients in a blender or food processor. Process until smooth and thick.**

Makes 1 cup.

Warm Bacon Dressing

6 slices bacon
½ cup olive oil
¼ cup apple cider vinegar
1 tablespoon sugar
Salt and pepper to taste

• In a medium sauté pan, cook bacon until crisp; drain fat, leaving bacon in pan. Crumble bacon, and add oil, vinegar, sugar, salt, and pepper. Bring mixture to a boil and remove from heat. Pour hot mixture over mixed salad greens, toss well, and serve immediately.

Makes 6 servings.

Dad's Garlic Dressing

Dad knows his stuff! This is creamy and wonderful!

½ cup sour cream

⅓ cup mayonnaise

¼ cup half-and-half

3 cloves garlic, chopped

2 tablespoons white wine vinegar

2 tablespoons vegetable oil

1½ teaspoons sugar

½ teaspoon salt

Freshly ground black pepper

• Combine all ingredients in a blender or food processor. Process until smooth and creamy. Cover and refrigerate at least 1 hour. Adjust seasonings before serving.

Makes 1 cup.

Picnic Wild Rice Salad

A salad of many contrasting tastes and textures. Very different and always enjoyed!

1½	cups uncooked wild rice	4	scallions or green onions, chopped
2	tablespoons chicken bouillon granules	¾	cup orange juice
1	cup dried cranberries		Grated rind of 1 orange
½	cup golden raisins	¼	cup olive oil
¼	cup chopped fresh mint leaves	1	cup pecan halves, lightly toasted

• **Cook wild rice in water and bouillon, according to package directions, until butterflied.**

• **While rice is cooking, combine cranberries, raisins, mint, onions, orange juice, and orange rind. Let stand.**

• **When rice is done, drain off excess water. Stir in oil and cranberry mixture; let stand for 2 hours. Serve at room temperature or chilled. Just before serving, top with pecans.**

Makes 8 servings.

Bleu Cheese Salad Dressing

Serve over thick slices of tomato and avocado.

1	small onion, finely chopped (can use less if milder taste is preferred)	2	tablespoons balsamic vinegar
		1	teaspoon salt
1	cup mayonnaise	1	teaspoon prepared yellow mustard
⅓	cup vegetable oil	½	teaspoon paprika
¼	cup ketchup	4	ounces bleu cheese crumbles
2	tablespoons sugar		Dash of ground black pepper

• **Place all ingredients in a blender and process for 2 minutes. Chill until ready to serve.**

This dressing may be refrigerated up to 4 days.

Makes about 2 cups.

Sandwiches and Soups

Soulful Sandwiches and Soups

Sandwiches and Soups

Gourmet Philly Steak Sandwich

2   tablespoons Dijon mustard
2   tablespoons Burgundy or other
     dry red wine
1¼   teaspoons coarsely ground
     black pepper, divided
¼   teaspoon garlic powder
1   pound lean, boneless sirloin
     steak, trimmed
     Nonstick cooking spray

1   small Vidalia or other sweet
     onion, thinly sliced and
     separated into rings
½   cup beef broth
1   tablespoon white wine vinegar
¼   teaspoon salt
2   (6-inch) French baguettes, split
1   (1-ounce) slices provolone
     cheese, divided
2   tablespoons creamy Dijon
     mustard blend, divided

- Combine Dijon mustard, red wine, 1 teaspoon pepper, and garlic powder; spread on both sides of steak. Place steak on a rack coated with cooking spray; place rack in broiler pan. Broil 4 inches from heat (with electric oven door partially opened) 4 to 5 minutes on each side or until a meat thermometer registers 150°. Let stand 5 minutes; wrap with plastic wrap, and cool at least 15 minutes. Chill 1 hour.

- Cook onion in a nonstick skillet coated with cooking spray, stirring constantly, until tender. Add broth, vinegar, salt, and ¼ teaspoon pepper; bring to a boil and cook until liquid evaporates. Set aside.

- Cut steak diagonally across grain into thin slices. Place slices evenly on bottom halves of baguettes; top evenly with onion mixture and cheese. Spread baguette tops evenly with Dijon mustard blend, and place on sandwiches. Cut in half, and serve immediately, or wrap in plastic wrap and refrigerate up to 4 hours.

Makes 4 servings.

In 1960, the Army Corps of Engineers completed work on Hartwell Dam, thereby finishing the first step toward creating Hartwell Lake, one of the largest man-made lakes east of the Mississippi. Hartwell Lake provides 962 miles of coastline in Georgia and South Carolina, and stretches through Anderson from Oconee to Abbeville Counties, our neighbors to the north and south respectively. It forms our western border with Georgia.

Flank Steak Sandwiches

These are the best for tailgating!

1	cup ketchup	3	tablespoons vegetable oil
1½	cups water	1½	teaspoons salt
	Dash of garlic salt	¼-½	teaspoon ground black pepper
2	tablespoons prepared yellow mustard	1	tablespoon onion powder
2	tablespoons Worcestershire sauce	2	(1-pound) flank steaks

Sandwich Spread

4	ounces blue cheese, crumbled	½	teaspoon salt
1	stick butter, softened		Dash of ground black pepper
½	clove garlic, minced		Sandwich buns of choice
2	tablespoons prepared yellow mustard	1	red onion, thinly sliced

• Combine ketchup and next 8 ingredients; stir until well blended.

• Place steaks in a large heavy-duty zip-top plastic bag. Pour ketchup mixture over steaks and seal. Refrigerate overnight, turning bag several times. Remove from bag and discard marinade. Grill steaks over medium-hot coals for 5 to 6 minutes on each side or until desired degree of doneness. Remove from grill and slice steak into ½-inch-thick strips. Cover and refrigerate, or keep warm, until serving.

• To prepare sandwich spread, combine blue cheese, softened butter, garlic, mustard, salt, and pepper. Mix until well blended and fairly smooth. Spread top half of buns with spread.

• Layer steak strips evenly over bottom halves of buns; layer sliced onions over steak, and top with spread-coated bun halves.

Makes 8 to 10 servings.

Chilled Smoked Turkey Burrito

Great for lunch or as an appetizer.

2	jalapeño peppers, seeded and minced	2	tablespoons lemon juice
1	(8-ounce) package cream cheese, firm	½	teaspoon onion powder
¼	cup sour cream	¼	teaspoon ground black pepper
4	ounces salsa	1	pound smoked turkey, cut into paper-thin slices
3	avocados, peeled	6	flour tortillas, warmed
			Salsa or corn relish

- In a small bowl, mix together jalapeños, cream cheese, sour cream, and salsa until well blended; set aside.

- In another small bowl, mash avocado with lemon juice until fairly smooth; add onion powder and pepper, and continue mashing until smooth.

- Thickly spread tortillas with jalapeño-cheese mixture out to edges. Top mixture with turkey slices, and spread mashed avocado on top of turkey.

- Roll up tortillas like jelly rolls; slice each diagonally into halves or fourths. Serve with salsa or corn relish.

Makes 6 servings.

To make appetizer servings, cut burritos diagonally into ¾-inch pinwheel slices; arrange on serving platter around small bowls of salsa and corn relish.

Notes

The Best Chicken Salad Sandwiches

These will disappear out of your refrigerator!

6	large chicken breasts	¼	cup sweet pickle relish
2	eggs, boiled and chopped	½-¾	cup mayonnaise
¼	cup fresh lemon juice	2	stalks celery, very finely chopped
¼	cup Worcestershire sauce		Salt and pepper
¼	cup Dijon mustard		

• Salt and boil chicken until done. When just cool enough to handle, remove skin and bones from chicken. Using a food processor or kitchen shears, cut chicken into small pieces. Add eggs, and using hands, mash together chicken, eggs, lemon juice, Worcestershire sauce, mustard, and pickle relish. Stir in mayonnaise, ¼ cup at a time, until desired consistency is reached. Stir in chopped celery, and salt and pepper to taste.

• To make sandwiches, scantly spread mayonnaise on both slices of bread. Use about ¼ cup of filling for each sandwich. Cut each sandwich in half, wrap in plastic wrap, and store in refrigerator.

Makes 10 to 12 sandwiches.

Traditional Southern Style Pimento Cheese Sandwich Spread

**This one has been passed down
through several generations of Southern belles!**

1	pound extra sharp Cheddar cheese	½	teaspoon vinegar
1	(4-ounce) jar sliced pimento, undrained	½	teaspoon sugar
			Ground black pepper
			Mayonnaise

• Finely grate cheese into a mixing bowl and set aside.

• Pour pimento and juice into a plate or shallow bowl; drizzle with vinegar and sprinkle with sugar. Using a fork, mash pimento. Mix grated cheese into mashed pimento, a handful at a time. Sprinkle with pepper. Add mayonnaise, a spoonful at a time, mixing well until desired creaminess is achieved.

Makes about 1 pint.

Spicy Mustard Cheese Spread

Great for sandwiches, but we loved this best when spread on good old-fashioned saltines.

3	pounds sharp Cheddar cheese, finely grated
1	quart mayonnaise
1	(8-ounce) jar hot jalapeño mustard
2-3	tablespoons spicy brown mustard
1	tablespoon chives
4	ounces diced pimento
	Ground red pepper to taste

• Mix all ingredients together and chill until serving.

Makes about 2 quarts.

This recipe makes quite a lot, which makes it perfect for a party. It also is easily halved for a smaller amount.

Gourmet Bacon Sirloin Burgers

1¼	pounds ground sirloin
½	teaspoon plus ⅛ teaspoon salt, divided
1	teaspoon plus ⅛ teaspoon coarsely ground black pepper, divided
⅓	cup sour cream
2½	teaspoons prepared white horseradish
4	English muffins, split and lightly toasted
4	strips bacon, cut in half and fried
4	Boston lettuce leaves

• Shape ground sirloin into 4 patties, each about ½ inch thick. Sprinkle patties with ½ teaspoon salt, and then with 1 teaspoon pepper, pressing the pepper lightly into the patties.

• Heat a 12-inch nonstick skillet over medium-high heat until hot. Add patties and cook until desired doneness (about 6 minutes for medium), shaking skillet occasionally and turning patties once.

• In a small bowl, combine sour cream, horseradish, ⅛ teaspoon salt, and ⅛ teaspoon pepper. Mix well.

• Serve patties on English muffins with bacon, lettuce, and horseradish sauce.

Makes 4 servings.

The first telephone service in Anderson began in 1855, using wires stretched between Pendleton and Belton along the railroad right-of-way.

Open-Faced Crab Cake Sandwiches with Roasted Red Pepper Sauce

1	pound fresh crabmeat	1	(7-ounce) jar roasted sweet red peppers, drained
2	cups soft breadcrumbs	3	tablespoons mayonnaise
1	small onion, finely chopped	1	clove garlic
½	green bell pepper, finely chopped	⅛	teaspoon dried crushed red pepper
⅓	cup mayonnaise		Nonstick cooking spray
1	large egg	6	lettuce leaves
¼	teaspoon salt	3	English muffins, split and lightly toasted
¼	teaspoon ground black pepper		
¼	teaspoon Paul Prudhomme's Seafood Magic		

- **Drain and flake crabmeat, removing any bits of shell.**

- **Stir together crabmeat and next 8 ingredients. Shape into 6 (3½-inch) patties. Chill 1 hour.**

- **While patties are chilling, prepare sauce. In a food processor, combine red peppers, mayonnaise, and garlic. Process until smooth. Stir in crushed red pepper. Set aside.**

- **Cook patties in a nonstick skillet coated with nonstick cooking spray over medium-high heat 5 minutes on each side or until lightly browned.**

- **Place lettuce on muffin halves. Top with crab patties; spoon red pepper sauce over patties. Serve immediately.**

Makes 6 servings.

Portobello Burgers
with Avocado Mayonnaise

To grill onion, push water-soaked skewers
crosswise through the whole onion at ½-inch intervals. Slice
between skewers, and place skewered slices on grill.

1	small avocado, peeled and chopped	2	red bell peppers, seeded and halved
½	cup mayonnaise	1	purple onion, cut into ½-inch-thick slices
2	tablespoons lemon juice		Garlic-flavored cooking spray
¼	cup fresh basil leaves	6	hamburger buns
1	clove garlic, minced		
6	portobello mushroom caps		

• In a food processor, combine avocado, mayonnaise, lemon juice, basil, and garlic. Process until smooth, stopping to scrape down sides. Cover and chill up to 2 hours, if desired.

• Coat mushrooms, bell peppers, and onion with cooking spray.

• Grill onion, covered with lid, over medium-high heat (350° to 400°) 8 minutes on each side. Grill mushrooms 5 minutes on each side. Place bell peppers on grill, skin side down, and grill 4 to 5 minutes or until skin is blistered.

• Peel bell peppers, and cut into strips.

• To serve, spread avocado-mayonnaise mixture on cut sides of buns; place on cooking grate, and grill 1 minute. Place mushrooms, bell pepper strips, and onion evenly on bottom halves of buns. Top each with avocado slices and top bun halves.

Makes 6 servings.

Cool Sunset Soup

Garnish with a light sprinkle of cinnamon and a mint sprig for a beautiful presentation.

1 large sweet cantaloupe, cut in chunks

2-3 fresh peaches

2 tablespoons orange-flavored liqueur

1 (6-ounce) can pineapple juice

1 (8-ounce) container vanilla yogurt

¼ teaspoon cinnamon

• Place cantaloupe and all remaining ingredients into a food processor or blender. Process until smooth. Chill for at least 3 hours to blend flavors before serving.

Serves 4.

Chilled Berry Soup

A creamy and refreshing summer treat.

1	quart strawberries, hulled	3	tablespoons clear cherry brandy
4	cups buttermilk, divided	½	pint blackberries
¾	cup sugar		Garnish: mint sprigs
1	(8-ounce) container vanilla yogurt		

- Combine strawberries, 1 cup buttermilk, and sugar in a food processor or blender. Process until smooth; set aside.

- Combine remaining buttermilk, yogurt, blackberries, and cherry liqueur in a large bowl. Pour the strawberry mixture into the blackberry yogurt mixture, stirring gently to combine. Cover and chill. Serve cold with mint sprigs, if desired.

Makes 4 to 6 servings.

Onion Soup Gratinée

**Serve with a tossed green salad
and fresh fruit for a delicious light lunch.**

4-5	large yellow onions, minced	1½	cups water
3	tablespoons butter	1	bay leaf
¼	teaspoon ground black pepper	6-8	slices French bread, toasted
1	tablespoon all-purpose flour	½	cup grated Swiss cheese
4	cups beef broth		

- Sauté onions in butter; add pepper. Cook until onions are lightly browned. Sprinkle onions with flour. Cook 1 minute, stirring constantly. Add beef broth, water, and bay leaf. Simmer 30 to 40 minutes. Discard bay leaf, and correct seasonings to taste if necessary.

- Turn soup into an ovenproof tureen or individual ovenproof dishes. Place toast on top and sprinkle with cheese. Place under broiler or in a 400° oven until cheese is golden.

Makes 6 servings.

Black-Eyed Pea Soup

**A pot of this soup simmering on the
stove is the perfect choice for a chilly autumn day.**

2	(10-ounce) boxes frozen black-eyed peas	1½	cups tomato sauce
1	medium onion, chopped	1	(8¾-ounce) can yellow corn, drained (optional)
1	bell pepper, chopped	1	(8-ounce) container sour cream
1	tablespoon vegetable oil	1	cup grated Cheddar cheese
2	medium tomatoes, chopped		Salt and pepper

• Cook peas according to package directions.

• Sauté onion and bell pepper in oil until tender and lightly browned.

• In a large saucepan, combine cooked peas, chopped tomatoes, and tomato sauce. Add onion and bell pepper. Add corn and sour cream, stirring until well blended. Simmer for 20 minutes or until well heated. Add salt and pepper to taste. To serve, top each bowl with shredded Cheddar cheese.

Makes 6 to 8 servings.

Quick and Easy Variation: In place of frozen peas, vegetables, and tomato sauce, combine 2 (15-ounce) cans black-eyed peas, 1 (14½-ounce) can stewed tomatoes with onions and peppers, and 1 cup tomato juice before adding corn and sour cream. Also, sour cream may be omitted from soup and used along with Cheddar cheese as garnish before serving.

On May 10, 1935, the "Quart of the Month" law was repealed, marking the end of prohibition in South Carolina. Our "Blue Laws," which limit the alcohol sales to daylight hours and completely prohibit sales of alcohol on Sundays, are a leftover vestige from the days of prohibition.

Crab and Leek Bisque

3	leeks (about 1½ pounds)	2	cups half-and-half
½	cup butter	3	tablespoons Worcestershire sauce
1	clove garlic, minced		
½	cup all-purpose flour	½	pounds crabmeat, flaked
4	cups chicken broth	¼	teaspoon salt
½	cup dry white wine	¼	teaspoon ground white pepper

- Remove roots, tough outer leaves, and green tops from leeks. Split white portions in half; wash halves and cut into thin slices.

- Melt butter in Dutch oven over medium-high heat. Add leeks and garlic; cook, stirring constantly, until tender. Add flour, stirring until smooth. Cook 1 minute, stirring constantly. Gradually add chicken broth and wine; cook 4 to 5 minutes over medium heat, stirring constantly, until mixture is thickened. Stir in half-and-half, Worcestershire sauce, crabmeat, salt, and pepper. Serve immediately.

Makes 6 servings.

Savory Italian Onion Soup

Serve with an antipasto salad and Italian bread.

1	large onion, halved and thinly sliced	1	tablespoon sugar
2	tablespoons margarine	1	tablespoon oregano
2	tablespoons olive oil		Salt and pepper
1	(14½-ounce) can chicken broth	½	cup cooking sherry
2	(28-ounce) cans whole tomatoes, puréed in blender		Thin lemon slices
			Grated Parmesan cheese

- Sauté onion in margarine and olive oil until clear and slightly browned. Add chicken broth, puréed tomatoes, sugar, oregano, and salt and pepper to taste. Simmer 30 minutes. Add sherry and cook 5 more minutes. Serve each bowl with a lemon slice and grated Parmesan cheese sprinkled on top.

Makes 4 to 6 servings.

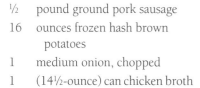

Hearthside Potato & Sausage Soup

**One spoonful of this creamy soup
will warm the coldest of winter days.**

½	pound ground pork sausage	1	(10¾-ounce) can cream of chicken soup, undiluted
16	ounces frozen hash brown potatoes	1	(10¾-ounce) can cream of celery soup, undiluted
1	medium onion, chopped	2	cups milk
1	(14½-ounce) can chicken broth		Shredded Cheddar cheese
2	cups water		

- Brown sausage in a large Dutch oven over medium heat, stirring until it crumbles and is no longer pink. Drain. Return to Dutch oven.

- Add potatoes and next 3 ingredients to sausage; bring to a boil. Cover, reduce heat, and simmer 30 minutes. Stir in soups and milk; cook, stirring often, until thoroughly heated. Garnish with Cheddar cheese, if desired.

Makes 8 servings.

Cream of Smoked Salmon Soup

**A wonderful choice when you want
something out of the ordinary, and easy to prepare.**

1	(8-ounce) package cream cheese, cut into cubes	1½	teaspoons chopped fresh dill weed or ½ teaspoon dried dill weed
1	cup milk	2	green onions, sliced
2	teaspoons Dijon mustard	1	(14½-ounce) can chicken broth
		12	ounces smoked salmon, flaked

- Heat cream cheese, milk, mustard, dill weed, onions, and chicken broth in a 2-quart saucepan over medium heat until cheese is melted and mixture is smooth. Stir in salmon; heat until hot and serve immediately.

Makes 4 servings.

**Make Your
Holidays Shine!**

*Tie a simple bow to the top
of an old chandelier crystal to
decorate your Christmas tree
or wreath. Unique crystals can
be found at garage sales
and antique stores.*

Dinner Party Tomato Bouillon

**This is wonderful to serve in pretty
mugs as a first course before seating guests.**

2	(46-ounce) cans tomato juice	½	stick margarine
2	(46-ounce) cans tomato-vegetable juice cocktail	3-4	(10½-ounce) measured cans water
2	(10¾-ounce) cans cream of tomato soup	1	tablespoon hot pepper sauce
3	(10½-ounce) cans beef bouillon or consommé	1	tablespoon dried oregano
		1	tablespoon dried parsley
2	(1¼-ounce) packages onion soup mix	1	tablespoon lemon pepper

• **Combine all ingredients in a large stockpot or Dutch oven. Simmer and serve.**

Makes 32 servings.

This recipe may be prepared one day ahead and refrigerated to blend flavors.

Good Grace's Vegetable Soup

An Anderson tradition!

1	pound lean ground round or sirloin	1	(10½-ounce) measured can burgundy wine
1	clove garlic, minced	5	beef bouillon cubes dissolved in 4 cups boiling water
1	jumbo onion, chopped		
2	(28-ounce) cans diced tomatoes	1	tablespoon dried parsley
		1	teaspoon dried basil
1	(10½-ounce) can beef consommé	½	teaspoon dried thyme
		2	(16-ounce) packages frozen soup mix vegetables

• **Brown beef, garlic, and onion in a Dutch oven. Drain excess liquid. Add remaining ingredients and simmer 3 to 4 hours.**

Makes 10 to 12 servings.

Delicious Chicken Chili

3	boneless chicken breasts, cut into small pieces	1	(14½-ounce) measured can frozen corn
1	(14½-ounce) can diced tomatoes	¼	cup sliced green onions or cilantro
1	tablespoon chili powder		Cooked rice (optional)
¼	cup chopped onion		Monterey Jack cheese
¼	cup chopped bell pepper (optional)		Diced avocado
1	(15½-ounce) can black beans		Green onions

- **In medium saucepan, combine chicken, tomatoes, and chili powder. Cook until chicken is done. Add remaining ingredients and simmer 5 to 7 minutes. Serve over rice, if desired, and top with Monterey Jack cheese, diced avocado, and green onions.**

Makes 4 servings.

Favorite Chili Beans

**The hands-down winner in our
chili cook-off. Our tasters couldn't get enough!**

2	(14½-ounce) cans diced tomatoes	1	jalapeño pepper, seeded and finely chopped
2	(16-ounce) cans pinto beans	2-3	teaspoons chili powder
2	pounds ground turkey, browned and drained	1	teaspoon cumin
1	large onion, chopped	¼	cup maple syrup
1-2	cloves garlic, minced	1	(6-ounce) can tomato paste
			Salt and pepper to taste

- **Put all ingredients in crockpot in the order listed. Stir once. Cover and cook on high 3 to 4 hours.**

Makes 4 servings.

To Clarify Butter

Start with unsalted butter, cut into 1 inch pieces. In a heavy saucepan melt the butter over low heat. Remove the saucepan from the heat and let it stand for 3 minutes. Skim the froth and discard it. Strain the butter through a sieve lined with a double thickness of rinsed and squeezed cheesecloth into a bowl, leaving the milky solids in the bottom of the pan. Pour the clarified butter into a jar or crock and store, covered, in the refrigerator. The butter keeps indefinitely, covered and chilled. When clarified, butter loses about one fourth of its original volume.

My Favorite Recipes

Vegetables
Sidelights

Vegetables

On the front:
Setting Sun on the Farm
Photograph by *Sabrina R. Dunn*

Asparagus Strudel

1	pound fresh asparagus spears	½	teaspoon salt
2	tablespoons minced shallots	¼	teaspoon ground white pepper
2	tablespoons butter, melted	¼	teaspoon ground nutmeg
2	tablespoons all-purpose flour	⅛	teaspoon hot pepper sauce
1	cup half-and-half	8	sheets frozen phyllo pastry, thawed
1	teaspoon lemon juice		
½	teaspoon dried dill weed	½	cup butter, melted and divided

- Snap off tough ends of asparagus. Remove scales from stalks with a knife or vegetable peeler, if desired. Cut stalks in half; arrange in a vegetable steamer over boiling water. Cover and steam 5 minutes. Place asparagus in ice water; set aside.

- Sauté shallots in 2 tablespoons butter in a heavy saucepan over medium heat until tender. Add flour, stirring until smooth. Cook, stirring constantly, 1 minute. Gradually add half-and-half; cook over medium heat, stirring constantly, until mixture is thickened. Stir in lemon juice and next 5 ingredients.

- Place 1 sheet of phyllo on a damp towel (keep remaining phyllo covered). Brush with 2 teaspoons melted butter. Layer second sheet of phyllo on first sheet; brush with 2 teaspoons butter. Cut stack in half lengthwise, making 2 rectangles.

- Drain asparagus. Place ⅛ of asparagus at short end of each rectangle; spoon ⅛ of sauce mixture over asparagus on each rectangle. Fold ends of rectangles over asparagus; roll up jelly roll style. Repeat with remaining phyllo, butter, asparagus, and sauce mixture. Brush phyllo packets with remaining melted butter; place on greased baking sheet.

- Bake at 350° for 30 minutes.

Makes 8 servings.

Asparagus is one of the South's oldest vegetables, elegant yet simple to serve. It is equally good hot or cold and doubles for a salad. Boiled, it is served with a variety of sauces, including butter, bread sauces, vinegar sauces and the famous Hollandaise. With a cream cheese sauce it becomes a delightful casserole, or it may be served on toast.

Lemon Butter Sauce

Serve with artichokes, asparagus, broccoli, Brussels sprouts, or spinach.

4 tablespoons lemon juice
¼ teaspoon salt
¼ pound butter
⅛ teaspoon ground white pepper

• Heat lemon juice and salt just to boiling; remove from heat. Beat in butter, 1 tablespoon at a time, until mixture is creamy. Beat in pepper.

Makes about ½ cup.

Roasted Asparagus

Roasting brings out the fullest flavor
of vegetables, and asparagus is no exception.

2	pounds fresh asparagus, trimmed		Pinch salt
			Shaved Parmesan cheese
2	tablespoons olive oil	¼	teaspoon ground black pepper

• Arrange oven racks to middle and lower third of oven. Heat oven to 400°.

• Divide asparagus and spread on 2 jelly-roll pans. Toss each with 1 tablespoon oil and salt.

• Roast 10 minutes. Switch pans between the racks and roast 10 minutes more, until stalks are tender. Sprinkle top with cheese, if desired, and pepper.

Makes 4 to 6 servings.

Green Beans with Pine Nuts and Goat Cheese

¼	cup pine nuts	1	tablespoon olive oil
2	(16-ounce) packages frozen French style green beans, thawed and well drained	4	plum tomatoes, chopped
		2	tablespoons lemon juice
		1	teaspoon salt
2	garlic cloves, minced	½	teaspoon ground black pepper
2	teaspoons dried Italian seasoning	1	(4-ounce) package crumbled goat cheese

• Bake pine nuts in a shallow pan at 350° for 6 to 8 minutes or until toasted. Set aside.

• In a large skillet over medium heat, sauté garlic and Italian seasoning in olive oil for 1 minute; add green beans and sauté 5 to 7 minutes. Add tomatoes and cook, stirring constantly for 2 minutes or until thoroughly heated.

• Stir in lemon juice, salt, and pepper. Sprinkle with cheese and pine nuts.

Makes 6 servings.

One 4-ounce package of feta cheese may be substituted for goat cheese.

Green Beans with Toasted Pecan Dressing

This dish is so versatile. It is wonderful as a cold side dish at a barbecue, or as an elegant accompaniment at a formal dinner.

2	pounds fresh green beans	1	teaspoon dried dill weed
½	cup chopped green onions	¾	teaspoon salt
⅓	cup olive oil	½	teaspoon ground black pepper
¼	cup cider vinegar	¾	cup chopped pecans, toasted

- Place green beans into large pot of boiling water and cook for 10 minutes. Drain and place into serving bowl.

- Combine onions, oil, vinegar, dill, salt, and pepper and pour over beans. Sprinkle with nuts. Serve warm or cold.

Makes 8 servings.

Frozen green beans may be substituted for fresh.

Sweet 'n Sour Green Beans

4	slices bacon	2	tablespoons sugar
1	large onion, chopped	¼	cup vinegar
2	large cans green beans		Dash of ground black pepper

- Cook bacon in heavy skillet until crisp. Remove bacon, drain, and crumble; set aside.

- Add chopped onion to bacon drippings in skillet, and sauté until tender. Add beans with liquid, sugar, vinegar, and pepper. Cover tightly and cook on low heat, stirring occasionally, until liquid is reduced and beans are tender, 1 to 2 hours. Place beans in serving bowl and sprinkle with bacon.

Makes 10 servings.

MaMa picked a "mess" of beans today for supper

A "mess" refers to a large bunch - usually more than enough to feed from 6 to 8 people. If it is a big mess, then most of it will probably be canned for later use.

Raspberry Green Beans

These are delicious served hot, cold, or at room temperature!

2 pounds fresh whole green beans

2 tablespoons sugar

1 cup vegetable oil

1 teaspoon salt

1 cup raspberry vinegar

1 teaspoon ground white pepper

- Cover green beans with water in a large saucepan and cook about 10 minutes or until tender. Drain and place in casserole dish; set aside.

- Combine remaining ingredients in a medium saucepan and cook over low heat until sugar dissolves. Pour mixture over green beans. Cover and refrigerate at least 4 hours before serving.

Makes 8 servings.

Crowd-Pleasing Baked Bean Medley

A big hit at any casual picnic or barbecue!

1	pound ground round or sirloin	1½	tablespoons chili powder
½	bell pepper, finely chopped	2	tablespoons Worcestershire sauce
1	large onion, chopped		
1	(16-ounce) can pork and beans, undrained	½	cup packed brown sugar
		2	tablespoons prepared mustard
1	(16-ounce) can lima or butter beans, undrained	1	teaspoon salt
		½	cup ketchup
1	(16-ounce) can light red kidney beans, undrained	6	strips bacon, fried and crumbled

- Brown ground meat with chopped pepper and onion; drain. Transfer to large bowl and stir in beans and next 6 ingredients.

- Pour bean mixture into 13 x 9-inch baking dish coated with nonstick cooking spray. Sprinkle bacon on top of beans.

- Bake at 350° for 45 minutes.

Makes 10 to 12 servings.

This recipe may also be prepared in a crockpot. After browning meat, pepper, and onions, place in crockpot and add all ingredients except bacon. Cook on low approximately 3 hours, adding bacon near the end of cooking.

Lima Beans with Red Pepper

1	(16-ounce) bag frozen lima beans	1-2	teaspoons chopped garlic
1	tablespoon olive oil	1	teaspoon salt
½	cup chopped onion	½	cup chicken broth
½	cup diced red pepper	1	teaspoon ground black pepper

- Cook limas in microwave oven according to package directions; drain well and set aside.

- Heat oil in skillet; add onion and cook 5 minutes. Stir in red pepper and cook 6 minutes. Stir in garlic and salt; cook until fragrant.

- Add lima beans and chicken broth; cook until beans are heated through, 3 to 5 minutes more. Stir in pepper.

Makes 4 servings.

Broccoli with Horseradish Sauce

This horseradish sauce can also be used as a flavorful dip for fresh veggies.

½	cup mayonnaise	1	tablespoon grated onion
2	tablespoons butter or margarine, melted	¼	teaspoon salt
1	tablespoon prepared horseradish	¼	teaspoon dry mustard
			Pinch of red pepper
		1	(1-pound) bunch of broccoli

- Combine first 7 ingredients in a small bowl, blending well. Cover and chill 3 to 4 hours.

- Trim large leaves from broccoli and cut 1 inch off stems. Steam in large Dutch oven, or microwave 6 to 8 minutes until tender. Serve with sauce.

Makes 4 servings.

Broccoli Walnut Sauté

1½	pounds fresh broccoli	1	cup thin onion strips (cut vertically)
½	cup water		
2	tablespoons balsamic vinegar	½	cup thin strips sweet red pepper
2	teaspoons cornstarch		
1	teaspoon chicken bouillon granules	2	teaspoons vegetable oil
1	clove garlic, minced	¼	cup chopped walnuts, toasted

- Wash broccoli. Cut into florets. Peel stems, removing tough ends, and slice thinly; set aside.

- Combine water and next 3 ingredients; set aside.

- Cook garlic, onion, and red pepper in oil in a large skillet over medium heat, stirring constantly, for 3 minutes. Add broccoli; cook additional 3 minutes until broccoli is crisp tender. Add cornstarch mixture and bring to a boil, stirring constantly. Cook for no longer than 5 minutes more.

- Toss broccoli mixture with walnuts.

Makes 6 servings.

Meet Me at the Fair!

In 1820, the Pendleton Farmers Society hosted the forerunner of today's modern Anderson County Fair. Exhibits featured farming techniques and livestock demonstrations. The Fair wasn't held during the Civil War years, and in 1867 the event moved to Anderson under the sponsorship of the Anderson Farmers Association.

Brussels Sprouts Timbales

1	(10-ounce) package frozen Brussels sprouts		Nonstick cooking spray
2	tablespoons butter or margarine	1	egg
½	small onion, chopped	1	cup whipping cream
½	small red pepper, diced	¼	teaspoon salt
		⅛	teaspoon ground nutmeg

- Prepare Brussels sprouts as label directs; drain well; cool slightly. Finely chop Brussels sprouts and set aside.

- In 2-quart saucepan over medium heat, in hot butter or margarine, cook onion and red pepper until tender. Remove skillet from heat; stir in Brussels sprouts.

- With cooking spray, grease 5 (6-ounce) molds or custard cups. In medium bowl, with fork, mix egg and whipping cream; stir in Brussels sprout mixture, salt, and nutmeg. Spoon into molds.

- Place molds in 12-inch skillet; pour water into skillet to come halfway up sides of molds. Over medium heat, heat water just to boiling. Reduce heat to low; cover and simmer 15 to 20 minutes until knife inserted in center of mixture comes out clean. Remove molds from skillet to wire rack; cool 5 minutes.

- To serve, unmold timbales onto warm platter.

Makes 5 servings.

Creole Cabbage

3	slices bacon, chopped	⅓	cup white vinegar
1	large head cabbage, coarsely shredded (about 12 cups)	2	teaspoons salt
2	(28-ounce) cans chopped tomatoes	2	teaspoons salt-free Creole seasoning
		¼	teaspoon ground red pepper

- Cook bacon in a large Dutch oven until crisp. Drain. Reserve drippings in Dutch oven.

- Stir cabbage and next 5 ingredients into hot drippings; bring to a boil. Cover, reduce heat, and simmer 45 minutes. Sprinkle bacon on top.

Makes 8 servings.

Cabbage Casserole

1	stick butter	1½	cups milk
1	medium-size head green cabbage (about 2½ pounds), cored and thinly sliced	4	eggs, lightly beaten
		30	saltine crackers, finely crushed
		1¼	teaspoons salt
1	large onion, finely chopped	½	teaspoon ground black pepper

- Melt butter in large pot. Add cabbage and onion; cook over medium heat until softened, about 20 minutes. Stir in milk; bring to boiling. Lower heat to medium-low; simmer for 5 minutes. Remove pot from heat. Let cool slightly.

- Gently stir in eggs. Add half of crushed crackers, salt, and pepper. Pour into buttered 11 x 7-inch baking dish. Dust top evenly with remaining crushed crackers.

- Bake at 325° for 30 minutes or until heated through and top is golden.

Makes 6 servings.

Bourbon Glazed Carrots

1	pound carrots, scraped and cut into ¼-inch-thick slices	2	teaspoons sugar
		½	teaspoon ground ginger
¾	cup canned ready-to-serve vegetable broth	⅛	teaspoon ground nutmeg
		2	tablespoons margarine
1½	tablespoons bourbon		

- Combine carrot slices, broth, and bourbon in a medium saucepan; bring to a boil. Cover, reduce heat, and simmer 10 minutes. Uncover and cook over high heat 5 minutes.

- Add sugar and remaining ingredients to carrot mixture, stirring well. Cook over medium heat and additional 2 to 3 minutes or until carrots are tender.

Makes 4 servings.

Local residents glimpsed into the future on Thanksgiving Day, November 28, 1912, as the first airplane passed over Buena Vista Park in Anderson.

Heavenly Carrot Soufflé

A delicious way to get kids to eat carrots. (Our tasters loved it, too!)
The taste is similar to a sweet potato casserole.

1	pound carrots, peeled and sliced	3	tablespoons all-purpose flour
1	stick butter	1	teaspoon baking powder
3	eggs	1	teaspoon vanilla extract
1	cup sugar		

- Cook carrots in small amount of salted water until tender; drain; put in blender with butter, and purée.

- Pour mixture into bowl.

- Add all other ingredients and mix well. Pour into greased soufflé dish (or deep casserole dish).

- Bake at 350° for 45 minutes or until firm.

Makes 8 servings.

Almond Cheese Cauliflower

1	small head cauliflower, cut into florets	½	cup blanched almonds, lightly toasted
2	tablespoons butter		Salt and freshly ground black pepper to taste
2	tablespoons all-purpose flour		Butter
1	cup milk		
1	cup grated sharp Cheddar cheese		

- Steam or boil cauliflower until crisp-tender.

- While cauliflower is cooking, melt butter in a small saucepan over low heat. Add flour, stirring constantly until smooth. Blend in milk and continue stirring until sauce thickens. Add cheese, stirring until melted. Remove sauce from heat.

- Place cauliflower in deep casserole dish. Add cheese sauce, almonds, salt, pepper, and butter (cut in small pieces). Stir mixture to blend.

- Bake at 200° for 30 minutes.

Makes 4 servings.

Confetti Cauliflower

7 cups cauliflower florets
   (about 1¾ pounds)
1 tablespoon olive oil
2 cloves garlic, minced
½ cup diced green bell pepper
½ cup diced red bell pepper
½ cup diced yellow pepper
2 tablespoons sliced green
   onions
¼ cup chopped fresh dill weed
1 teaspoon lemon pepper
2 teaspoons white wine vinegar

- In a steamer, cover the cauliflower and steam for 8 minutes or until crisp-tender. Drain and set the cauliflower aside.

- In a medium skillet, heat oil over medium-high heat. Add garlic, peppers, and onion; sauté for 2 minutes. Stir in dill, lemon pepper, and vinegar; cook for 1 minute. Spoon over cauliflower.

Makes 6 to 8 servings.

Collards with Apples

2 pounds fresh collard greens,
   cleaned and chopped
2 cloves garlic, minced
3 green onions, chopped
1 tablespoon olive oil
1 cooking apple, diced
½ cup dry white wine
1 teaspoon sugar
1 teaspoon Greek seasoning
½ teaspoon salt
¼ teaspoon ground black pepper

- Cover greens with water in a Dutch oven and bring to a boil. Cook for 30 minutes; drain.

- Sauté garlic and green onions in hot oil in Dutch oven over medium-high heat until tender; add collards, apple, and remaining ingredients. Bring to a boil; cover, reduce heat, and simmer 15 minutes or until apple is tender, stirring occasionally.

Makes 6 servings.

Guests love the aroma of napkins stored in an airtight container with simmering-type potpourri chips or dried flower petals.

Notes

Company Corn

2	tablespoons butter	1	(16-ounce) bag frozen corn
2	tablespoons chopped onion	8	strips bacon, fried crisp,
2	tablespoons all-purpose flour		crumbled, and divided
½	teaspoon salt	1	tablespoon chopped parsley
1	(8-ounce) carton sour cream		

- **In a large skillet, melt butter and sauté onion until tender. Blend in flour and salt. Add sour cream gradually, stirring until smooth. Bring to a low boil.**

- **Add corn to mixture and cook until corn is heated through. Add half of crumbled bacon.**

- **Pour into greased 11 x 7-inch baking dish. Top with parsley and remaining bacon.**

- **Bake at 350° for 30 to 45 minutes or until bubbly.**

Makes 8 servings.

Scalloped Corn Bake

This dish is easy-fixing and man-pleasing!

2	cups corn kernels, fresh or frozen	¼	cup butter or margarine, melted
1	(14¾-ounce) can creamed corn	1	(4-ounce) jar diced pimentos, drained
1	(8-ounce) container French onion sour cream dip	¼	teaspoon ground red pepper
1	egg, lightly beaten	¾	teaspoon salt
1	(8½-ounce) box corn muffin mix	¼	teaspoon ground black pepper
			Nonstick cooking spray

- **In a large bowl, mix together corn kernels, creamed corn, onion sour cream dip, egg, corn muffin mix, and butter. Fold in pimentos, red pepper, salt, and black pepper. Place mixture into deep 8-cup casserole dish that has been coated with nonstick cooking spray.**

- **Bake at 350° for 1½ hours or until set and lightly golden. Serve immediately.**

Makes 12 servings.

Cajun Spiced Corn on the Cob

20	ears of fresh corn	¾	teaspoon ground black pepper
2	cups butter, melted	¾	teaspoon dried basil
1	tablespoon kosher salt	¾	teaspoon dried thyme
1½	teaspoons garlic powder	½	teaspoon (scant) dried oregano
1½	teaspoons cayenne pepper		Chopped parsley to taste
¾	teaspoon ground white pepper		

- Shuck the corn and remove silk. Cut ears of corn into halves.

- Fill an 8-quart stockpot ¾ full of water. Bring to a boil. Add corn. Bring back to a boil, and boil for 30 seconds. Cover and turn off heat. Let corn sit for 10 minutes. Drain.

- Pour butter over corn in stockpot.

- In a sealable plastic bag, combine kosher salt, garlic powder, cayenne powder, white pepper, black pepper, basil, thyme, and oregano; shake well. Add 2 to 3 tablespoons of mixture to corn, turning to coat corn well. (Reserve remaining spice mix for another purpose.) Place corn in large serving bowl and sprinkle with parsley.

Makes 20 to 25 servings.

Eggplant Fritters

2	eggplants, peeled and cubed	4	tablespoons dried parsley
1	cup all-purpose flour	4	tablespoons minced onion
2	teaspoons baking powder	1½	teaspoons garlic salt
2	large eggs, beaten		Salt and pepper to taste
2½	cups shredded Cheddar cheese		Peanut oil
4	tablespoons sugar		

- Boil cubed eggplant in just enough water to cover until tender; drain and mash.

- Combine flour, baking powder, eggs, cheese, sugar, parsley, onion, garlic salt, salt, and pepper; combine with mashed eggplant.

- Drop by spoonfuls into hot peanut oil and cook until golden brown. Drain on paper towels and serve immediately.

Makes 4 servings.

The Anderson Country Club was founded in 1918 by a group of about fifty public-spirited men, who wanted the community to have a country club with a golf course and tennis courts.

Notes

Cheesy Eggplant Pie

We loved this recipe! Wonderful and different!

2	(9-inch) pie shell pastries	1	teaspoon sugar
1	small eggplant, pared and cubed	¼	teaspoon salt
½	cup chopped onion	⅛	teaspoon dried oregano, crushed
¼	cup chopped green pepper		Dash of ground black pepper
2	tablespoons butter	3	eggs, beaten
1	tablespoon flour	1	tomato, peeled and chopped
1	can condensed cream of chicken soup	1	cup shredded sharp Cheddar cheese

- Use one pie crust to cut shapes or cutouts for top of pie. Partially bake crust and cutouts at 450° for about 5 minutes, watching carefully not to overbake.

- In a saucepan, cook eggplant, covered in boiling salted water, for 8 to 10 minutes until tender; drain.

- Cook onion and green pepper in butter until tender. Blend in flour; stir in soup, sugar, salt, oregano and pepper. Heat and stir until bubbly. Remove from heat.

- Stir half of the hot mixture into eggs; return all to saucepan.

- Fold in tomato, cheese, and eggplant; turn into partially baked crust and top with cutouts.

- Bake at 350° for 30 to 35 minutes.

Makes 6 to 8 servings.

Kale That's Cooking!

| 2 | bunches fresh kale (about 1 pound) | 1 | small onion, chopped |
| 6 | slices bacon, chopped | 1-2 | tablespoons cider vinegar |

- Remove stems and discolored spots from kale; rinse with cold water, and drain. Tear kale into bite-size pieces.

- Place kale in a steamer basket over boiling water. Cover and steam 5 minutes.

- Cook bacon in a skillet until crisp; remove and drain on paper towels, reserving 2 tablespoons drippings in skillet.

- Sauté onion in hot drippings until tender. Stir in kale and bacon. Drizzle with vinegar.

Makes 4 to 6 servings.

Stewed Mushrooms

Another all-around favorite, these mushrooms can be spooned over toast for a delicious light supper, or served as a nice accompaniment to steak or lamb.

½	cup unsalted butter	½	cup chopped onion
1	tablespoon all-purpose flour	4	large garlic cloves, chopped
3	pounds fresh mushrooms	2	teaspoons Worcestershire sauce
2	cups dry red wine		Chopped fresh parsley
2	cups canned vegetable broth		

- Melt butter in heavy large Dutch oven over medium heat. Add flour and stir to blend. Add mushrooms, wine, broth, onion, garlic, and Worcestershire sauce; cook until mushrooms are tender and sauce thickens, stirring occasionally, about 40 minutes.

- Season to taste with salt and pepper. Transfer to bowl; sprinkle with parsley and serve.

Makes 6 to 8 servings.

This recipe can be prepared 1 day ahead. Cover and refrigerate after seasoning with salt and pepper. Rewarm, sprinkle with parsley and serve.

Mild greens such as kale and Swiss chard retain their flavor better when cooked quickly, just until tender.

Fresh Okra and Tomatoes

8	slices bacon	3	cups peeled, chopped tomato
3	tablespoons all-purpose flour	½	teaspoon salt
4	cups sliced okra (about 1 pound)	½	teaspoon ground black pepper
¾	cup chopped onion	⅛-¼	teaspoon ground red pepper
2	cloves garlic, minced		Hot cooked rice

- Cook bacon in a large skillet over medium heat until crisp. Remove from heat; crumble bacon, and set aside. Reserve 3 tablespoons bacon drippings in skillet; discard remaining drippings.

- Stir flour into remaining drippings, and cook over medium heat, stirring constantly, until roux is caramel colored (about 10 to 15 minutes). Add okra, onion, and garlic; cook 2 minutes, stirring constantly. Stir in tomato and next 3 ingredients. Cover and simmer 10 to 15 minutes or until okra is tender, stirring occasionally.

- Serve okra and tomatoes over cooked rice. Sprinkle with reserved crumbled bacon.

Makes 6 to 8 servings.

Baked Whole Onions

4	medium Vidalia onions	4	teaspoons sugar, divided
4	teaspoons teriyaki sauce, divided	2	tablespoons margarine, divided
4	beef bouillon cubes, divided		Salt and pepper to taste

- Peel onions and scoop out a small cavity in the top of each onion, about 1 inch in diameter and ½ inch deep. Place in a deep casserole dish.

- In each onion cavity, place 1 teaspoon teriyaki sauce, 1 bouillon cube, 1 teaspoon sugar, and ½ tablespoon margarine. Pour 1 inch of water into bottom of dish.

- Bake at 400° for 1 hour.

Makes 4 servings.

Hearty Black-Eyed Peas

1	(16-ounce) package dried black-eyed peas	¾	teaspoon salt
4	cups water	1	(1-pound) ham steak, cut into ½-inch cubes, or 1 ham hock
1	medium onion, chopped	4	whole jalapeño peppers (optional)
½	teaspoon ground black pepper		

• Bring first 6 ingredients and, if desired, jalapeños to a boil in a Dutch oven; cover, reduce heat, and simmer 1 hour or until peas are tender.

Makes 8 servings.

Cajun Black-Eyed Peas

Enjoy a bowl of these tasty peas with cornbread or saltine crackers for a light lunch or dinner.

1	cup chopped onion	1	(14½-ounce) can diced tomatoes, undrained
½	cup chopped green bell pepper	1	(14½-ounce) can black-eyed peas, undrained
1	cup chopped celery	½	teaspoon Cajun seasoning
1	tablespoon oil		Salt and pepper to taste

• In a large skillet, sauté onion, bell pepper, and celery in oil until tender. Add tomatoes, black-eyed peas, Cajun seasoning, salt, and pepper. Simmer over low heat for approximately 30 minutes.

Makes 6 to 8 servings.

New Year's Day is a special time for many Southern families and their friends to gather around the table for a traditional meal of ham, collard greens, hoppin' john and sweet potatoes. Tradition holds that eating these foods on January 1st will bring fortune and good luck in the coming year. Some might say we are superstitious, but here's what we eat: black-eyed peas for "coins", collard greens for our "green backs" (paper money), and ham to focus on the future. (Pigs only move forward and won't turn back.) Sweet potatoes (or any root vegetable) are eaten because they provide strength and support for the coming year. Whatever your beliefs, you can be certain that it will be oh, so good!

Peas with Prosciutto

2	minced shallots	¾	cup chicken stock
3	tablespoons butter	3	ounces prosciutto ham, sliced
2	(10-ounce) packages frozen		into thin strips
	small green peas		Salt and pepper to taste
2	teaspoons sugar		

- **In a medium saucepan, sauté shallots in butter over medium heat until softened. Stir in peas, sugar, and chicken stock; cook until peas are warmed through and tender. Add prosciutto and cook for 1 minute. Drain pea mixture in a colander over bowl.**

- **Return liquid to saucepan and reduce over high heat until thickened to a glaze. Add salt and pepper to taste. Place peas in serving bowl and pour glaze over the top. Serve immediately.**

Makes 6 servings.

Dilled Peas and Potatoes Vinaigrette

8	small red potatoes (about 1½ pounds)	½	teaspoon salt
1	pound fresh sugar snap peas	½	teaspoon freshly ground black pepper
½	cup olive oil	6	green onions with tops, chopped
6	tablespoons white wine vinegar		
1½	tablespoons minced fresh dill weed		

- **Cook potatoes in a Dutch oven in boiling water to cover 25 to 30 minutes or until tender; drain. Thinly slice.**

- **Cook snap peas in boiling water 2 minutes or until crisp-tender; drain. Plunge peas into ice water to stop cooking process; drain.**

- **Whisk together oil and next 4 ingredients in a large bowl. Add sliced potato, snap peas, and onions, tossing gently to coat. Chill 2 hours, or serve immediately.**

Makes 6 to 8 servings.

1 (16-ounce) package frozen sugar snap peas may be substituted for fresh peas.

Baked Sweet Red and Yellow Pepper Wedges

2   medium-size sweet red peppers

2   medium-size sweet yellow peppers

1   medium-size onion, finely chopped

1   (28-ounce) can crushed tomatoes, well drained

¼   cup chopped fresh parsley

¼   cup plus 2 tablespoons olive oil

3   tablespoons pine nuts

4   cloves garlic, finely chopped

1   teaspoon salt

¼   teaspoon ground black pepper, or to taste

¼   cup fresh breadcrumbs

• Trim tops off peppers; discard stems and finely chop tops. Cut each pepper lengthwise into sixths. Place wedges, inner side up, in oiled 13 x 9-inch baking pan; set aside.

• In a medium bowl, combine chopped pepper tops, onion, tomatoes, parsley, ¼ cup olive oil, pine nuts, garlic, salt, and pepper. Spoon equal amount of mixture into each pepper wedge.

• Bake at 375° for 25 to 30 minutes or until just tender. Sprinkle breadcrumbs and remaining 2 tablespoons oil over all. Bake 10 minutes longer.

Makes 6 to 8 servings.

Roasted Potatoes

3   pounds baking potatoes, peeled and cut into strips

1   tablespoon salt

2   tablespoons dried oregano

2   tablespoons lemon juice
    Vegetable cooking spray
    Paprika

• Place potatoes, salt, oregano, and lemon juice in a large plastic freezer bag. Spray cooking spray into bag and shake well.

• Spray large baking sheet with cooking spray; pour potato mixture onto sheet in a single layer. Sprinkle with paprika.

• Bake at 425° for approximately 35 minutes.

Makes 6 to 8 servings.

Selecting and Storing Potatoes

Choose fresh potatoes with clean, smooth skins, a firm texture and good shape for the variety. Avoid potatoes with green spots, soft or moldy areas, or wilted skins. Store fresh potatoes in a well-ventilated, dark place that's cool and humid, but not wet. Lengthy exposure to light will cause greening of the skin, resulting in a bitter flavor. Avoid refrigerating potatoes because they become overly sweet and may darken when cooked. Home freezing of potatoes is not recommended.

Three-Cheese Mashed Potatoes

4	large potatoes, peeled and cubed	½	cup (1 ounce) shredded Muenster cheese
1	cup sour cream	2	teaspoons salt
2	(3-ounce) packages cream cheese, softened	1	teaspoon ground black pepper
4	tablespoons butter or margarine, softened	2	tablespoons butter or margarine, cut into small pieces
⅔	cup milk		Garnish: minced fresh chives
½	cup (1 ounce) shredded Cheddar cheese		

- Cook potatoes in boiling water to cover 15 minutes or until tender. Drain.

- Beat potatoes, sour cream, cream cheese, and 4 tablespoons butter at medium speed of electric mixer until smooth. Stir in milk and next 4 ingredients. Spoon into a lightly greased 2-quart baking dish; dot with 2 tablespoons butter. Cover and chill for 8 hours.

- Remove from refrigerator and let stand for 30 minutes.

- Bake at 400° for 25 to 35 minutes or until thoroughly heated. Garnish, if desired.

Makes 4 servings.

Creamed Spinach

1	pound fresh spinach	½	cup sour cream
1	medium onion, chopped		Dash of salt
1	clove garlic, crushed	¼	teaspoon ground black pepper
¼	cup butter or margarine, melted		Pinch of ground nutmeg
			Paprika

- Remove stems from spinach; wash leaves thoroughly, and tear into large pieces. Cook spinach in a small amount of boiling water 5 to 8 minutes or until tender. Drain; place on paper towels, and squeeze until barely moist.

- In a large skillet, sauté onion and garlic in butter until tender. Stir in sour cream, salt, pepper, and nutmeg. Add spinach, and cook over low heat until thoroughly heated; sprinkle with paprika and serve immediately.

Makes 4 servings.

Orange Sweet Potato Cups

4½ cups peeled, cubed sweet
     potatoes
3   tablespoons margarine
½   cup unsweetened orange juice
¼   cup whipping cream
1   tablespoon brown sugar
1   tablespoon orange-flavored
     liqueur

¼   teaspoon salt
¼   teaspoon ground nutmeg
¼   cup firmly packed brown
     sugar
1½   tablespoons all-purpose flour
1½   tablespoons margarine,
     softened
¼   cup finely chopped pecans

• Cook sweet potatoes in boiling water to cover 15 minutes or until
  tender; drain. In a bowl, combine sweet potatoes and 3 tablespoons
  margarine; mash. Add orange juice and next 5 ingredients; stir
  well. Spoon mixture into 4 lightly greased ramekins; set aside.

• Combine ¼ cup brown sugar, flour, 1½ tablespoons margarine,
  and chopped pecans; sprinkle evenly over sweet potato mixture
  in ramekins.

• Bake, uncovered, at 350° for 20 minutes or until bubbly.

Makes 4 servings.

*Simple and elegant
decorations and centerpieces
can be created by placing votive
candles in wine goblets
or crystal glasses of
differing sizes.*

Stuffed Sweet Potatoes

6	medium sweet potatoes, scrubbed	2	tablespoons butter or margarine
1	(8-ounce) package Neufchâtel cheese, softened	1-2	tablespoons cream sherry
¼	cup firmly packed brown sugar	¾	teaspoon salt
		½	teaspoon ground black pepper
		⅓	cup coarsely chopped pecans, toasted

- With fork, prick potatoes all over; lightly rub with salad oil. Place on jelly-roll pan; bake at 375° for 1 hour or until tender. Cool potatoes slightly.

- With sharp knife, trim a lengthwise strip, about ¼-inch thick, from one side of each potato. With spoon, scoop out cooked potatoes, leaving ¼-inch-thick shell (do not break skin); set shells aside.

- Place cooked potato in large bowl of electric mixer. At medium speed, beat until smooth. Add cheese, sugar, butter, sherry, salt, and pepper; beat until smooth. Spoon mixture into pastry bag fitted with large star tip; pipe into reserved skins. Sprinkle potatoes evenly with pecans and place on jelly-roll pan.

- Bake at 350° for 30 minutes, or until heated through.

Makes 6 servings.

Crusty Broiled Tomatoes

4	large tomatoes	1	teaspoon dried thyme
2	tablespoons spicy brown mustard	¼	teaspoon salt
½	cup Italian seasoned breadcrumbs	¼	teaspoon coarsely ground black pepper
½	cup shredded Parmesan cheese	¼	teaspoon ground red pepper
		¾	cup butter, melted

- Slice tomatoes into ½-inch slices; place slices in a single layer on a baking sheet or in a shallow baking pan.

- Combine remaining ingredients in a bowl and mix well; spoon mixture on top of tomatoes.

- Broil on high for 2 to 4 minutes or until lightly browned.

Makes 6 servings.

Acorn Squash with Glazed Fruit

2   (1-pound each) acorn squash
Vegetable oil
Salt and pepper
¼   cup butter or margarine
2   pears, cored and coarsely
      chopped

½   cup pecan halves
½   cup sugar
1½ cups cranberries
½   cup golden raisins
½   teaspoon ground cinnamon

• Cut acorn squash in half lengthwise; remove and discard seeds. Place squash, cut side up, in baking dish; add ½-inch water to dish. Brush cut sides of squash with oil; sprinkle with salt and pepper. Cover baking dish with aluminum foil.

• Bake at 400° for 30 minutes.

• While squash is baking, prepare glazed fruit. In a large skillet over medium-high heat, melt butter. Add pears, pecans, and sugar; cook for 8 minutes, stirring constantly, until fruit is glazed and tender. Add cranberries, raisins, and cinnamon; cook until slightly thickened.

• Uncover squash and fill each with fruit mixture, dividing evenly.

• Return to oven and bake, uncovered, for 15 minutes, or until squash is tender. Cut each squash in half lengthwise. Serve immediately.

Makes 8 servings.

Basil-Marinated Tomatoes

3   large tomatoes
⅓   cup olive oil
¼   cup balsamic vinegar
3   tablespoons dried basil
2   tablespoons chopped onion

1   teaspoon salt
¼   teaspoon ground black pepper
½   teaspoon concentrated
      chopped garlic

• Cut tomatoes into ¼-inch slices; arrange in thin layer in shallow baking dish.

• Combine oil and remaining ingredients in a bowl and whisk vigorously; pour mixture over tomato slices and marinate in refrigerator for at least 8 hours.

Makes 6 servings.

Garden-Stuffed Yellow Squash

The curvy crookneck squash makes an interesting presentation for stuffed shells.

6	medium-size yellow squash		Dash of freshly ground black pepper
1	cup chopped onion		
1	cup chopped tomato	1¼	cups shredded extra sharp Cheddar cheese
½	cup finely chopped green pepper	2	tablespoons butter or margarine
1	tablespoon chopped fresh basil	3	slices bacon, cooked and crumbled
¼	teaspoon salt		

- **Wash squash thoroughly; cover with water and bring to a boil. Cover, reduce heat, and simmer 8 to 9 minutes or until squash is tender but still firm. Drain and cool slightly. Cut squash in half lengthwise; remove and discard seeds, leaving a firm shell.**

- **In a bowl, combine onion, tomato, green pepper, basil, salt, and pepper. Stir in cheese.**

- **Place squash shells in a 13 x 9-inch baking dish. Spoon vegetable mixture into shells; dot with butter. Sprinkle with bacon.**

- **Bake, uncovered, at 400° for 20 minutes. Serve immediately.**

Makes 6 servings.

Southern Fried Green Tomatoes

⅔	cup cornmeal	1	egg, beaten
¼	teaspoon salt	¼	cup plus 2 tablespoons vegetable or olive oil, divided
¼	teaspoon ground black pepper		
3	large green tomatoes, sliced		

- **Combine cornmeal, salt, and pepper in a small bowl; stir well. Dip tomato slices in beaten egg; dredge in cornmeal mixture, coating well on both sides.**

- **Heat 2 tablespoons oil in a large skillet over medium-high heat until hot. Add one layer of coated tomato slices, and fry 3 to 5 minutes or until browned, turning once. Remove tomato slices from skillet. Drain; set aside, and keep warm. Repeat procedure twice with remaining oil and tomato slices. Serve immediately.**

Makes 6 servings.

"South of the Border" Squash

1	cup chopped onion	½	cup grated Monterey Jack cheese
1½	pounds yellow squash, washed and sliced	1	egg
2	tablespoons butter	1	cup cottage cheese
1	(4-ounce) can green chilies	2	tablespoons chopped parsley
2	tablespoons all-purpose flour	½	cup Parmesan cheese
	Salt and pepper		

- In a large skillet, sauté onion and squash in butter until tender. Stir in chilies, flour, salt, and pepper. Pour into greased 13 x 9-inch baking dish. Sprinkle cheese on top.

- Stir together egg, cottage cheese, and parsley; spread on top of cheese.

- Sprinkle Parmesan cheese on top and bake at 375° for 30 minutes. Serve immediately.

Makes 8 to 10 servings.

Turnip Greens with Turnips

2	pounds fresh turnip greens	1	tablespoon sugar
6	slices bacon, chopped	½	teaspoon salt
4	cups water	¼-½	teaspoon ground black pepper
3	medium turnips, peeled and diced		

- Remove stems from turnip greens. Wash leaves thoroughly, drain, and tear into bite-size pieces.

- Cook bacon in a Dutch oven until browned. Drain bacon, and set aside; reserve drippings in Dutch oven. Add greens and water. Cover and simmer 20 minutes. Stir in turnips, sugar, and salt. Cover and cook an additional 20 minutes or until desired degree of doneness. Spoon into serving dish; sprinkle bacon over top. Serve immediately.

Makes 6 servings.

Grilled Summer Vegetable Seasoning

3 tablespoons salt

3 tablespoons packed light brown sugar

2 tablespoons paprika

1½ tablespoons chili powder

1 tablespoon ground black pepper

2¼ teaspoons garlic powder

1½ teaspoons cayenne pepper

1½ teaspoons dried basil

Assorted vegetables for grilling, cut into ½-inch thick slices (zucchini, peppers, onions, portobello mushrooms, squash, cherry tomatoes, etc.)

Vegetable or other desired oil

- Process first 8 ingredients in a food processor for 15 seconds; store in tightly covered container.

- Place vegetables on skewers; lightly brush with oil and sprinkle generously with spice mixture. Lay skewers directly on grill and cook until desired tenderness is achieved.

Oiled and seasoned vegetables may also be placed in a foil packet with all sides folded shut and placed on heated grill until done.

Baked Brown Rice

This quick and easy dish is a delicious accompaniment for any meat.

1 cup uncooked brown rice (not instant)

1 (10¼-ounce) can beef broth

1 (10½-ounce) can beef consommé

1 small onion, finely chopped

1 tablespoon dried parsley (optional)

1 stick butter

• Combine rice, broth, consommé, onion, and parsley; place mixture in casserole dish.

• Cut butter into small pats and place on top of rice mixture.

• Cover and bake at 350° for 45 minutes

Makes 6 to 8 servings.

St. Paul Rice

1	pound sausage	¾	cup uncooked rice
1	medium onion, chopped	2	(2.1-ounce) packages chicken noodle soup mix
1	medium bell pepper, chopped		
½	cup chopped celery	1	(2¼-ounce) package sliced almonds
4½	cups water		

• In a large skillet brown sausage, onion, pepper, and celery; drain.

• Bring water to a boil; add rice and soup mix. Boil for 7 minutes.

• Add sausage mixture and almonds to rice. Pour into casserole dish and cover lightly with foil.

• Bake at 350° for 1 hour.

Makes 8 servings.

Vegetables Jardiniere

In this simple recipe, vegetables "from the garden" are served with a light coating of fresh sweet butter. Carrots, celery, turnips, and peas are recommended here, but most fresh vegetables would be suitable for this delightful dish.

1	cup matchstick cut carrots	3	ounces unsalted butter
3	celery stalks, matchstick cut	1	tablespoon chopped parsley
1	cup matchstick cut white turnips		Salt and pepper
1	cup fresh peas	½	teaspoon sugar (optional)

• Blanch vegetables separately in boiling salted water, shock, and drain them.

• In a large skillet, reheat the vegetables by tossing them in the butter over medium heat.

• Add parsley, salt and pepper to taste, and sugar, if desired. Serve immediately.

Makes 8 to 10 servings.

Stuffed Zucchini

2	medium zucchini	¾	cup cracker crumbs
1	small onion, chopped	1	egg
1	cup coarsely chopped fresh mushrooms	½	cup grated Cheddar cheese
½	cup chopped celery	2	tablespoons Parmesan cheese
1	medium tomato, chopped	½	teaspoon salt
1	tablespoon butter or margarine, melted	⅛	teaspoon ground black pepper
		½	teaspoon paprika

- Cut zucchini in half lengthwise. Remove and save pulp, leaving ¼-inch shell.

- Chop zucchini pulp; add onion, mushrooms, celery and tomatoes. Cover and microwave on high for 4 to 6 minutes, stirring once. Drain off excess liquid and stir in all remaining ingredients except paprika.

- Fill zucchini shells with mixture and sprinkle with paprika. Place filled shells in glass dish and cover with plastic wrap.

- Microwave on high for 5 to 7 minutes. Serve immediately.

Makes 4 servings.

Favorite Macaroni and Cheese

2	cups small curd cottage cheese	2	cups shredded sharp Cheddar cheese
1	(8-ounce) carton sour cream	1	(8-ounce) package small elbow macaroni, cooked
1	egg		Paprika
¾	teaspoon salt		
½	teaspoon ground black pepper		

- In a large bowl combine first 6 ingredients. Stir in macaroni. Spoon mixture into a lightly greased 2-quart casserole dish; sprinkle with paprika.

- Bake at 350° for 45 minutes. Let stand 10 minutes before serving.

Makes 8 to 10 servings.

Delicious Zucchini Pie

2 cups shredded zucchini
¾ cup biscuit baking mix
¾ cup shredded Cheddar cheese
1 small onion, finely chopped
½ teaspoon salt
¼ teaspoon ground black pepper
¼ teaspoon rubbed sage
2 large eggs, lightly beaten
¼ cup oil

- Stir together all ingredients. Pour into greased 9-inch pie plate.

- Bake at 350° for 45 minutes. Cool 10 minutes before serving.

Makes 4 to 6 servings.

Couscous with Raisins, Almonds, and Lemons

1	(14½-ounce) can vegetable broth	1	(2.25-ounce) package slivered almonds
¼	cup water	1	tablespoon lemon juice
3	tablespoons olive oil, divided	2	small celery ribs, diced
1	(4.8-ounce) package Israeli couscous	3	garlic cloves, pressed
½	cup raisins	4	skinned and boned chicken breast halves, cut into strips
⅓	cup chopped fresh Italian parsley		

- Bring broth, ¼ cup water, and 1 tablespoon oil to a boil in a saucepan over medium heat.

- Stir in couscous and seasoning packet. Cover, reduce heat, and simmer 15 minutes or until liquid is absorbed and couscous is tender. Fluff with a fork. Stir in raisins and next 4 ingredients.

- Heat remaining 2 tablespoons oil in a large skillet over medium heat. Add garlic, and sauté 2 to 3 minutes or until tender. Add chicken, and sauté 8 minutes or until browned.

- Spoon couscous onto a serving platter; top with chicken.

Makes 4 servings.

Mushroom Pesto Pasta

7	ounces uncooked linguine, broken in half	½	cup drained and thinly sliced canned roasted red peppers
4	ounces fresh shiitake mushrooms, thinly sliced	2	ounces oil-packed sun dried tomatoes
½	cup chopped onion	2	tablespoons dried parsley flakes
3	tablespoons olive oil	⅓	cup grated Parmesan cheese
½	cup commercial pesto sauce		

- Cook pasta according to package directions; drain and set aside.

- Sauté mushrooms and onion in hot olive oil until tender. Add pesto, red peppers, tomatoes, and parsley; stir well. Add pasta and simmer over low heat for approximately 4 minutes. Sprinkle with Parmesan cheese and serve immediately.

Makes 4 servings.

Creamy Rice and Squash Casserole

5	tablespoons butter or margarine, divided	4	cups cooked rice, seasoned as directed on package
2	cups chopped yellow squash	½	cup whipping cream
1	cup chopped onion	1	tablespoon dried basil
2	(14½-ounce) cans diced tomatoes, drained	1	tablespoon dried parsley flakes
¼	cup all-purpose flour	½	teaspoon ground black pepper
2	cups chicken broth	¼	cup grated Parmesan cheese
			Salt and pepper
		½	cup Cheddar cheese

- Melt 1 tablespoon butter in large skillet over medium heat; add squash, onion, and tomatoes. Cook, stirring often, until squash is tender. Set vegetables aside.

- Melt remaining 4 tablespoons butter in medium saucepan over low heat; add flour, stirring until smooth. Cook 1 minute, stirring constantly. Gradually add chicken broth; cook over medium heat, stirring constantly, until mixture is thickened. Stir in vegetables, rice, and next 5 ingredients. Add salt and extra pepper to taste. Pour into lightly greased 11 x 7 x 1½-inch baking dish. Sprinkle with Cheddar cheese.

- Bake at 350° for 30 minutes or until thoroughly heated.

Makes 8 to 10 servings.

Notes

Simple Salt

Table salt contains ingredients, such as dextrose, to maintain its pure white color and to keep it from clumping. Generally, it is iodized to help provide iodine, an essential mineral in the diet. (Pickling or canning salt is a finer grind than table salt. Free of additives, it won't cloud pickling liquids or brines.)

Kosher Salt

A coarse-ground and additive-free salt, kosher salt tastes about half as salty as table salt.

Rock Salt

An inedible coarse-grain salt, rock salt is often used in freezing homemade ice cream.

Sea Salt

Sea salt is formed by evaporating sea water. It may contain slightly more trace minerals than table salts, but has no other nutritional advantages.

Seasoned Salts

Celery, garlic, or onion salt, are blends of salt and other seasonings.

Spinach Manicotti

**A great dish that can be prepared
ahead of time to accommodate a busy schedule!**

1	tablespoon vegetable oil	1	egg
1	(10-ounce) box frozen chopped spinach, thawed	1	cup cottage cheese
		1	(16-ounce) jar pasta sauce
1	tablespoon finely chopped onion	8	manicotti shells
			Parmesan cheese

- In medium saucepan sauté spinach and onion in oil until heated through. Remove from heat; stir in egg. Add cottage cheese, mixing thoroughly. Set aside.

- Cook manicotti according to package directions; drain.

- Place ½ cup of pasta sauce in bottom of ungreased 9 x 9-inch baking dish. Stuff manicotti shells with spinach mixture and place in sauce in dish. Pour remaining sauce over manicotti.

- Cover and bake at 350° for 25 to 30 minutes. Garnish with Parmesan cheese.

Makes 4 servings.

Pasta with Basil, Capers, and Pine Nuts

Top with crumbled feta cheese to further tantalize your palate.

1	tablespoon olive oil		½	cup pine nuts
2-3	tablespoons minced garlic		1	cup chicken broth
3	cups chopped tomatoes		½	teaspoon salt
¾	cup sun-dried tomatoes packed in oil, drained and thinly sliced		¼	teaspoon freshly ground black pepper
½	cup chopped fresh basil		1	pound vermicelli pasta, cooked al dente
2	tablespoons capers			

- Heat oil in a large skillet. Add garlic and sauté until translucent. Add tomatoes, basil, capers, and pine nuts. Cook 2 to 3 minutes. Add chicken broth, salt, and pepper. Cook until heated thoroughly.

- Place cooked pasta in serving bowl, add sauce, and toss. Serve immediately.

Makes 6 servings.

"Pasta-bilities"

Spaghetti pasta is cut in long, thin strands (the name means "strings"). According to the The National Pasta Association, it's America's favorite.

Capellini (Angel Hair, Fine Hairs) is the thinnest type of spaghetti.

Linguine pasta is cut in long, flat strands (the name means "little tongues").

Fusilli (Twisted Spaghetti, Fusilli Lungi) is a tightly curled spiral pasta, either long like spaghetti or short like penne.

Rigatoni is a large, tubular pasta with grooves (the name means "big grooves").

Penne Rigati is also a tubular pasta with grooves, the ends of which are cut on the diagonal to resemble a pen point.

Sage and Cornbread Dressing

This classic Southern favorite takes a bit of time, but is well worth the effort. The batter can be made one day ahead and refrigerated until ready to bake.

3	cups self-rising cornmeal
¼	cup all-purpose flour
1	tablespoon sugar
1	teaspoon salt
	Pinch of baking soda
3	cups buttermilk
2	eggs, well beaten
1	cup finely chopped celery
¾	cup finely chopped onion
3	tablespoons bacon drippings
1¾	cups herb seasoned stuffing mix
½	teaspoon rubbed sage
1	(10½-ounce) can cream of chicken soup, undiluted
3	cups chicken or turkey broth

- Combine cornmeal, flour, sugar, salt, and baking soda, stirring lightly. Add buttermilk and eggs; mix well. Stir in chopped celery and onion.

- Heat bacon drippings in a 10-inch cast iron or oven proof skillet on stove until very hot. Add 1 tablespoon hot drippings to batter, mixing well. Pour batter into hot skillet, and bake at 450° for 30 minutes or until bread is lightly browned. When bread is cool enough to handle, crumble into a large mixing bowl; add stuffing and sage. Set aside.

- Place soup in a medium saucepan; slowly stir in broth. Cook until thoroughly heated, stirring constantly. Pour over crumb mixture and stir well. Spoon into well greased 13 x 9-inch baking dish.

- Bake at 375° for 35 to 40 minutes or until thoroughly heated.

Makes 12 to 15 servings.

Entrées

Electric City Entrées

Entrées

On the front:
Fireside in our Backyard
Photograph by *Sabrina R. Dunn*

Celebration Roast

A tender rib-eye roast is always a
hit for a lavish feast, and is easy to slice and serve.

2	tablespoons cream-style prepared horseradish	½	teaspoon salt	
4	cloves garlic, minced	1	(4 to 6-pound) boneless beef rib-eye roast	
4-5	teaspoons cracked pink and black peppercorns, (or cracked black pepper), divided	12	medium onions	
		6	small red and/or white onions	
		1	tablespoon olive oil	

• Combine horseradish, garlic, 3 teaspoons of the cracked peppercorns, and salt; rub mixture onto meat. Place beef roast, fat side up, on a rack in a shallow roasting pan. (Do not add liquid.) Insert a meat thermometer into center of roast. Roast, uncovered, at 350° for 1½ to 2 hours or until thermometer registers 135° (rare) or 150° (medium). (The meat's temperature will rise about 10° while standing.)

• Meanwhile, slice root ends from onions to allow them to stand upright. Leave about 1 inch of onion top, if desired. Brush onions with olive oil. Sprinkle with remaining cracked peppercorns. During the last 1¼ hours of roasting time, arrange onions, standing upright, around meat. If desired, serve with Horseradish-Peppercorn Cream.

Makes 12 to 16 servings.

Horseradish-Peppercorn Cream

½ cup whipping cream
2 tablespoons cream-style prepared horseradish
1 teaspoon Dijon mustard
1-2 tablespoons cracked pink and black peppercorns

• In a chilled mixing bowl, beat whipping cream just until soft peaks form. Fold in horseradish and Dijon mustard. If not using immediately, cover and store in refrigerator up to 6 hours. To serve, sprinkle each serving of cream with cracked peppercorns.

Makes about 1 cup.

To crack pepper, enclose peppercorns in a clean kitchen towel or in a heavy-duty sealable plastic bag. Pound with a mallet or the bottom of a heavy skillet until the pepper-corns are lightly crushed. You can also use an electric spice grinder or crush them in a mortar with a pestle. Of course, you could always use your pepper mill!

Many of the early settlements in Anderson County have vanished. One of the most memorable ones was Andersonville, a manufacturing town. Founded in 1901 not far from the convergence of the Seneca and Tugaloo Rivers, it was home to a cotton gin, a wool mill, an iron foundry, a gun factory, a tailor shop, a shoe shop, several stores and liveries, and even an academy for young ladies. Andersonville's growth was stunted by a great flood in 1840. After another great flood in 1852, and the rebuilding town being bypassed by the railroad, Andersonville never recovered. When Hartwell Lake was created, the flooding of the rivers resulted in the low-lying ruins of Andersonville being almost completely covered by water. Andersonville Island is a reminder of that vestige of Anderson County's early pioneer history.

Marinated Roast Beef

So easy and so good!

1	tablespoon sesame seeds		½	cup soy sauce
1½-2	tablespoons butter		1	large onion, chopped
½	cup strong coffee		1	tablespoon Worcestershire
1	tablespoon apple cider			sauce
	vinegar		1	(3 to 5-pound) chuck roast

- Brown sesame seeds in butter in skillet. Add coffee, vinegar, soy sauce, onion, and Worcestershire sauce. Simmer 5 minutes, stirring frequently. Remove from heat.

- Place roast in large heavy-duty zip-top bag. Pour marinade over roast and seal bag. Refrigerate all day or overnight, turning bag every few hours. Remove roast from bag, and discard marinade. Grill over medium-hot coals for about 45 minutes or until done.

Makes 6 to 8 servings.

Cajun Smoked Heavenly Brisket

½	cup packed dark brown sugar		1	tablespoon Worcestershire
2	tablespoons Cajun seasoning			sauce
2	tablespoons salt		1	(5 to 6-pound) beef brisket
1	tablespoon lemon pepper			Hickory wood chips
	seasoning			

- Combine first 5 ingredients in a shallow dish; add brisket, turning to coat both sides. Cover and chill 8 hours or overnight.

- Soak hickory chips in water for 1 hour.

- Prepare charcoal fire in smoker; burn 20 minutes.

- Drain hickory chips, and place on coals. Place water pan in smoker, adding water to pan up to fill line.

- Remove brisket from marinade; place on lower food rack. Pour remaining marinade over meat. Cover with smoker lid, and cook 5 hours or until a meat thermometer inserted in thickest portion registers 170°.

Makes 12 servings.

Pear and Cheese Stuffed Tenderloin

1¾ cups finely chopped fresh pears

½ cup minced green onions

3 tablespoons crumbled blue cheese

1 tablespoon lemon juice

1 teaspoon cracked black pepper

1 (4½-pound) beef tenderloin

Nonstick cooking spray

¼ cup port wine

- Combine first 5 ingredients in a small bowl and set aside.

- Trim fat from tenderloin. Slice tenderloin lengthwise, cutting to, but not through, the center, leaving one long edge intact.

- Spoon pear mixture into opening of tenderloin. Bring sides of meat together, enclosing pear mixture, and secure at 2-inch intervals with heavy string. Place tenderloin, seam side down, on a rack in a roasting pan coated with cooking spray. Insert meat thermometer into thickest part of tenderloin, if desired. Brush wine over tenderloin.

- Heat oven to 500°. Place tenderloin in oven. Reduce heat to 350° and bake, uncovered, for 1 hour or until meat thermometer registers 140° (rare) or 160° (medium). Remove from oven and let stand 10 minutes. Remove string and cut tenderloin diagonally across grain into ¼-inch-thick slices; arrange on serving platter.

Makes 15 to 18 servings.

Bourbon Peppered Beef in a Blanket

8	(6 to 8-ounce) beef tenderloin steaks, cut to 1½ inches in thickness)	1	pound portobello mushrooms, thinly sliced
2	leeks, chopped	3	tablespoons Worcestershire sauce
¾	cup bourbon	2	(8-ounce) cans refrigerated crescent rolls
¼	cup freshly cracked black pepper	1	egg white, lightly beaten
			Garnish: fresh chives

- Combine first 3 ingredients in a shallow dish or large heavy-duty zip-top plastic bag. Cover or seal, and chill 8 hours, turning occasionally.

- Remove steaks from marinade, reserving marinade. Press pepper evenly onto both sides of steaks.

- Cook steaks in a large nonstick skillet over medium-high heat 4 to 5 minutes on each side. Set aside; cool completely.

- Bring reserved marinade to a boil in a medium saucepan over medium heat. Stir in mushrooms and Worcestershire sauce; reduce heat, and simmer 10 minutes. Keep warm.

- Unroll crescent rolls, and separate into 8 rectangles; press perforations to seal. Roll rectangles to 6-inch squares.

- Place 1 steak in the center of each pastry square. Bring corners of 1 pastry square to center, pinching to seal. Repeat with remaining steaks and pastry. Brush with egg white.

- Bake, seam side down, on a lightly greased rack in a broiler pan at 375° for 13 minutes.

- Spoon warm sauce evenly onto serving plates; top with steaks. Garnish, if desired.

Makes 8 servings.

The steaks and sauce may be prepared 1 day ahead. Follow the recipe up to baking the steaks. Remove steaks and sauce from refrigerator, and let stand 30 minutes before completing the recipe.

Italian Crock Pot Roast with Linguine

2	tablespoons olive oil	⅔	cup water
1	(3¾-pound) chuck or top round roast	2	teaspoons dried basil
½	large onion, sliced	2	teaspoons hot pepper sauce
1	cup beef broth	1	teaspoon coarsely ground black pepper
1	cup dry red wine	1	tablespoon sugar
2	teaspoons concentrated chopped garlic	12	ounces linguine
1½	(6-ounce) cans tomato paste with Italian seasonings	½	cup Parmesan cheese (optional)

- Pour oil into crockpot and place roast on top. Combine next 10 ingredients in a bowl and mix well. Pour over roast and cook on high for 3½ hours or until tender.

- Cook linguine according to package directions. Drain and serve with juice from roast on top of linguine and sliced roast on the side. Sprinkle with Parmesan cheese.

Makes 6 servings.

Saucy Chuck Roast

1	(8-ounce) can tomato sauce	¼	cup ketchup
½	cup beef broth	2	teaspoons Worcestershire sauce
1	medium onion, chopped	1	teaspoon prepared yellow mustard
1	(3 to 4-pound) chuck roast		
2	tablespoons vegetable oil	1	teaspoon paprika
½	cup apple cider vinegar	⅛	teaspoon garlic powder

- Combine first 3 ingredients in a shallow dish; add roast. Cover and marinate in refrigerator for 8 hours or overnight.

- Remove roast from marinade, reserving marinade. Place roast in a Dutch oven. Combine marinade and remaining ingredients; pour over roast. Cover and bake at 350° for 2½ to 3 hours or until roast is tender. Skim fat from sauce and serve sauce with roast.

Makes 6 to 8 servings.

Cowboy Grilling Sauce

Use this tasty sauce to baste any type of grilled meat.

1 cup ketchup
1 cup strong black coffee
½ cup Worcestershire sauce
¼ cup butter
2 tablespoons sugar
1 tablespoon cracked black pepper
½-1 tablespoon salt
1 small jalapeño pepper, seeded and finely chopped

- Combine all ingredients in a saucepan over medium heat and bring to a boil. Reduce heat and simmer for 30 minutes.

Makes about 3 cups.

Crispy Onions

Try these with steak for some crunchy seasoning!

*3 large sweet onions, cut into
¼-inch slices and divided into rings*

1 egg

1 cup buttermilk

1 cup flour

½ teaspoon baking powder

½ teaspoon salt

Vegetable oil

• Soak onion rings in ice water for 2 hours, adding additional ice as it melts.

• Combine egg, buttermilk, flour, baking powder, and salt in a medium bowl and mix well.

• Drain onion rings and pat dry. Dip rings into the batter and deep-fry a few at a time in vegetable oil at 375° until brown. Drain on paper towels and keep warm until all onions are cooked. Serve immediately.

Makes 6 servings.

Balsamic-Basted Steaks

3	tablespoons olive oil
2	tablespoons balsamic vinegar
2	tablespoons coarse mustard
1	teaspoon salt
½	teaspoon freshly ground black pepper
6-8	long fresh rosemary sprigs (optional)

Kitchen twine or string

4 (6-ounce) filet mignon or tenderloin steaks, 1 inch thick

Nonstick cooking spray

4 small red onions, halved

4 plum tomatoes, halved

Vegetable Oil

• Mix together oil, vinegar, mustard, salt, and pepper in a large, shallow dish.

• If desired, wrap a rosemary sprig around edge of steak and tie ends securely with kitchen string. Repeat with other steaks. Place steaks in marinade and turn to coat. Cover with plastic wrap and refrigerate 30 minutes or overnight.

• Lightly coat clean grids of grill with cooking spray. Heat grill to medium-high heat.

• Lightly brush onion and tomato halves with oil. Place onions on grill, cut side down, and grill 10 minutes with the lid down. Turn and cook 5 minutes more; transfer to a plate and keep warm.

• Place steaks on grill and cook, without turning, 4 minutes with the lid down. Turn steaks and place tomatoes, cut side down, on grill. Cook steak and tomatoes, with lid down, 4 minutes. Transfer steak to plates along with the onions and tomatoes.

Makes 4 servings.

Flank Steak
with Orange Papaya Butter

1   (1-pound) lean flank steak
2   tablespoons soy sauce
2   tablespoons vegetable oil
2   tablespoons peeled, minced gingerroot
⅛   teaspoon hot pepper sauce
1   clove garlic, minced
¼   cup butter, softened

¼   cup flaked coconut
3   tablespoons finely chopped papaya
2   teaspoons finely minced fresh parsley
¾-1 teaspoon curry powder
2   teaspoons freshly grated orange peel

- Trim fat from steak.

- Combine soy sauce and next 4 ingredients in a heavy-duty zip-top plastic bag; seal bag, and shake until steak is well coated. Add steak to bag and marinate in refrigerator 12 to 24 hours, turning bag occasionally.

- Place greased rack on grill over medium hot coals.

- Remove steak from marinade; discard marinade. Place steak on rack; grill with lid down 6 minutes on each side or to desired degree of doneness. Remove steak from grill and let stand 10 minutes.

- Meanwhile, combine butter and remaining ingredients in a small mixing bowl; beat with electric mixer on medium speed until fluffy.

- Cut steak diagonally across the grain and serve with butter mixture.

Makes 4 servings.

Basic Steak Marinade

¾ cup oil
¼ cup soy sauce
¼ cup honey
2 tablespoons vinegar
1 clove garlic, minced
1½ teaspoons ground ginger
2 green onions, chopped

• Mix all ingredients together. Pour over meat and marinate 8 hours, or overnight, turning occasionally. Remove meat from marinade, and broil or cook on grill.

Makes about 1¼ cups.

Savory Spaghetti Sauce

You may want to double this easy recipe and freeze in containers for a quick supper.

2 pounds ground beef or 1 pound each ground beef and ground veal

2 tablespoons olive oil

4 cups canned diced tomatoes

1 cup tomato purée

½ cup tomato paste

½ cup sliced fresh mushrooms

1 medium onion, chopped

1-2 cloves garlic, minced

½ teaspoon dried basil

½ teaspoon dried oregano

1 tablespoon salt

½ teaspoon ground black pepper

• Brown beef in oil and add tomatoes, tomato purée, and tomato paste.

• Place mushrooms and remaining ingredients in a blender or food processor and process until smooth. Add to tomato mixture and mix well. Bring to a boil, reduce heat, and simmer for 30 to 45 minutes. Serve over cooked pasta.

Makes 6 to 8 servings.

Oriental Sirloin with Asparagus and Wild Rice Pilaf

Omit the red pepper from this recipe if you prefer a less spicy entrée.

1	pound fresh asparagus spears	1	(1-pound) top sirloin steak
⅓	cup low-sodium soy sauce	4	cups sliced spinach
¼	cup dry sherry	2	cups cooked wild rice
½	teaspoon ground black pepper	⅔	cup chopped green onions
⅛	teaspoon ground red pepper	½	cup finely chopped celery
1	clove garlic, minced	2	teaspoons dark sesame oil

• Snap off tough ends of asparagus. Cook asparagus in boiling water for 2 minutes or until crisp-tender. Drain well, and chill.

• Combine soy sauce and next 4 ingredients. Reserve ⅓ cup of the soy sauce mixture, and place remaining mixture, along with steak and asparagus, in a large heavy-duty zip-top bag; seal. Marinate in refrigerator for 1 hour, turning the bag occasionally.

• Remove the asparagus and steak from bag, and discard the marinade. Heat a grill pan or skillet over medium-high heat. Add the asparagus and steak, and cook steak for 3 minutes on each side or until desired degree of doneness, turning asparagus as needed. Place steak on a platter and asparagus on a plate, and cover both with foil. Let stand for 5 minutes. Cut the steak diagonally across the grain into thin slices.

• Combine ⅓ cup of reserved soy sauce mixture, spinach, rice, green onions, celery, and oil; toss to coat. Divide asparagus, steak, and wild rice pilaf evenly among 4 plates. Serve immediately.

Makes 4 servings.

Reuben Meat Loaf

2	pounds ground beef	¼	cup Thousand Island salad dressing
2	cups soft rye breadcrumbs	1	teaspoon caraway seeds
1	(10-ounce) can shredded sauerkraut, drained	1	teaspoon dry mustard
½	cup chopped onion	2	eggs, beaten
¼	cup whole milk	5	slices bacon
		½	cup shredded Swiss cheese

- Combine first 9 ingredients in a medium bowl; stir well. Shape mixture into a 9 x 5-inch loaf; place on a rack in a lightly greased roasting pan. Arrange bacon slices over loaf. Bake at 350° for 1½ hours. Sprinkle cheese over meat loaf, and bake an additional 5 minutes. Let stand 10 minutes before serving.

Makes 10 servings.

Family Night Shepherd's Pie

**You will never have any leftovers
when you make this wonderful dish!**

1	(22-ounce) package frozen mashed potatoes	1	(10½-ounce) can beef broth
1	pound ground beef	2	teaspoons salt, divided
1	medium onion, chopped	½	teaspoon ground black pepper, divided
½	cup frozen sliced carrots or mixed vegetables, thawed	1	large egg, lightly beaten
2	tablespoons all-purpose flour	½	cup shredded Cheddar cheese
			Garnish: chopped fresh parsley

- Cook potatoes according to package directions; set aside.

- Cook beef and onion in a large skillet over medium-high heat 5 to 6 minutes, stirring until beef crumbles and is no longer pink. Drain and return to skillet; add vegetables, flour, broth, 1 teaspoon salt, and ¼ teaspoon pepper. Cook, stirring constantly, 3 minutes or until slightly thickened. Spoon mixture into a lightly greased 11 x 7-inch baking dish.

- Stir together potatoes, egg, remaining 1 teaspoon salt, and remaining ¼ teaspoon pepper. Spoon over beef mixture. Bake at 350° for 25 minutes. Sprinkle with cheese, and bake 5 more minutes. Garnish, if desired.

Makes 6 servings.

Meatballs – not just with spaghetti anymore!

Add any of the following to your basic meatloaf or meatball recipe - with 2 pounds of meat

Greek Meatballs:
Add 1 teaspoon dried oregano and 2 tablespoons dried dill.

Spanish Meatballs:
Add 1 teaspoons dried oregano and 2 tablespoons chopped green or red pepper.

Italian Sausage Meatballs:
Add 1 teaspoon each crushed red pepper and fennel seeds.

Mexican Meatballs:
Add 1 tablespoon chili powder, 1 teaspoon each dried oregano and cumin.

Method:
1. Preheat oven to moderate (350°). 2. Combine all ingredients in mixing bowl. Divide mixture evenly into 64 small balls. Place on rack that fits inside a baking pan. 3. Bake 40 minutes or until meatballs are cooked through. These may be made ahead and frozen. Note: Mix and shape meatballs in the morning. Put them into the oven about 15 minutes before you expect your guests. By the time the crowd gathers (about 45 minutes), the meatballs will be ready.

Autumn Pumpkin Meatloaf

**Make this a Halloween family tradition! This meatloaf
is very kid-friendly since it's tasty but not too spicy. The
cooked pumpkin is quite good as well!**

1	small pumpkin (3 to 4 pounds)	1	tablespoon Worcestershire sauce
	Salt and pepper		
3	tablespoons prepared yellow mustard	½	teaspoon salt
		1½	pounds lean ground beef
2	tablespoons brown sugar	½	cup fine dry breadcrumbs
1	egg		

- Cut off top of pumpkin and discard along with seeds and strings. (Cut off just enough so that pumpkin resembles a serving bowl.)

- Place whole pumpkin in a 13 x 9-inch baking dish. Add enough hot water to dish to cover 1 inch around pumpkin. Cover pumpkin and dish with foil. Bake at 400° for 45 minutes or until pumpkin is tender. Remove from oven, uncover, and pour off water; season inside of pumpkin with salt and pepper.

- In a small bowl, combine mustard and brown sugar; using a brush, generously coat inside of pumpkin. (Any that is left over can be spread or brushed on top of meatloaf before cooking.)

- Combine remaining ingredients. Mix well and spoon into pumpkin shell, packing lightly.

- Bake, uncovered, at 400° for 45 minutes to 1 hour, or until meatloaf is cooked. To serve, cut slices of pumpkin and meatloaf as if cutting slices of a cake.

Makes 6 to 8 servings.

Grilled Veal Chops
with Mustard-Herb Butter

4	tablespoons (½ stick) unsalted butter	1	tablespoon chopped fresh chervil or tarragon
1½	tablespoons Dijon mustard	1	tablespoon chopped chives
1	shallot, minced		Freshly ground black pepper
1	tablespoon chopped fresh flat-leaf parsley	2	(1½-inch-thick) veal chops

- **To prepare butter, combine butter, mustard, shallot, parsley, chervil, and chives; add pepper to taste. Mix well and set aside at room temperature.**

- **Cook veal chops on grill over hot coals, turning every 2 minutes and brushing with the mustard-herb butter. Check for doneness after 10 to 12 minutes; the veal should be light pink.**

Makes 2 servings.

Veal Scaloppine with Mushrooms

3	tablespoons all-purpose flour	6	tablespoons butter, divided
½	teaspoon salt	1	bunch green onions, sliced
	Dash of ground white pepper	1	cup sliced fresh mushrooms
⅛	teaspoon paprika	½	cup dry white wine, divided
1½	pounds veal scallops, thinly cut and pounded	1	teaspoon chopped parsley
			Pinch of dried tarragon

- **Combine flour, salt, pepper, and paprika in a medium bowl. Add veal scallops and toss to lightly coat.**

- **Sauté veal, a few pieces at a time, in 3 tablespoons butter in a very hot skillet, about 2 minutes on each side. Remove veal to platter.**

- **Add onions and mushrooms to pan drippings and cook over low heat until tender. Add ¼ cup wine and simmer 2 minutes. Add parsley, tarragon, and remaining ¼ cup wine. Stir in remaining 3 tablespoons butter, cooking until thoroughly heated. Pour over veal and serve immediately.**

Makes 4 servings.

For parties, buy large quantities of inexpensive, attractive glassware. Once purchased, you can use it again and again.

Baked Curried Bananas

A deliciously different side dish for lamb or pork.

4 large, firm bananas
¼ cup butter
1 teaspoon curry powder
2 tablespoons light brown sugar

• Cut bananas lengthwise, then in half crosswise.

• Melt butter in baking dish in oven at 350°; stir in curry powder. Place bananas in baking dish, turning to cover with butter mixture. Sprinkle with brown sugar and return to oven and bake 12 to 15 minutes.

Makes 8 servings.

Peppercorn Lamb Chops

Even our tasters who don't like lamb loved this!

2	tablespoons plus 1 teaspoon coarse-grain mustard	1	green onion, finely chopped
1	tablespoon plus 1 teaspoon cracked blacked pepper	1½	teaspoons concentrated garlic
1	tablespoon soy sauce		Nonstick cooking spray
		8	(4-ounce) lean lamb chops

• Combine mustard, pepper, soy sauce, green onion, and garlic in a small bowl.

• Coat one side of lamb chops with mustard-pepper mixture.

• Spray grill rack with cooking spray and heat grill to medium-hot temperature. Place lamb chops, coated side up first, and grill 5 minutes on each side.

Makes 4 servings.

Lamb with Mustard Glaze

½	cup Dijon mustard	1	teaspoon crushed dried rosemary
1	tablespoon soy sauce	¼	cup olive oil
1	clove garlic, minced	1	(6½-pound) leg of lamb, boned
1	(½-inch) slice gingerroot, minced		

• Combine mustard, soy sauce, garlic, ginger, and rosemary in a small mixing bowl. Gradually whisk in olive oil. Using a brush, coat lamb thickly and evenly with mixture; let stand at room temperature 2 to 3 hours. (If all glaze is not used, baste with the remainder while lamb is roasting.)

• Place lamb on a rack in roasting pan, and roast at 325° for 1 hour and 45 minutes or until done to taste.

Makes 6 servings.

Tuscany Lamb

2	pounds lean lamb, cut into ½-inch cubes	½	teaspoon dried oregano
		½	teaspoon dried basil
3	tablespoons vegetable oil	½	cup dry red wine (optional)
¾-1	cup chopped onion		Salt and pepper
1	green bell pepper, cut into ½-inch squares	¼	pound fresh mushrooms, sliced
1	(8-ounce) can tomato sauce		Cooked rice

• In a heavy skillet or saucepan, quickly brown lamb in oil over medium-high heat. Add onions and cook until limp, stirring frequently. Add green pepper and cook for about 2 minutes. Add tomato sauce, oregano, basil, wine, salt, and pepper. Add mushrooms and simmer for 1 minute. Serve lamb in sauce over cooked rice.

Makes 4 servings.

Pork Tenderloins with Pineapple Stuffing

A wonderful choice for a dinner party.

6	slices wheat bread	¾	teaspoon dried sage
½	cup crushed pineapple in juice, drained	½	teaspoon poultry seasoning
		1	teaspoon salt
½	cup chopped water chestnuts	¾	teaspoon ground black pepper
½	cup finely chopped onion	2	egg whites, lightly beaten
½	cup finely chopped celery	3	(1-pound) pork tenderloins

• Tear bread slices into blender; process into small crumbs. Place breadcrumbs in a medium bowl. Add crushed pineapple, water chestnuts, onion, celery, and seasonings. Toss well. Add egg whites and toss to combine. Set aside.

• Split each tenderloin lengthwise, not cutting all the way through. Spread stuffing mixture evenly into each tenderloin; tie together with kitchen string, if necessary.

• Coat a roasting pan with cooking spray. Lay tenderloins 2 inches apart. Bake at 350° for about 50 minutes or until no longer pink. Slice ½ inch thick. Serve immediately.

Makes 12 servings.

Notes

Pear Chutney

4½ pounds firm ripe pears,
peeled and chopped

1 small green bell pepper, minced

1 cup raisins

4 cups sugar

1 cup crystallized ginger, chopped

3 cups white vinegar

1 cup water

1½ teaspoons salt

½ teaspoon ground cinnamon

¼ teaspoon ground cloves

¼ teaspoon ground nutmeg

¼ teaspoon ground allspice

1 (3-ounce) package liquid pectin

• Bring first 12 ingredients to a boil in a large Dutch oven. Reduce heat; simmer, stirring occasionally, 2 hours or until tender.

• Stir in liquid pectin; return mixture to a boil. Boil, stirring constantly, 1 minute.

• Remove from heat; skim off foam with a metal spoon. Pour hot chutney into hot, sterilized jars, filling to ¼ inch from top; wipe jar rims. Cover at once with metal lids, and screw on bands. Process jars in boiling-water bath 5 minutes.

Makes 11 (6-ounce) jars.

Rosemary Pork Tenderloins with Parmesan-Pepper Biscuits

The pork tenderloins can be prepared ahead and even served cold. The rounds can also be made a day ahead and stored in an airtight container. An autumn picnic beckons!

Tenderloins

2   (¾-pound) pork tenderloins

1½ tablespoons freshly ground black pepper

2   tablespoons chopped fresh rosemary

Parmesan-Pepper Biscuits

2   cups self-rising soft-wheat flour

⅓   cup refrigerated shredded Parmesan cheese

1   teaspoon coarsely ground black pepper

¼   cup butter or margarine, cut into pieces

⅔   cup buttermilk

• Sprinkle tenderloins with pepper and rosemary. Grill, covered with grill lid, over medium-high heat (350° to 400°) 14 to 17 minutes or until a meat thermometer inserted into thickest portion registers 160°, turning occasionally. Cut into 24 slices.

• To prepare biscuits, combine flour, Parmesan cheese, and coarse black pepper. Cut butter into flour mixture with a pastry blender until crumbly; add buttermilk, stirring until dry ingredients are moistened.

• Turn dough out onto a lightly floured surface; knead 3 to 4 times. Roll dough to ¼-inch thickness; cut with a 2-inch round cutter, and place on baking sheet. Reroll and cut trimmings, if necessary, to make 2 dozen. Bake at 425° for 8 to 11 minutes or until lightly browned.

• To serve, place tenderloin slices on top of biscuits. Top with pear or other chutney, if desired.

Makes 6 to 8 servings.

Herb-Crusted Pork Tenderloin with Horseradish-Roasted New Potatoes

2	pounds new potatoes	1	tablespoon freshly ground black pepper
¼	cup butter or margarine, melted	1	teaspoon kosher salt (or 1¼ teaspoons table salt)
2	tablespoons prepared horseradish	3	tablespoons chopped fresh thyme
½	teaspoon salt	1½	pounds pork tenderloins
½	teaspoon freshly ground black pepper	2	tablespoons chopped fresh parsley
½	cup fine, dry breadcrumbs		Garnish: fresh herb sprigs
⅓	cup chopped fresh basil		
3	tablespoons olive oil		

• Peel a 1-inch strip around center of each potato. Place potatoes in a large bowl. Add butter and next 3 ingredients, tossing gently to coat. Place potatoes on a lightly greased rack in a broiler pan. Bake at 425° for 20 minutes; remove from oven.

• Stir together breadcrumbs and next 5 ingredients. Moisten tenderloins with water; press crumb mixture over tenderloins, and place on rack with potatoes. Bake at 425° for 25 more minutes or until potatoes are tender and a meat thermometer inserted into the thickest portion of tenderloins registers 160°. Sprinkle potatoes with parsley, and slice tenderloins. Garnish, if desired.

Makes 4 to 6 servings.

Pepper Chutney

This chutney also makes a great topping for hot dogs and hamburgers!

6 medium-size red and green bell peppers, seeded and chopped

2-3 fresh jalapeño peppers, seeded and minced

1 medium onion, chopped

1½ cups packed light brown sugar

1½ cups apple cider vinegar

1 teaspoon salt

• Combine all ingredients in a medium saucepan. Bring to a boil. Reduce heat, and simmer, uncovered, 1 to 2 hours or until syrupy. Transfer chutney to a serving bowl. Cover and chill thoroughly.

Makes about 1 quart.

Jezabel sauce is a wonderful companion to beef or pork dishes, and it also doubles as a wonderful appetizer when poured over cream cheese and served with crackers. The recipes usually make a fairly large amount, but can easily be divided in half. We have included two of our favorites:

Jazzy Jezebel Sauce

1 cup apple jelly
1 cup pineapple-orange marmalade
1 (6-ounce) jar prepared yellow mustard
1 (5-ounce) jar prepared horseradish
¼ teaspoon ground black pepper

• Mix all ingredients together at medium speed of electric mixer until well blended and smooth.

Makes 3 cups.

Marinated Pork Tenderloin

Serve this wonderful dish as a dinner entrée, or take to a tailgate party. You'll be a hit either way! Make sure to pair it with Jezebel Sauce for the ultimate in taste!

¼	cup soy sauce	8	drops hot pepper sauce
¼	cup dry sherry	2	cloves garlic, minced
1	tablespoon dry mustard	1	(1½-pound) pork tenderloin
2	tablespoons olive oil	½	cup apple cider vinegar
1	teaspoon sesame oil	3	dozen party rolls

• Combine first 7 ingredients in a large heavy-duty zip-top plastic bag. Add tenderloin; seal and chill 8 hours or overnight, turning bag occasionally.

• Remove tenderloin from bag, reserving ½ cup of marinade. Combine reserved marinade and apple cider vinegar.

• Grill tenderloin over medium-hot coals until meat thermometer inserted in thickest portion registers 140°, turning and basting with marinade during first 15 minutes of cooking. (Tenderloin may also be cooked in oven at 400° for about 30 minutes.) Slice tenderloin; serve warm or chilled with rolls and Jezebel Sauce.

Makes 12 servings.

Roast Pork Loin with Fruit

We recommend serving this with brown rice.

1	(3-pound) pork loin	¼	cup lemon juice
2	tablespoons canola oil	2	tablespoons dark corn syrup
2	teaspoons salt	1	pound small white onions
½	teaspoon ground ginger	1	cup dried apricots
¼	teaspoon ground black pepper	1	cup pitted prunes
¼	teaspoon dry mustard	1	tablespoon cornstarch
¾	cup orange juice		

- Trim excess fat from pork. Brown on all sides in oil in a large Dutch oven. Sprinkle with salt, ginger, pepper, and mustard.

- Stir together orange juice, lemon juice, and corn syrup. Pour over pork and heat to boiling. Reduce heat, cover, and simmer 1½ hours.

- Add onions, apricots, and prunes; simmer approximately 1 hour longer or until pork is tender.

- Remove pork from Dutch oven and place on serving platter. Remove onions, apricots, and prunes; arrange around pork on platter.

- Skim fat from remaining sauce in Dutch oven. Mix cornstarch with a small amount of water and add to sauce, stirring to combine. Cook, stirring constantly, until sauce thickens and bubbles, about 3 minutes. Serve with pork.

Makes 4 servings.

Cranberry Jezabel Sauce

1 cup water
½ cup sugar
½ cup firmly packed brown sugar
1 (12-ounce) bag fresh or frozen cranberries
3 tablespoons prepared horseradish
1 tablespoon Dijon mustard
Garnish: fresh mint sprigs

• Combine the first 3 ingredients in a medium saucepan; stir well. Bring to a boil over medium heat; add cranberries. Return to a boil, and cook 10 minutes, stirring occasionally. Spoon into a bowl; let cool at room temperature.

• Stir in horseradish and mustard; cover and chill. Garnish with fresh mint, if desired.

Makes 2½ cups.

Pork Curry

A flavorful and interesting combination.

2	pounds pork tenderloin, cut into cubes	½	teaspoon cumin (optional)
3	tablespoons margarine, melted and divided	1½	cups chicken broth
¾	cup sliced celery	⅓	cup cream of coconut
1	clove garlic, crushed	⅓	cup tomato sauce
1½	cups chopped cooked apples	4	cups cooked long grain rice
1	tablespoon curry powder	¼	cup sliced green onions
¼	teaspoon ground ginger	½	cup coarsely chopped dry roasted peanuts
1½	teaspoon all-purpose flour	½	cup raisins (optional)
¼	teaspoon ground red pepper	½	cup flaked coconut (optional)

- Cook half of pork in 1 tablespoon margarine in a large skillet over medium heat 5 to 6 minutes or until lightly browned. Remove pork from skillet. Drain, set aside, and keep warm. Repeat procedure with remaining pork and 1 tablespoon melted margarine.

- Sauté celery and garlic in remaining 1 tablespoon margarine in skillet over medium-high heat until tender. Add apples, curry powder, and ginger; sauté over medium heat 6 minutes or until apple is crisp tender. Stir in flour, red pepper, and cumin. Gradually add chicken broth, cream of coconut, and tomato sauce. Return pork to skillet. Bring to a boil; reduce heat, and simmer, uncovered, 10 minutes or until pork is tender, stirring frequently. To serve, spoon pork mixture over rice; sprinkle with onions, peanuts, raisins, and coconut.

Makes 6 servings.

Baby Back Ribs with Onion Sauce

4-6	pounds spare ribs		2	tablespoons lemon juice
2	onions, diced		2	tablespoons Worcestershire sauce
2	cloves garlic, minced		3	tablespoons brown sugar
1	tablespoon vegetable oil		1½	teaspoons salt
½	cup apple cider vinegar		1	teaspoon dry mustard
½	cup water			
¼	cup chili sauce			

- Place ribs in Dutch oven; cover with salted water. Bring to a boil, cover, and reduce heat to low. Simmer for 1 hour.

- Sauté onions and garlic in oil in large saucepan until tender. Add remaining ingredients and simmer 10 minutes.

- Place ribs on foil-lined baking sheets. Brush ribs with sauce. Cover baking sheets with foil. Bake at 350° for 2 hours, turning once and basting again with sauce after first hour. Remove foil during last 15 minutes of cooking.

Makes 4 to 6 servings.

One Pot German Style Pork with Apples

2	cups shredded red cabbage		1	teaspoon caraway seeds
1	medium onion, chopped		1	teaspoon salt
3	Granny Smith apples, peeled and sliced		½	teaspoon ground black pepper
3	tablespoons apple jelly		1	(2-pound) boneless pork butt, cut into 6 steaks
2	tablespoons apple cider vinegar			

- In a large bowl, combine cabbage, onion, apple slices, apple jelly, cider vinegar, caraway seeds, salt, and pepper. Mix well. Place mixture in a slow cooker. Add pork steaks on top of mixture. Cover and cook on low for 5 to 5½ hours or until pork is tender. To serve, lift pork, cabbage, and apples with a slotted spoon. Discard liquid.

Makes 6 servings.

When purchasing ribs, plan on 1 pound per person.

Quick and Easy Rib Sauce

1 cup ketchup
¼ cup Worcestershire sauce
¼ cup brown sugar
1 teaspoon celery seed
¼ cup vinegar
2 teaspoons salt

• Bring ketchup and remaining ingredients to a boil in a saucepan. Reduce heat and simmer for 15 minutes.

Makes 1¾ cups, enough for 4 pounds of ribs.

Broiled Pineapple with Basil

Serve with pork or lamb for a wonderful combination.

¼ cup honey

2 tablespoons apple cider vinegar

1 teaspoon ground ginger

1 teaspoon dried basil

1 pineapple, peeled, cored, and cut into slices or wedges

• Combine honey, vinegar, ginger, and basil in a small saucepan. Cook over low heat for 3 minutes.

• Arrange pineapple evenly in a shallow baking dish. Drizzle with honey mixture. Broil until pineapple is lightly browned. Serve immediately.

Makes 4 to 6 servings.

Pan-Roasted Pork Chops with Garlic Potatoes

4	(4-ounce) boneless pork loin chops	8	small red potatoes (about ¾ pound), cut into ⅛-inch-thick slices
1	teaspoon dried rosemary leaves, crushed	3	cloves garlic, minced
¼	teaspoon salt	1	teaspoon olive or vegetable oil
¼	teaspoon ground black pepper		Nonstick cooking spray
		½	cup chicken broth

• Sprinkle both sides of pork chops with rosemary, salt, and pepper.

• In a large bowl, combine potatoes, garlic, and oil; toss to coat.

• Spray large nonstick skillet with cooking spray. Heat over medium-high heat until hot. Add pork chops; cover and cook 3 minutes on each side. Remove pork chops from skillet.

• In same skillet, combine potato mixture and chicken broth; stir to coat potatoes with liquid. Spread potatoes evenly over bottom of skillet. Place pork chops over potatoes. Cover; cook over medium heat for 12 to 18 minutes or until pork is no longer pink in center and potatoes are tender.

• Remove pork chops from skillet; cover to keep warm. Increase heat to high and cook until liquid is slightly thickened. Serve pork chops and potatoes immediately.

Makes 4 servings.

Carolina Country Ham

1	(10 to 12-pound) country ham, with hock removed	1	cup bourbon or sherry
1	cup brown sugar	1	cup water

• Soak ham overnight in cold water and scrub ham with a stiff brush. Change water 2 or 3 times to remove excess salt.

• Mix sugar, bourbon, and water. Coat ham, pressing into the fat of the ham. Cover ham tightly with foil in roasting pan. Bake at 200° for 8 hours.

Makes 12 servings.

Damn Good Ham

The devil made us eat...and eat...and eat!

1	(16 to 20-pound) ham with bone	2	teaspoons prepared yellow mustard
1	(1.5-liter) bottle sherry	1	cup brown sugar
1	cup any flavor fruit preserves	1	(1-ounce) bottle whole cloves

- Remove all fat and hard skin from ham. Score the top in a diamond pattern and make some large slices through ham. Place cloves in diamond centers. Place ham on a rack in a shallow pan. Slowly pour half of the bottle of sherry over ham. Cook at 325° 20 minutes per pound, basting every 45 minutes with juices and sherry. (Reserve ½ cup sherry for glaze.) If ham starts to look too dark, cover with foil tent. Temperature should be 160°.

- 30 minutes before ham should be done, prepare glaze by mixing the reserved ½ cup sherry, preserves, mustard, and brown sugar. Slowly pour mixture over top of ham. Increase oven temperature to 400° for remainder of baking time to allow the glaze to harden.

Makes 16 to 20 servings.

Apricot Glazed Ham

½	cup apricot preserves	1	teaspoon Worcestershire sauce
2	tablespoons prepared yellow mustard	⅛	teaspoon ground cinnamon
1	tablespoon water	1	(1½-pound) fully cooked center cut 1-inch-thick ham slice
2	teaspoons lemon juice		

- Combine preserves and next 5 ingredients in a saucepan, and cook over medium-low heat, stirring frequently, until preserves melt.

- Place ham in shallow dish and pierce several times with fork. Slowly pour preserves mixture over ham; cover and marinate 2 to 3 hours in refrigerator. Remove ham from dish, discarding marinade. Grill or cook until heated thoroughly. Serve immediately.

Makes 6 servings.

Apricot Casserole

Serve this delicious accompaniment with your next ham or turkey.

3 (20-ounce) cans apricots, drained

1-1½ sticks margarine

1 (16-ounce) package brown sugar

2 sleeves Ritz crackers, crushed

- Arrange apricots evenly in a 13 x 9-inch casserole dish, and cover with sugar. Cut margarine into pats and place over sugar. Top with crushed crackers. Bake at 325° for 1 hour.

Makes 16 to 20 servings.

Notes

Capital Chicken

A delicious combination of flavors that your guests will love.

¼ cup butter	½ cup whipping cream
1 tablespoon vegetable oil	1 teaspoon salt
3 pounds skinless, boneless chicken breasts	¼ teaspoon ground black pepper
8 ounces fresh mushrooms, sliced	¼ teaspoon dried tarragon
1 (10-ounce) can cream of chicken soup	1 (15-ounce) can artichoke hearts, drained
1 cup dry white wine	6 green onions with tops, chopped
1 cup water	2 tablespoons chopped fresh parsley
1 tablespoon all-purpose flour	

- **Heat butter and oil in a large skillet over medium heat until butter is melted. Add chicken breasts and cook for 10 minutes or until chicken is browned on all sides, turning occasionally. Using slotted spoon, remove chicken to baking dish and reserve pan drippings.**

- **Sauté mushrooms in reserved pan drippings for 5 minutes or until tender. Add soup, wine, water, and flour; mix well. Simmer 10 minutes or until thickened, stirring frequently. Stir in cream, salt, pepper, and tarragon. Pour over chicken. Bake at 350° for 1 hour.**

- **Remove chicken from oven and stir in artichokes, green onion, and parsley. Return to oven and bake 5 minutes longer or until chicken is cooked through.**

Makes 6 to 8 servings.

Cheese-Stuffed Chicken in Phyllo

Very elegant!

8	skinless, boneless chicken breast halves	½	cup crumbled feta cheese
4	cups chopped fresh spinach	½	cup shredded Cheddar cheese
1	cup chopped onion	1	egg yolk, beaten
2	tablespoons olive oil	1	tablespoon all-purpose flour
4	ounces cream cheese, cubed and softened	½	teaspoon ground nutmeg
		½	teaspoon ground cumin
1	cup shredded mozzarella cheese	16	sheets phyllo dough
		⅔	cup margarine, melted

- Place each chicken breast half between 2 sheets of heavy plastic wrap; pound with flat side of a meat mallet until ⅛ inch thick. Season with salt and pepper; set aside.

- In a large skillet cook spinach and onion in hot oil until onion is tender. Remove from heat. Add cream cheese, stirring until blended. Stir in remaining cheeses, egg yolk, flour, nutmeg, and cumin.

- Place about ½ cup of spinach mixture on each chicken breast half; roll up jelly roll style. Place one sheet of phyllo on work surface, keeping remaining sheets covered with a damp towel to prevent drying out. Brush phyllo sheet with melted margarine. Place one chicken roll near a short side of phyllo; roll chicken and phyllo over once to cover chicken. Fold in long sides; continue rolling from short side. Place in shallow baking pan. Repeat with remaining chicken, phyllo, and margarine. Bake, uncovered, at 350° for 30 to 35 minutes or until chicken is no longer pink.

Makes 8 servings.

Young Chicken
Pounds: 4-5
Temperature: 300°
Minutes per pound: 30
Time: 2 to 2½ hours

Turkey
Pounds: 10-16
Temperature: 300°
Minutes per pound: 18-20
Time: 3½ to 4½ hours

Pounds: 18-23
Temperature: 300°
Minutes per pound: 16-18
Time: 4½ to 6 hours

Pounds: 24-30
Temperature: 300°
Minutes per pound: 15-18
Time: 6 to 7½ hours

Rum Raisin Chicken

**Company coming? They'll think you
slaved for hours on this incredible dish!**

3	tablespoons light rum	¾	teaspoon salt
2	tablespoons dark seedless raisins	¼	teaspoon ground black pepper
¼	cup butter	¾	cup chicken broth
⅓	cup slivered almonds	1	tablespoon cornstarch
3	whole chicken breasts, halved, skinned, and boned	½	cup half-and-half
			Fresh curly mustard greens

- Combine raisins and rum in a small bowl; set aside.

- In a large skillet, melt butter over medium heat; add almonds and cook, stirring constantly, until almonds are toasted. With slotted spoon, remove almonds to small dish.

- In same skillet, place chicken and sprinkle evenly with salt and pepper. Cook over medium heat, turning often, about 20 minutes or until fork can be easily inserted into thickest part of chicken. Remove chicken to a platter and keep warm.

- Add broth to skillet and bring to a boil.

- In a small bowl, mix cornstarch and half-and-half until smooth; slowly add to broth, stirring constantly until smooth. Reduce heat and simmer 2 minutes. Stir in rum and raisins; cook 1 minute. To serve, pour sauce over chicken; top with almonds. Garnish with mustard greens.

Makes 6 servings.

Moroccan Chicken Kabobs

This is wonderful and low in fat. Serve over couscous.

¼ cup nonfat plain yogurt

¼ cup chopped fresh parsley

2 tablespoons chopped fresh cilantro

2 tablespoons lemon juice

1 tablespoon olive oil

3 cloves garlic, finely chopped

1½ teaspoons paprika

1 teaspoon ground cumin

¼ teaspoon salt

¼ teaspoon ground black pepper

1 pound boneless, skinless chicken breasts, cut into cubes

2 small bell peppers (red and yellow), cored, seeded, and cut into 1½-inch strips

1 zucchini, cut into ¼-inch rounds

- Combine yogurt and next 9 ingredients in a medium bowl, stirring until blended. Add chicken and toss to coat. Cover bowl with plastic wrap and marinate in refrigerator 20 minutes.

- Soak wooden skewers in water.

- Blanch peppers in boiling salted water 3 minutes. Drain peppers and refresh with cold water.

- Blanch zucchini in boiling salted water 1 minute. Drain and refresh with cold water.

- Alternate chicken, peppers, and zucchini on skewers. Grill or broil until chicken is no longer pink.

Makes 4 servings.

Notes

Chicken with Tarragon Sauce

1¼	pounds chicken breast tenderloins, cut into bite-size cubes	½	small yellow pepper, cut into julienne strips
¼	cup sherry wine	1	scallion, cut into ½-inch slices
4	tablespoons olive oil, divided	2	cups chicken broth
1	(6 to 8-ounce) package fresh mushrooms, thinly sliced	⅓	cup Marsala wine
1	medium Vidalia or other sweet onion	1	heaping tablespoon cornstarch
		1	tablespoon butter
½	small red pepper, cut into julienne strips	½	cup flour
		2	teaspoons dried tarragon, crushed between fingers
			Cooked white rice

- Marinate chicken pieces in sherry wine overnight in refrigerator. Remove from refrigerator to gain room temperature.

- In a 10-inch skillet, with a cover available, heat a tablespoon of olive oil. Sauté mushrooms over medium heat until lightly golden. Transfer to a bowl.

- Add another tablespoon olive oil to skillet. Add onions and peppers, stirring briefly until well coated. Reduce heat to very low and cover; cook for 20 to 25 minutes until onions and peppers are soft, stirring occasionally.

- Meanwhile, in a medium bowl, combine broth and Marsala wine; stir in dissolved cornstarch, and set aside.

- Transfer onions and peppers to bowl containing mushrooms; place sliced scallions on top and set aside.

- Combine and heat 2 tablespoons olive oil and butter in skillet. While skillet is heating, drain sherry from chicken pieces and dredge chicken in the flour. Turn heat to medium-high and brown the chicken on all sides, turning constantly.

- As soon as chicken is browned and sizzling, stir broth mixture to remix. Pour mixture over the chicken. Immediately add onions, peppers, scallions, and mushrooms. Add tarragon; add salt and pepper to taste, stirring all ingredients to mix well. Reduce heat to low and cook covered 30 to 45 minutes. Serve over cooked rice.

Makes 4 servings.

Seasoned Chicken Roll-Ups

Very easy and fun to prepare, and good!

2	tablespoons lemon juice	1	teaspoon celery salt
1	teaspoon garlic salt	1	teaspoon paprika
⅛	teaspoon ground black pepper	½	cup butter, melted
½	teaspoon salt	6-8	boneless, skinless chicken breasts
1	(8-ounce) container sour cream		
2	teaspoons Worcestershire sauce	1	(6-ounce) package herb-seasoned stuffing mix

- Mix first 8 ingredients in a large bowl; add chicken and marinate overnight in refrigerator.

- Remove chicken and discard marinade. Dredge chicken in crushed stuffing mix and roll each piece jelly roll style. Place in glass baking dish and drizzle with melted butter. Bake at 350° for 30 minutes or until chicken is done.

Makes 6 to 8 servings.

Crockpot Chicken Brunswick Stew

2	large Vidalia or other sweet onions, chopped	¼	cup Worcestershire sauce
6	boneless, skinless chicken breast halves	4	tablespoons butter
2	(15-ounce) cans white corn, drained	2	tablespoons apple cider vinegar
1	(28-ounce) can crushed tomatoes	1	teaspoon prepared yellow mustard
1	(12-ounce) bottle chili sauce	½	teaspoon salt
1	(14½-ounce) can chicken broth	½	teaspoon ground black pepper
		½	teaspoon hot pepper sauce

- Combine all ingredients in crockpot and cook on high for 4 hours. Remove chicken; shred and return to stew.

Makes 6 servings.

Chicken Picante

Need dinner in a hurry? This is the meal for you!

1½ cups picante sauce

3 tablespoons packed light brown sugar

1 tablespoon Dijon mustard

4 boneless, skinless chicken breast halves

3 cups hot cooked rice

- Mix picante sauce, brown sugar, and mustard.

- Coat a 2-quart shallow baking dish with cooking spray; add chicken. Pour picante sauce mixture over chicken. Bake at 400° for 20 minutes or until chicken is done. Serve over rice.

Makes 4 servings.

Lemon Drumsticks

Great for snacking or as a take-along item for a picnic.

½ cup apple cider vinegar

2 tablespoons cracked black pepper

1 teaspoon salt

¼ cup brown sugar

¼ cup lemon juice

2 cups oil

18 drumsticks

Soy sauce (optional)

• Bring vinegar, pepper, salt, and brown sugar to a boil in a medium saucepan. Remove from heat; add lemon juice and oil. Reserve ⅓ cup and pour remainder over drumsticks; cover, and marinate 3 to 4 hours in refrigerator. Remove drumsticks, discarding used marinade. Place drumsticks on a rack over a broiler pan; Broil, basting with reserved marinade, about 10 minutes on each side. Serve with soy sauce, if desired.

Makes 18.

Margarita Grilled Chicken

Great with grilled corn and a fresh green salad.

6	boneless chicken breasts	¼	cup tequila
⅔	cup olive oil	2	tablespoons Triple Sec
½	cup fresh lime juice	¼	cup minced fresh cilantro

• Place chicken in a shallow non-metallic baking dish.

• Combine olive oil and remaining ingredients. Reserve ⅓ cup and pour the remainder over chicken. Cover and marinate in refrigerator for 4 hours, turning occasionally. Remove from refrigerator 30 minutes before cooking and discard used marinade.

• Grill chicken on both sides, basting frequently with reserved marinade, until chicken is cooked throughout. Serve with salsa.

Makes 6 servings.

Greek Chicken Bake

This is actually better if made the day before serving and reheated.

2	whole breast chicken fillets	1	tablespoon dried oregano
	Salt and pepper	½-1	teaspoon basil
1	medium eggplant	1	(28-ounce) can Italian tomatoes
	Flour		Red pepper bits to taste
	Olive oil		Feta cheese crumbles
1	medium onion, sliced		Cooked rice
3	cloves garlic, chopped		

• Season chicken with salt and pepper; set aside.

• Cut eggplant lengthwise into 4 (¾-inch-thick) slices; salt and pepper slices, and coat lightly with flour. Brown eggplant in olive oil and place in bottom of a 2-quart casserole dish.

• Brown chicken breasts in olive oil and place on top of eggplant.

• Sauté onion and garlic until onions are transparent. Add oregano, basil, tomatoes, and red pepper bits. Pour over chicken, and top with crumbles of feta cheese. Bake at 425° for 20 to 25 minutes or until tender. Serve over rice.

Makes 4 servings.

Southern Fried Kickin' Chickin'

Don't be afraid to try this unusual fried chicken recipe.
It is scrumptious and you will be asked for the recipe every time!

4	boneless, skinless chicken breast halves	½	teaspoon ground red pepper
2¼	teaspoons salt, divided	1¼	cups all-purpose flour
1	tablespoon ground black pepper	2	tablespoons powdered sugar
			Vegetable oil

- Place chicken breasts in a bowl of cold water with 1 teaspoon salt; cover and chill for 1 to 3 hours.

- In a small bowl, combine remaining 1¼ teaspoon salt, black pepper, and red pepper; set aside.

- In a bowl, combine flour and powdered sugar. Dredge chicken in flour mixture.

- Cover bottom of a large skillet with vegetable oil and heat to medium/medium-high. Place each chicken breast in skillet and sprinkle with salt and pepper mixture. Cook, covered, over medium heat for approximately 7 minutes on each side or until both sides are lightly browned.

Makes 4 servings.

Baked Chicken Reuben

4	whole chicken breasts, halved, skinned, and boned	1	(16-ounce) can sauerkraut, well drained
¼	teaspoon salt	4	(6 x 4-inch) slices Swiss cheese
⅛	teaspoon ground black pepper	1¼	cups Thousand Island salad dressing

- Place chicken in a single layer in a greased baking pan; sprinkle with salt and pepper.

- Press excess liquid from sauerkraut; spoon over chicken. Arrange cheese slices over sauerkraut. Pour dressing evenly over the top. Cover pan with aluminum foil. Bake at 325° about 1½ hours or until chicken is tender.

Makes 6 to 8 servings.

Traditional Fried Chicken

Since no two fried chicken recipes are alike,
we decided to include a tried and true one, guaranteed to
please any fried chicken connoisseur!

3	quarts water	1	teaspoon ground black pepper
1	tablespoon plus 1 teaspoon salt, divided	1	cup all-purpose flour
1	(2 to 2½-pound) broiler-fryer chicken, cut up	2	cups vegetable oil
		¼	cup bacon drippings

- Combine water and 1 tablespoon salt in a large bowl; add chicken. Cover and chill 8 hours.

- Drain chicken; rinse with cold water and pat dry with paper towels.

- Combine 1 teaspoon salt and pepper; sprinkle half of mixture over all sides of chicken. Combine remaining half with flour in a large heavy-duty zip-top plastic bag.

- Place 2 pieces of chicken in plastic bag, seal, and shake to coat completely. Remove. Repeat procedure with remaining pieces.

- Combine oil and drippings in a cast iron skillet, electric skillet, or stainless frying pan. Heat to 360°. Add chicken, a few pieces at a time, skin side down. Reduce heat to 300° to 325°, keeping oil sizzling. Cover and cook 6 minutes; uncover and cook 9 more minutes.

- Turn chicken pieces; cover and cook 6 more minutes. Uncover and cook 5 to 9 more minutes, turning pieces during the last 3 minutes for even browning, if necessary. Remove and drain on paper towels.

Makes 4 servings.

In place of the saltwater solution used to soak the chicken, 2 cups of buttermilk may be used. Soak for 8 hours and proceed as directed.

Brown Sugar Crusted Chicken

The secret to this recipe is marinating the chicken in the lemon juice overnight. Serve with mashed potatoes and carrots.

2	chickens, cut into quarters	½	cup corn oil
2	cups fresh lemon juice	2	tablespoons lemon zest
2	cups flour	¼	cup brown sugar
2	teaspoons salt	¼	cup chicken broth
2	teaspoons paprika	1	teaspoon lemon extract
1	teaspoon freshly ground black pepper	2	lemons, sliced paper thin

- Combine chicken pieces and lemon juice in a bowl. Cover and marinate in the refrigerator overnight, turning occasionally.

- Drain chicken thoroughly and pat dry.

- In a large heavy-duty zip-top bag, combine flour, salt, paprika, and pepper. Put 2 pieces of chicken into bag at one time and shake, coating completely.

- Heat corn oil in frying pan until hot and fry chicken a few pieces at a time, until well browned and crisp.

- Arrange chicken in a single layer in a large shallow baking dish. Sprinkle evenly with brown sugar and top with lemon zest.

- Mix chicken broth and lemon extract together; pour around chicken pieces. Top each piece of chicken with a thin lemon slice. Bake at 350° for 35 to 40 minutes.

Makes 8 servings.

Basic Turkey Gravy

Pan drippings from roasted turkey

Melted unsalted butter, as needed

6 tablespoons all-purpose flour

Salt and freshly ground
black pepper, to taste

4 cups hot turkey or chicken broth

- After removing turkey from pan, skim off all but ½ cup pan drippings. If there is less than ½ cup in the pan, add melted butter to make ½ cup.

- Heat pan over medium heat and using wooden spoon, stir and scrape browned bits from bottom of pan. Add flour, whisking constantly to mix well, and cook until lightly browned, 3 to 4 minutes.

- Season with salt and pepper. Slowly pour in hot broth, whisking constantly. Cook, whisking constantly, until smooth and thickened, about 2 minutes. Simmer for about 10 minutes to allow flavors to blend.

Makes 8 servings.

Roasted Turkey with Fresh Sage Stuffing

Sage Stuffing

8	tablespoons unsalted butter, divided	3	tablespoons finely chopped fresh sage
1½	cups finely chopped yellow or white onion	⅓-½	cup finely chopped flat-leaf parsley
1¼	cups finely chopped celery	1	teaspoon salt
8	cups dry bread cubes	1	teaspoon freshly ground pepper
		½-1	cup turkey or chicken broth

Turkey

1	(12-pound) turkey, at room temperature	Salt and freshly ground black pepper, to taste
1	stick unsalted butter, softened	

- To prepare stuffing, melt 2 tablespoons of the butter in a skillet over medium heat. Add onion and celery. Cook, stirring often, 6 to 8 minutes or until vegetables are soft but not browned.

- In a small saucepan over low heat, melt remaining 6 tablespoons butter. In a large mixing bowl, combine bread cubes and next 4 ingredients. While tossing mixture, slowly add just enough broth to moisten the stuffing. (To test for correct seasonings and moisture, melt a small amount of butter in a skillet. Add a tablespoon of the stuffing and stir until light golden. Taste, and adjust seasonings, if desired.)

- Remove giblets from turkey and discard. Rinse turkey inside and out and pat dry with paper towels. Stuff body and neck cavities loosely with stuffing mixture.

- Tie legs together with kitchen twine. Using 2 turkey lacers, pin loose skin down to keep stuffing from coming out. Fold wings underneath body.

- Rub softened butter over turkey, thoroughly coating entire body. Season turkey with salt and pepper. Place the turkey, breast side down, on a thoroughly greased rack in a roasting pan that has been lined with foil. Roast at 325° for 1 hour. Using paper towels to protect hands, turn turkey breast side up. Roast an additional 2 hours or until an instant-read thermometer inserted into the thickest part of the breast, away from the bone, registers 165° to 170°, and the thigh registers 175° to 185°.

Roasted Turkey with Fresh Sage Stuffing, continued

- Transfer turkey to a warmed serving platter, and remove stuffing to a warmed serving bowl. Cover turkey loosely with foil or clean towel, and let rest 30 to 45 minutes before carving.

Makes 6 to 8 servings.

Mom's Chicken Pot Pie

Comfort food at it's best.

1	(4-pound) whole chicken		Nonstick cooking spray
1	carrot, sliced	1½	tablespoons flour
2	stalks celery, chopped	1	cup milk
1	small onion, chopped	1	(10½-ounce) can cream of chicken soup
1	teaspoon salt		
	Ground black pepper, to taste		Biscuits, uncooked and rolled to ½ inch thick
1	whole clove		
⅛	teaspoon ginger		

- Place chicken in large stockpot and cover with water; bring to a boil. Add carrots, celery, onion, salt, pepper, clove, and ginger. Simmer until meat falls from the bone. Remove chicken, discarding bones. Cut chicken into small pieces and arrange in casserole dish that has been coated with cooking spray.

- Strain stock, remove clove, and add vegetables to chicken in casserole dish.

- In a small bowl, blend flour and milk until smooth. Combine with chicken soup in a saucepan. Heat slowly to boiling and cook until thickened. Slowly pour gravy over chicken and vegetables. Top with biscuits. Bake at 400° for 20 to 25 minutes

Makes 6 to 8 servings.

Big Birds
Buying Tips:

With birds that weigh 12 pounds or less, allow 1 pound per adult family member. With birds that weigh more than 12 pounds, count on ¾ pound for each serving. If you're serving boneless turkey breast, figure ½ pound per person. For leftovers, buy a bird that is 2 to 4 pounds larger than you need.

Big Birds
Thawing Tips:

Allow plenty of time to thaw the bird. For a whole frozen turkey, leave the bird in its wrapping and place on a tray in the refrigerator for 2 to 5 days. Plan on at least 24 hours for every 5 pounds - and remember, don't count the day you will be roasting the bird. Thawed birds will keep for 1 or 2 days in the refrigerator.

Marinated Cornish Game Hens

Serve with wild rice.

¾	cup chopped onion	1	bay leaf
¼	pound butter	1	cup beef bouillon
1	clove garlic, minced	2	tablespoons dry sherry
1	teaspoon salt	2	hens, split and flattened
¼	teaspoon thyme	1	cup fresh mushrooms
1	tablespoon chopped fresh parsley		

- Sauté onions in butter until soft. Add next 6 ingredients. Simmer, add sherry, and taste to adjust seasonings.

- Rinse hens; dry inside and out. Salt entire bird. Coat hens with marinade, cover, and soak overnight, turning occasionally.

- Place hens, mushrooms, and marinade in a baking pan and bake at 350° for 1½ hours, basting occasionally.

Makes 4 servings.

Quail with Grapes and Almonds

8	quail	1	cup chicken broth
	Salt and pepper	1	cup small white grapes
	Flour	4	tablespoons sliced almonds, lightly browned in butter
5	tablespoons butter		
¼	cup white wine		

- Rinse quail and pat dry. Salt and pepper quail, and roll in flour. Sauté in butter until browned. Add wine and broth and simmer 15 minutes, turning several times. Add grapes and heat just until grapes are warmed. Place quail on a hot plate and spoon sauce over them. Arrange grapes around quail. Sprinkle with almonds.

Makes 4 servings.

Grilled Venison Tenderloin

1   (2 to 2½-pound) venison
    tenderloin
2   tablespoons Worcestershire
    sauce
3   cups Burgundy wine
8   strips bacon

- Marinate venison 3 to 4 hours in Worcestershire sauce and Burgundy; wrap in bacon.

- Place venison on preheated grill and cook 15 to 20 minutes, turning frequently. Venison should be pale pink inside when done. Serve immediately, keeping unused portion warm and covered.

Makes 4 servings.

Venison Stew

**This is delicious served with
cooked rice or noodles. It also freezes well.**

½   cup bacon drippings
1   onion, chopped
1   pound fresh mushrooms,
    sliced
2   pounds boneless venison stew
    meat, cut into ¾-inch cubes
5   tablespoons all-purpose flour
2   cups beef broth
1¾ cups Burgundy wine
½   teaspoon garlic salt (optional)
½   teaspoon salt
¼   teaspoon ground black pepper
2   stalks celery, finely chopped
    (optional)

- Sauté onions and mushrooms in bacon drippings; remove from drippings and set aside, leaving drippings in pan.

- Brown venison, small portions at a time, in bacon drippings until browned on all sides. Remove venison to a Dutch oven. Stir in flour. Add broth, wine, and seasonings. Simmer 3 hours. Add sautéed onions and mushrooms; simmer 1 additional hour.

Makes 6 servings.

Notes

Smoked Wild Duck

4	wild ducks, cleaned and gutted	¼	cup water
	Hickory chips	1½	tablespoons salt
4	tablespoons butter	2	tablespoons sugar
¾	cup vinegar	1½	tablespoons hot pepper sauce

- Cut ducks in half down backside. Simmer in salted water, covered, for 2 hours or until tender.

- Soak hickory chips in water for 1 hour.

- Combine butter and next 5 ingredients in a small saucepan; bring to a boil. Cover, reduce heat, and simmer for 20 minutes.

- Place wet hickory chips on slow charcoal fire. Brush oil on grill. Place ducks on grill and brush with sauce. Smoke ducks in covered grill for 1 hour, basting frequently with sauce. (Be sure to keep chips wet while cooking.)

Makes 4 servings.

Barbecued Duck Breasts

½	pound butter	1	teaspoon salt
½	cup ketchup	¼	teaspoon ground black pepper
1	tablespoon sugar	1	clove garlic, pressed
1½	tablespoons lemon juice	1	small onion, chopped
1	tablespoon Worcestershire sauce	½	teaspoon hot pepper sauce
		4	duck breast halves

- Combine butter and next 9 ingredients in a saucepan; cover and simmer 5 minutes.

- Place duck breasts on rack in flat pan and bake at 375° for 1 hour, basting with barbecue sauce every 10 to 15 minutes.

Makes 2 servings.

Sole Fillets in White Wine Sauce

This is simple to prepare and very elegant.

6	fillets of sole	2	shallots, chopped
1	cup water or fish stock	½	cup dry white wine
	Salt and pepper	1	tablespoon flour
6	tablespoons butter, divided	½	cup whipping cream

- Cut fillets in half lengthwise. Roll each half and secure with toothpicks; place in a large skillet. Add water or fish stock, salt, pepper, 3 tablespoons butter, shallots, and wine. Bring to a boil; reduce heat and simmer until fish is white in center, about 12 to 15 minutes. Remove fish to hot platter to keep warm, leaving liquid in pan.

- Boil liquid in skillet and reduce to one third.

- Blend flour and cream, and add to liquid. Add remaining butter. Heat, stirring until smooth. Strain liquid and pour over fish.

Makes 6 servings.

Grouper with Pecan Sauce

4	(1-inch-thick) grouper fillets (about 1½ to 2 pounds)	3	tablespoons vegetable oil
1	tablespoon plus 1 teaspoon soy sauce, divided	1	cup whipping cream
		1	tablespoon dark corn syrup or molasses
¼	cup all-purpose flour	½	cup pecan pieces, toasted

- Place fillets in a shallow baking dish. Brush with 1 tablespoon soy sauce. Cover and chill 10 minutes.

- Dredge fillets in flour, shaking off excess flour.

- Heat oil in a nonstick skillet over medium-high heat until hot. Add fish; cook 6 to 8 minutes on each side or until browned and fish flakes easily when tested with a fork. Remove fish from skillet and keep warm. Wipe skillet dry with a paper towel.

- Add whipping cream and corn syrup to skillet; bring to a boil over medium heat. Boil until mixture is reduced to ¾ cup, about 6 minutes. Stir in 1 teaspoon soy sauce and pecans. Spoon sauce over fish.

Makes 4 servings.

During the late 1800's and early 1900's, horse-drawn ice wagons made their way through the streets of Anderson, providing a much-needed source of refrigeration for local residents. Routes were covered twice every day except Sunday. Another popular service provider was the driver of the meat wagon, who also served as the meat cutter. Accompanied by a ringing bell announcing its arrival, the meat wagon was usually surrounded by swarms of flies and stray dogs.

Lemon Soy Swordfish

Lemony and lucious!

8	small swordfish steaks, or 4 large, cut in half	1	clove garlic, crushed
⅓	cup soy sauce	2	teaspoons Dijon mustard
¼	cup lemon juice	½	cup vegetable oil
1	teaspoon lemon zest		Garnish: lemon wedges and fresh parsley sprigs

- **Pierce the fish with a fork and place in a shallow 13 x 9-inch baking dish.**

- **In a small bowl combine soy sauce, lemon juice, lemon zest, garlic, Dijon mustard, and oil; mix well. Pour over fish. Cover, and refrigerate 1 to 3 hours, turning fish occasionally and again piercing with fork.**

- **Drain fish, discarding marinade, and place in a preheated broiler pan. Broil for 5 to 6 minutes on each side or until fish flakes easily when tested with a fork. To serve, garnish with lemon and parsley.**

Makes 8 servings.

To grill, reserve marinade. Grill fish over medium coals for 5 to 6 minutes on each side, brushing occasionally with marinade.

Tuna Nantucket

½	cup capers, drained and chopped	1	tablespoon Worcestershire sauce
3	green onions, finely chopped	8	tuna steaks
¾	cup sour cream	2	tablespoons Parmesan cheese
¾	cup mayonnaise		

- **Mix capers, green onions, sour cream, and mayonnaise in a medium bowl. Add Worcestershire sauce, stirring to blend.**

- **Rinse tuna steaks and pat dry. Place steaks on a broiler pan and cover with sour cream mixture. Sprinkle Parmesan cheese over sour cream mixture. Bake at 325° for 20 to 25 minutes or until tuna is no longer pink.**

Makes 8 servings.

Grouper Spectacular

3	pounds grouper fillets		2	medium tomatoes, diced
⅓	cup lemon juice			Salt and pepper
1	medium onion, diced		2½	cups shredded mozzarella cheese
1	medium-size green bell pepper, diced		½	cup sliced black olives
3	tablespoons butter, melted			

- Place fish fillets in a shallow container. Pour lemon juice over fish, cover, and refrigerate 2 hours.

- Sauté onion and green pepper in butter 5 minutes. Add tomatoes, and cook an additional 2 minutes; remove from heat, and set aside.

- Remove fish from lemon juice; place, skin side down, in a lightly greased 13 x 9 x 2-inch baking dish. Sprinkle with salt and pepper. Bake, uncovered, at 350° for 30 minutes. Spoon vegetable mixture over fish; sprinkle with cheese. Return to oven and bake at 350° for an additional 15 minutes or until fish flakes easily when tested with a fork. Sprinkle with olives.

Makes 6 servings.

Creole Barbecued Shrimp

**Peel, eat, and enjoy! Have plenty of
French bread for dipping in the sauce!**

3	sticks butter, melted		1	tablespoon chili sauce
3	cloves garlic, minced			Hot pepper sauce to taste
½	teaspoon paprika		1	(12-ounce) can beer or 1 cup white wine, at room temperature
1	teaspoon salt			
½	teaspoon ground black pepper		1	pound unpeeled fresh shrimp
½	teaspoon dried oregano			

- Combine all ingredients in a large bowl. Cover and refrigerate for 1 hour.

- Pour ingredients into large baking dish. Bake at 300° for 30 minutes. Do not overcook.

Makes 2 to 3 servings.

Reusable cloth napkins are a cost-saver and are more elegant than paper.

The word "crumbs" in a recipe indicates crackers or cookies that are crushed finely for cheesecake, tart crusts, or coatings. This is done using a rolling pin, food processor, or blender. "Cubed" refers to uniform pieces, usually ½ inch on all sides. "Chopped" means cut into medium-size irregular pieces. "Coarsely chopped" indicates slightly larger pieces. "Snipped fresh herbs" signifies that scissors should be used to cut the leaves into tiny pieces. For ease, put herbs in a cup, and then snip. "Minced" means cut into tiny irregular pieces. (Garlic can be minced by squeezing through a press.) "Diced" means cut into uniform pieces about ¼ inch on each side. "Until pieces are the size of small peas" refers to shortening, margarine, or butter worked into dry ingredients with a pastry blender, until the largest pieces are about ½ inch in diameter. "Matchsticks" or "julienne" refers to strips about 2 inches long and about ¼ inch thick. "Sliced" means cut crosswise about ¼ inch thick.

Savory Salmon Florentines

These individual casseroles make a beautiful presentation.
Serve on a plate with fresh fruit and crusty bread.

2	cups salmon, cooked or canned, undrained	¼	teaspoon salt
	Milk	¼	teaspoon hot pepper sauce
¼	cup butter	1½	cups grated mild Cheddar cheese, divided
¼	cup flour	2	cups cooked and drained spinach
½	teaspoon dry mustard		

- Drain and flake salmon, reserving liquid. Add enough milk to liquid to make 1½ cups.

- In a saucepan, melt butter and add flour, whisking until blended.

- Bring milk mixture to a boil and add to flour and butter, whisking until smooth and thick. Season with mustard, salt, hot sauce, and 1 cup cheese.

- Layer spinach evenly in 4 individual greased casseroles; top with salmon, sauce, and remaining cheese. Bake uncovered at 425° for 15 minutes.

Makes 4 servings.

Greek Shrimp with Orzo

2	tablespoons olive oil		2-3 tomatoes, chopped
1	medium onion, chopped	½	cup dry white wine
1	clove garlic, minced	1	green bell pepper, chopped
1	pound fresh mushrooms, chopped	1	pound peeled shrimp
2	tablespoons Greek seasoning	½-¾	block feta cheese
			Cooked orzo pasta

- In heated olive oil, sauté onion, garlic, mushrooms, Greek seasoning, and tomatoes. Add wine and simmer. Stir in peppers and simmer. Add shrimp and cook until pink. Stir in feta cheese to taste. Serve over orzo.

Makes 4 servings.

Highlands Shrimp Casserole

Our tasters gave this rave reviews!

1⅔	pounds fresh shrimp
8	tablespoons butter, divided
½	pound fresh mushrooms, sliced
1	(19-ounce) can artichoke hearts, drained
4½	tablespoons all-purpose flour
¾	cup milk
¾	cup whipping cream
¼	cup plus 1 tablespoon dry cooking sherry
½-¾	teaspoon salt
¾	teaspoon ground black pepper
1	tablespoon Worcestershire sauce
1	cup freshly grated Parmesan cheese
	Paprika
½	cup finely chopped fresh parsley
	Cooked rice

- Boil and shell shrimp.

- Melt 2½ tablespoons butter in skillet and sauté mushrooms approximately 6 minutes.

- In a buttered 2-quart casserole dish make one layer each of artichokes, shrimp, and mushrooms.

- In a heavy saucepan, melt 5½ tablespoons butter over low heat. Stirring with wire whisk, add flour until well blended and smooth. Add milk, then cream, whisking constantly until mixture thickens. Remove from heat; add sherry, salt, pepper, and Worcestershire sauce. Pour mixture over layered ingredients. Sprinkle with Parmesan cheese, paprika, and parsley. Bake at 350° for about 45 minutes. To serve, spoon over cooked rice.

Makes 4 servings.

Traditional Tartar Sauce

1 cup mayonnaise
⅓ cup chopped dill pickle
⅓ cup chopped onion
1½ teaspoons chopped capers
½ teaspoon prepared yellow mustard
½ teaspoon lemon juice

• Mix all ingredients together and refrigerate at least 1 hour before serving with seafood.

Makes about 1⅔ cups.

Low Country Crab Cakes with Jalapeño Tartar Sauce

A wonderful combination!

Crab Cakes

1	pound white crabmeat	1	teaspoon Worcestershire sauce
1	cup finely chopped green onions	½	teaspoon salt
1½	cups fresh breadcrumbs, divided	⅛	teaspoon ground black pepper
2	eggs	1	tablespoon Dijon mustard
¼	cup milk	¼	cup cooking oil

Jalapeño Tartar Sauce

1	cup mayonnaise	3	tablespoons chopped sweet pickle
¼	cup chopped fresh dill weed		
1	medium bottled jalapeño pepper, seeded and minced	1	heaping tablespoon small capers
		1	tablespoon chopped chives

• Mix crab, onions, and ¾ cup of breadcrumbs in a mixing bowl.

• In another bowl, beat eggs; add milk, Worcestershire sauce, salt, pepper, and mustard. Pour over crab mixture and mix. Shape into round cakes, and dredge in remaining ¾ cup of breadcrumbs.

• In a medium skillet, heat oil to medium-high. Fry cakes, turning once, about 5 minutes per side. Drain and serve hot.

• To prepare tartar sauce, combine mayonnaise and next 5 ingredients in a bowl, mixing well. Serve with crab cakes.

Makes 6 servings.

Triple Seafood Casserole

1 pound unpeeled medium-size fresh shrimp
1 cup dry white wine
1 tablespoon chopped fresh parsley
4 tablespoons butter or margarine, divided
1 teaspoon salt
1 medium onion, thinly sliced
1 pound fresh bay scallops
3 tablespoons all-purpose flour

1 cup half-and-half
½ cup (2 ounces) shredded Swiss cheese
2 teaspoons lemon juice
⅛ teaspoon ground black pepper
½ pound fresh crabmeat, flaked
1 (4½-ounce) can sliced mushrooms, drained
1 cup soft homemade breadcrumbs
¼ cup grated Parmesan cheese

- **Peel and devein shrimp.**

- **Combine wine, parsley, 1 tablespoon butter, salt, and onion in a large Dutch oven; bring to a boil. Add shrimp and scallops; cook 3 to 5 minutes or until shrimp turn pink, stirring often. Drain, reserving ⅔ cup cooking liquid.**

- **Melt 3 tablespoons butter in Dutch oven over low heat; add flour, stirring until smooth. Cook 1 minute, stirring constantly. Gradually add half-and-half; cook over medium heat, stirring constantly, until thickened and bubbly. Stir in Swiss cheese. Gradually stir in reserved cooking liquid, lemon juice, and pepper. Stir in shrimp mixture, crabmeat, and mushrooms.**

- **Spoon mixture into a lightly greased 11 x 7-inch baking dish. Cover and bake at 350° for 40 minutes or until bubbly. Combine breadcrumbs and Parmesan cheese; sprinkle over casserole. Return to oven, uncovered, and bake 5 more minutes. Let stand 10 minutes before serving.**

Makes 6 to 8 servings.

Notes

Notes

Family Favorite Lasagne

A fresh twist on a classic entrée that will please even picky eaters.

4	medium zucchini, divided	1	pound lean ground beef
4	red and/or yellow bell peppers, halved through the stems and seeded	1	large onion, finely chopped
		1½	teaspoons dried oregano
2	large eggplants, each cut lengthwise into 8 (¼-inch-thick) slices	2	(8-ounce) cans tomato sauce, divided
	Nonstick cooking spray	1	(15-ounce) container part-skim ricotta cheese
2	tablespoons olive oil	1¾	cups shredded part-skim mozzarella cheese, divided
4	cloves garlic, minced and divided	1	cup grated Parmesan cheese, divided
1½	teaspoons salt, divided	¾	cup thinly sliced fresh basil
1	teaspoon ground black pepper, divided	1	large egg
		½	cup seasoned dry breadcrumbs

- Cut 1 zucchini in half lengthwise. Using small spoon, scoop out center portion and coarsely chop. Reserve both.

- Dice 2 pepper halves and set aside.

- Cut remaining 3 zucchini, along with 1 reserved, lengthwise into ¼-inch-thick slices. Arrange sliced eggplant and zucchini, along with pepper halves in single layers on baking sheets. Coat both sides of all pieces with cooking spray. In a small bowl, combine oil and 2 teaspoons garlic. Brush vegetables lightly with garlic oil. Sprinkle with ¼ teaspoon salt and ¼ teaspoon pepper. Broil, turning once, until vegetables are softened and browned, about 10 to 12 minutes; set aside.

- In a large nonstick skillet over medium-high heat, cook beef 8 minutes or until browned. Add reserved diced pepper and diced zucchini center; add onion, remaining garlic, oregano, ½ teaspoon salt, and ½ teaspoon pepper. Cook, stirring occasionally, until softened, about 6 to 8 minutes. Add all but ⅔ cup tomato sauce to mixture and simmer 5 minutes.

- For cheese layer, combine ricotta cheese, 1¼ cups mozzarella cheese, ½ cup Parmesan cheese, basil, egg, and remaining salt and pepper.

- To make lasagne, spread ⅓ cup reserved plain tomato sauce on the bottom of a 13 x 9-inch baking dish. Top with half of the eggplant slices. Sprinkle with 2 tablespoons breadcrumbs. Top with half of the meat mixture, and sprinkle with 2 more tablespoons breadcrumbs. Top with layer of zucchini and peppers, and sprinkle with 2 tablespoons breadcrumbs. Top with cheese mixture and remaining meat mixture. Sprinkle with 2 tablespoons breadcrumbs. Top with remaining eggplant slices. Spread remaining plain tomato sauce over eggplant. Sprinkle with ½ cup mozzarella cheese and remaining Parmesan cheese. Cover with aluminum foil. Bake at 425° for 30 minutes. Remove foil; bake 10 more minutes or until cheese is melted and bubbly. Let stand 15 minutes before cutting.

Makes 12 servings.

Thanksgiving Oyster Pie

A favorite of our oyster lovers!

2	frozen deep dish pie shell pastries	1	cup chopped fresh parsley
6	tablespoons bacon drippings or vegetable oil, divided	3	tablespoons all-purpose flour
1	cup chopped onion	2	pints oysters, drained
1	cup chopped celery		Salt and pepper
1	cup chopped green bell pepper		Pepper
			Hot pepper sauce
			Worcestershire sauce

• Bake pie shells according to package directions; set aside.

• Sauté onions in 3 tablespoons bacon drippings. Add celery, bell pepper, and parsley; sauté until tender.

• In a separate pan, brown flour in 3 tablespoons bacon drippings, whisking constantly. Add to vegetables. Add oysters and simmer until oysters begin to shrink.

• Season with salt and pepper, 2 shots of Worcestershire, and 2 dashes of hot pepper sauce. Stir to mix. Pour into pie crust and top with second crust. Bake at 350° for 1 hour.

Makes 6 servings.

Early in Anderson's history, boundary streets defined the city's limits. On the north was Orr Street, in recognition of Governor J. L. Orr. The southern boundary was formed by Belton Street, which later changed to River Street because several of the local boys claimed it led to their swimming hole on the Rocky River. Fant Street, on the east, was named after George W. Fant who lived there. A. B. Towers, prominent merchant and leader in the First Presbyterian Church, gave his name to the western boundary street.

Notes

Lobster Tortellini

2 (1½-pound) lobsters, boiled and shelled (1 pound lobster meat)

1 (9-ounce) package fresh tortellini with cheese

¼ cup butter or margarine

1 clove garlic, minced

1 shallot, minced

2 tablespoons chopped fresh basil or 2 teaspoons dried basil

⅓-½ cup grated Parmesan cheese

Garnish: fresh basil

• Cut lobster meat into chunks; set aside.

• Cook pasta according to package directions; drain and set aside.

• Melt butter in a large skillet over medium-high heat; add lobster, garlic, shallot, and basil. Cook about 5 minutes, stirring constantly. Add pasta and cheese. Toss gently, and garnish, if desired, with fresh basil.

Makes 4 servings.

Kids

Fireflies and Mudpies

Kids

*The Kids section features the winning artwork from an art contest sponsored
by the Junior League for all third graders in Anderson County public and private schools.*

On the front:
Fireflies
Artwork by *Tia Tomco*

On the back:
Christmas Candlelight
Artwork by *Redmond Donald*

and

Still Life
Artwork by *Gerome Telford*

Berry Fizz

3 tablespoons frozen raspberry juice concentrate

1 cup ginger ale

• Put juice concentrate in a tall glass.

• Add ginger ale and ice.

Makes 1 serving.

Breakfast in a Glass

A great and healthy breakfast-on-the-run that is simple enough for children to prepare themselves.

1	(8-ounce) carton lemon yogurt (or other flavor)	1	small banana, peeled
1	tablespoon frozen orange juice concentrate, undiluted	1	tablespoon wheat germ

• **Combine all ingredients in a blender. Process on high speed for about 20 seconds or until smooth. Pour into a tall glass and serve immediately.**

Makes 1 serving.

Lemonade For Sale!

Perfect for a lemonade stand!

6	large lemons	2	quarts cold water
1	cup sugar		

• **Cut lemons in half and squeeze juice (need 1½ cups); remove seeds. Add sugar and stir to dissolve. Add water and stir. Serve over ice.**

Makes 8 to 10 servings.

Crockpot Cider

1	gallon apple cider	2	whole nutmegs
10	whole cloves		Pinch of ginger
4	cinnamon sticks		

• **Combine all ingredients in a large crockpot; cook on low for 2 hours. To serve, ladle into mugs.**

Makes 16 to 20 servings.

Banana Pop Freeze

A great summer snack!

3-4 bananas, peeled and cut in half crosswise

Wooden or plastic sticks

2-3 tablespoons orange juice

1 (6-ounce) bag chocolate chips

1 tablespoon margarine

Finely chopped pecans, unsalted peanuts, or coconut

• Insert sticks in cut ends of bananas.

• Brush bananas with orange juice; place on waxed paper on cookie sheet. Freeze until firm.

• Combine chocolate chips and margarine in the top of a double boiler. Cook until chocolate melts. Allow to cool slightly.

• Spoon chocolate over frozen bananas and immediately roll in chopped nuts. Eat at once, or wrap in waxed paper and keep in freezer.

Makes 6 to 8 servings.

Peanut Butter & Jelly French Toast

No more picky eaters at breakfast when this is served!

12 slices bread

¾ cup peanut butter

6 tablespoons jelly or jam

3 eggs

¾ cup milk

¼ teaspoon salt

2 tablespoons butter or margarine

• Spread peanut butter on 6 slices of bread; spread jelly on other 6 slices. Put one slice of each together to form sandwiches.

• In a mixing bowl, lightly beat eggs; add milk and salt, mixing well.

• Melt butter in a large skillet over medium heat.

• Dip sandwiches in egg mixture, coating well. Place in skillet and brown both sides. Serve immediately.

Makes 6 servings.

Once when my oldest daughter was about 16 months, I said to her, "Let's cook dinner". She ran to the microwave and looked up at it with a big grin on her face.

Strawberry Yogurt Pops

Easy to make, and nutritious, too.

1¼	cups trimmed and sliced ripe strawberries, divided	4	small (5-ounce) paper cups
1	(8-ounce) container low-fat strawberry yogurt	4	lollipop sticks

- **In a blender, purée 1 cup strawberries and yogurt. Stir remaining ¼ cup strawberries into puréed mixture. Divide mixture evenly among paper cups. Insert lollipop stick into center of each cup. Freeze at least 4 hours. Peel away paper cup and enjoy!**

Makes 4 servings.

Honey Light Bunny Bright Pancakes

3	cups all-purpose flour	2	eggs
2	tablespoons baking powder	¼	cup honey
½	teaspoon salt	¼	cup vegetable oil
3	cups milk	12	drops food coloring (optional)

- Combine flour, baking powder, and salt in a large bowl.

- Combine milk and remaining ingredients; add to flour mixture, stirring until smooth.

- For each pancake, pour ¼ cup batter onto lightly greased hot griddle. Turn pancakes when tops begin to bubble. Remove to platter when edges are lightly browned. Serve with butter and syrup.

Makes 6 servings.

Egg In a Nest

We wouldn't be surprised if Mom cooks
this for herself after the kids have left for school!

1   slice bread   Butter
1   egg

- Using a 2-inch round cutter, cut a circle from the center of the slice of bread. Butter both sides of the slice and the circle.

- Place bread in frying pan on medium-high heat and drop a small amount of butter into hole to prevent egg from sticking. Place circle in pan with bread slice.

- Crack egg and carefully place in the hole. Fry for a few minutes until egg begins to set. Carefully turn and cook other side. Turn circle also. Fry until desired doneness.

Makes 1 serving.

Fun & Easy Soft Pretzels

Children will love to help mix and shape these pretzels.
Add food coloring to the dough or salt for extra fun!

1   package active dry yeast   4   cups all-purpose flour
1½   cups warm water   1   egg, beaten
1   teaspoon salt   Coarse salt
1   tablespoon sugar

- In a large mixing bowl, dissolve yeast in warm water. Add salt and sugar. Blend in flour to form dough. Knead until smooth. Form into desired shapes and place on lightly greased cookie sheet.

- Brush pretzels with egg; sprinkle with salt.

- Bake at 425° for 12 to 15 minutes.

Makes 16 to 18 servings.

Dog Gone Good

**Delicious after
a hard day at play!**

½ cup Thousand Island dressing
8 whole grain hot dog buns, split
2 cups shredded lettuce
16 (1-ounce) turkey slices
8 string cheese sticks

- Spread dressing on insides of hot dog buns. Add shredded lettuce evenly to each.

- Wrap 2 turkey slices around each cheese stick, and place in buns. Pack chilled dogs in lunchbox next to a frozen drink box.

Makes 8.

Chunky Cinnamon Applesauce

| 8 | medium tart apples, peeled and quartered | 1 | cup sugar |
| 1 | cup water | ¼ | cup red hot cinnamon candies |

- Place apples and water in a 5-quart saucepan. Cover and cook over medium-low heat for 20 minutes or until tender.

- Mash apples; add sugar and candies. Cook, uncovered, over low heat until sugar and candies are dissolved. Remove from heat; cool. Refrigerate until serving.

Makes about 6 cups.

Baby Burgers

Moms will love having these on hand for lunches and snacks.

1	pound lean ground beef	5	slices American process cheese slices, quartered
2	tablespoons ketchup		Condiments: mustard, ketchup, mayonnaise, minced onion, dill pickle slices, tomato slices, lettuce leaves
¼	teaspoon salt		
¼	teaspoon pepper		
1	(7½-ounce) package party rolls		

- Combine first 4 ingredients. Shape mixture by tablespoonfuls into patties, and place on a rack in a broiler pan.

- Bake at 350° for 15 to 17 minutes or until done.

- Split rolls horizontally, and place a piece of cheese and a meat patty in each. Serve with desired condiments.

Makes 20 servings.

Note: Place in heavy-duty zip-top plastic bags; seal and freeze. Remove desired number of burgers from freezer and pack frozen in lunchbox. Sandwiches will thaw in approximately 2½ to 3 hours.

Toddler Trail Mix

Those little hands will grab this up!

1	cup gummy bears	½	cup raisins
1	cup pretzel goldfish	1	cup Honey Nut Cheerios
1	cup miniature marshmallows	1	cup Fruit Loops

• Combine all ingredients in a large zip-top plastic bag. Shake to mix and serve for a great snack!

Makes 10 to 12 servings.

Baked Chicken Nuggets

Kids will love these crispy nuggets!

3-4	skinless, boneless chicken breasts	1	teaspoon dried thyme
½	cup Parmesan cheese	1	teaspoon salt
1	cup Italian breadcrumbs	1	teaspoon dried basil
		½	cup margarine, melted

• Cut chicken into 2-inch pieces; set aside.

• In a medium bowl, combine Parmesan cheese, breadcrumbs, thyme, salt, and basil. Stir to blend.

• Put melted margarine in a separate small bowl.

• Dip each chicken piece into the margarine, then into the breadcrumb mixture. Place on lightly greased cookie sheet.

• Bake at 400° for about 20 minutes. Serve with bottled honey-mustard dressing, honey, or ranch dressing for dipping.

Makes 4 servings.

Cherry Fruit Dip

1 (7-ounce) jar whipped marshmallow cream

1 (10-ounce) jar red maraschino cherries (juice only)

• Mix marshmallow cream and cherry juice together and serve with slices of apple, pear, pineapple, peach, etc. and grapes.

Makes about 1 pint.

Kid's Favorite Cheese Fondue

1 (10½-ounce) can
Cheddar cheese soup
1½ cups grated
sharp Cheddar cheese

• Cook soup according to
directions on can. Add grated
cheese; stirring until melted. Serve
with breadsticks, bread cubes,
carrots, celery, broccoli,
cauliflower, or apple slices.

Makes 8 servings.

Chicken on a Stick

Fun to eat!

4 skinless, boneless chicken breasts, cut into 1-inch cubes	¼ cup maple syrup
1 (20-ounce) can pineapple chunks in juice, undrained	½ cup cooking sherry
½ cup brown sugar	¼ cup teriyaki sauce
	Bamboo skewers, cut in half

• **Combine chicken and next 5 ingredients in a large bowl, stirring to mix well. Cover and refrigerate for 1 to 2 hours.**

• **Using skewers, alternate chicken and pineapple chunks, making kabobs.**

• **Grill for approximately 20 minutes or until chicken is done.**

Makes 10 to 12 servings.

Shake It Up Baby!

You don't need a fancy ice cream maker to whip up this frozen dessert - just a couple of plastic zip-lock bags.

1 cup whole milk	12 ice cubes
1 teaspoon vanilla extract	2 tablespoons table salt
1 tablespoon sugar	

• **Pour milk into a small zip-lock bag. Add vanilla and sugar. Seal the bag.**

• **Place ice cubes into a large zip-lock bag. Sprinkle salt on the ice cubes.**

• **Put the small bag into the larger bag and seal the outer bag.**

• **Let everyone take turns vigorously shaking the bag. Within 10 minutes, you should see ice crystals forming in the milk mixture. Once it reaches the consistency of soft-serve ice cream, scoop the ice milk into a bowl and serve immediately. Top with candy, nuts, or fruit, if desired.**

Makes 1 cup.

Caribbean Dessert Pizza

1 (20-ounce) package refrigerated
   rolled sugar cookie dough
1 (3.4-ounce) package instant
   vanilla pudding
1¾ cups milk
1 mango, peeled, seeded, and
   thinly sliced

½ cup strawberries, sliced
1 kiwi, peeled, halved, and sliced
1 banana, sliced
1 (10-ounce) container frozen
   nondairy whipped topping,
   thawed
¼ cup shredded coconut

• Slice cookie dough into ¼-inch-thick slices. Arrange ¾ of the
  dough slices in a lightly greased 12-inch pizza pan. Press dough
  into sides of pan to make crust. Bake at 350° for 14 minutes, or
  until slightly browned. (Remaining dough slices may be baked
  according to directions on package.)

• While crust cools, prepare filling by blending milk and pudding.
  Spread over crust. Arrange fruit slices on top of filling. Pizza may be
  chilled up to 2 hours before serving. To serve, cut pizza and serve
  slices with a dollop of whipped topping. Sprinkle coconut on top.

Makes 8 servings.

Frosted Brownie Pizza

½ cup butter
2 (1-ounce) squares unsweetened
   chocolate
1 cup sugar
¾ cup all-purpose flour
2 eggs, beaten
1 cup powdered sugar

⅓ cup creamy peanut butter
1½ teaspoons vanilla extract
2-4 tablespoons milk
¾ cup plain M & M's
½ cup flaked coconut, toasted
½ cup chopped pecans, toasted

• In a saucepan over low heat, melt butter, chocolate, and sugar.
  Remove from heat; stir in flour until smooth. Add eggs and beat
  until smooth. Spread batter onto a greased 12-inch pizza pan.

• Bake at 350° for 15 minutes, or until a wooden pick inserted in
  center comes out clean. Cool completely.

• In a mixing bowl, combine powdered sugar, peanut butter, and
  vanilla. Beat, adding enough milk to achieve desired spreading
  consistency. Spread over cooled pizza. Top with M & M's,
  coconut, and pecans. Slice to serve.

Makes 8 servings.

Pinwheel Sandwiches
Peanut butter and jelly with a twist!

1 flour tortilla
Peanut butter
Apple, strawberry, or grape jelly

• Spread tortilla with peanut butter and then jelly. Roll up tortilla as tight as possible and slice into pinwheels.

Makes 1 serving.

Gingerbread Men

Make these a holiday tradition.

1	cup butter	6	cups all-purpose flour
1	cup sugar	1½	teaspoons baking soda
½	teaspoon salt	4	teaspoons ground ginger
2	eggs	1	teaspoon cinnamon
1	cup molasses		Raisins
2	tablespoons vinegar		Red candied cherries

- Combine butter, sugar, and salt in a large bowl and cream well.

- Beat eggs in a separate bowl. Add to butter mixture. Add molasses and vinegar.

- Combine flour and baking soda; gradually blend into butter mixture. Add ginger and cinnamon.

- Chill dough for 2 hours. (If mixture becomes sticky while you are working with it, just place back in refrigerator.)

- Place dough on a floured surface and roll as thin as you like. Dip cookie cutter into flour, and cut out gingerbread men. Place on baking sheet, and bake at 350° for 10 to 12 minutes.

- Remove from pan before cookies are completely cooled. Decorate with raisins for eyes and buttons, and candied cherries for mouth.

Makes 2 to 3 dozen.

Desserts

Sweet Reflections

Desserts

On the front:
Sunset at River Forks Hartwell Lake, Anderson, South Carolina
Photograph by *Sabrina R. Dunn*

Molten Chocolate Cakes

These delicious individual cakes are great by themselves or garnished with a dollop of whipped cream and fresh berries.

1	stick (4 ounces) unsalted butter	2	egg yolks
6	ounces premium bittersweet chocolate	¼	cup sugar
			Pinch of salt
2	eggs	2	tablespoons all-purpose flour

• Butter and lightly flour 4 (6-ounce) ramekins. Tap out excess flour and set ramekins on a baking sheet.

• In a double boiler, melt butter and chocolate over simmering water.

• In a medium bowl, beat the eggs, egg yolks, sugar and salt at a high speed until thickened and pale.

• Whisk the chocolate until smooth. Quickly fold it into the egg mixture along with the flour.

• Spoon the batter into the prepared ramekins and bake at 450° for 12 minutes, or until the sides of the cakes are firm and the centers are soft. Let the cakes cool in the ramekins for 1 minute.

• Cover each ramekin with an inverted dessert plate. Carefully turn each one over, let stand for 10 seconds and unmold. Serve immediately.

Makes 4 servings.

The batter can be prepared ahead and refrigerated for several hours. Bring to room temperature before baking.

Tips for making cakes, cookies and more from standard cake mixes

• *Use salted butter, not unsalted. If you must use margarine for health reasons, make sure it's a stick version with more than 65% vegetable oil.*

• *If whole milk is called for, don't substitute. But if the recipe just says "milk," any kind is fine.*

• *For best results, buy large eggs and let them come to room temperature before preparing the recipe.*

• *If a recipe requires vegetable oil, use a light, flavorless one like soybean or canola.*

• *Add more chocolate! Drop mini chips into batter before baking; intensify devil's food with a spoonful of unsweetened cocoa powder.*

*Use a purchased doily,
a purchased stencil, or make
your own stencil from
lightweight cardboard. Place
the stencil on top of the dessert
surface. Sift powdered sugar or
cocoa powder over stencil.*

Banana Dream Cake

Cake

3	cups all-purpose flour	2	eggs
1½	teaspoons baking powder	1½	teaspoons vanilla extract
1½	teaspoons baking soda	1	cup plus 2 tablespoons buttermilk
½	teaspoon salt	1½	cups mashed ripe bananas
¾	cup margarine		
2	cups sugar		

Frosting

½	cup butter, softened	1	cup chopped pecans (optional)
8	ounces cream cheese, softened	2	bananas, sliced
2	teaspoons vanilla extract		Garnish: pecans
1	(16-ounce) package powdered sugar		

- In a medium bowl, sift together flour, baking powder, baking soda, and salt. Set aside.

- In a large bowl, cream margarine and sugar until light and fluffy. Add eggs, one at a time, beating well after each addition. Stir in vanilla.

- Add flour mixture and buttermilk, alternately, to the creamed mixture, beating well.

- Stir in mashed bananas.

- Spoon into 3 greased and floured 8-inch round cake pans.

- Bake at 325° for 30 minutes, or until layers are light brown and spring back gently to touch. (Do not overbake.) Remove to wire racks to cool.

- While cake layers are cooling, prepare frosting. Beat butter and cream cheese together until smooth. Add the vanilla and mix well. Beat in powdered sugar. Stir in chopped pecans.

- Spread frosting over bottom layer. Top with sliced bananas. Add next layer and repeat.

- Add top layer. Frost top and sides of cake. Garnish with pecans, if desired.

Makes 16 servings.

Lemon-Raspberry Cake with Lemon Buttercream Frosting

The lemony flavor of this cake is complemented by the raspberry preserves.

Prevent a cake from sticking to its serving platter by first sprinkling the platter with powdered sugar.

Cake

1	cup shortening	1	cup milk
2	cups sugar	1	teaspoon almond extract
4	large eggs	1	teaspoon vanilla extract
3	cups cake flour, sifted	1	(10-ounce) jar seedless
2½	teaspoons baking powder		raspberry preserves
½	teaspoon salt		

Lemon Buttercream Frosting

1¼	cups butter or margarine, softened	3	tablespoons lemon juice
2	teaspoons grated lemon rind	3	cups sifted powdered sugar

- Grease 3 (9-inch) round cake pans; line with wax paper. Grease and flour wax paper. Set pans aside.

- Beat shortening at medium speed of an electric mixer until creamy; gradually add sugar, beating well. Add eggs one at a time, beating well after each addition.

- Combine flour, baking powder, and salt; add to shortening mixture alternately with milk, beginning and ending with flour mixture. Mix after each addition. Stir in flavorings.

- Pour batter into prepared pans. Bake at 350° for 16 to 18 minutes or until a wooden pick inserted in center comes out clean.

- While cake is baking, prepare frosting. Combine butter or margarine, lemon rind and lemon juice. Beat at medium speed of electric mixer until creamy. Gradually add powdered sugar, beating until frosting is spreading consistency.

- Cool cake layers in pans on wire racks 10 minutes; remove from pans, and let cool completely on wire racks. Slice cake layers in half horizontally to make 6 layers. Place 1 layer, cut side up, on a cake plate; spread with about 2½ tablespoons preserves. Repeat procedure with remaining 5 layers and preserves, omitting preserves on top of last layer.

- Reserve ¾ cup frosting; spread remaining frosting on top and sides of cake. Using a star tip, pipe reserved frosting on top of cake. Garnish with lemon slice wedges, if desired. Store in an airtight container in refrigerator.

Makes 16 servings.

Chocolate Godiva Mousse Cake with Buttercream Frosting

Sinful never tasted so good.

Cake

½	cup butter, softened	2	teaspoons baking soda
2¼	cups brown sugar		Pinch of salt
3	eggs, at room temperature	1	cup sour cream
3	ounces unsweetened chocolate, melted	1	cup boiling water
		1	teaspoon vanilla extract
2¼	cups all-purpose flour	¼	cup Godiva liqueur

Mousse Filling

2	cups heavy cream	½	teaspoon vanilla extract
3	tablespoons powdered sugar	½	cup Godiva liqueur

Buttercream Frosting

½	cup butter, softened	¼	cup cocoa powder
1	(16-ounce) package powdered sugar	½	cup Godiva liqueur
1	teaspoon vanilla extract	1-2	tablespoons heavy cream

- Grease 2 (9-inch) cake pans. Dust with cocoa and line with parchment paper. Set aside.

- Beat butter and sugar together until creamy. Add eggs, one at a time. Add melted chocolate.

- Combine flour, baking soda, and salt. Add to creamed mixture, alternating with sour cream, starting and ending with flour mixture.

- Slowly pour boiling water into mixture, gently mixing, just until combined. Add vanilla and ¼ cup liqueur.

- Spread batter in cake pans and bake at 350° for 25 to 30 minutes, or until a wooden pick comes out clean. Cool completely.

- To prepare filling, combine heavy cream, powdered sugar, vanilla, and liqueur. Whip until stiff peaks form.

- To prepare frosting, cream together butter and powdered sugar. Add vanilla, cocoa, and liqueur. Whip until smooth. Add heavy cream as needed to reach spreading consistency.

- Slice cake layers in half horizontally to make 4 layers. Spread 3 layers with mousse filling. Frost top and sides with frosting.

Makes 16 servings.

Nana's Orange Chiffon Cake

A wonderful family tradition.

Cake

2¼	cups sifted cake flour		3	tablespoons grated orange rind
1½	cups sugar		¾	cup orange juice
3	teaspoons baking powder		8	egg whites, at room temperature
1	teaspoon salt			
½	cup vegetable oil		½	teaspoon cream of tartar
5	medium egg yolks, at room temperature			

Orange Buttercream Frosting

½	cup butter		⅛-¼	cup orange juice or milk
⅛	teaspoon salt		1	teaspoon grated orange rind
3½	cups sifted powdered sugar		½	teaspoon vanilla extract

- In a large bowl, sift together flour, sugar, baking powder, and salt. Make a well in the flour mixture and pour in vegetable oil. Add egg yolks, orange rind, and orange juice. Beat on medium speed of mixer until smooth.

- In another large bowl pour egg whites and add cream of tartar. With mixer on high speed, beat until very stiff peaks form and hold. (Do not underbeat!)

- Slowly pour egg yolk mixture over whites, folding mixture gently with rubber spatula or spoon. Continue folding until mixture is just blended.

- Turn batter into ungreased 10-inch tube pan. Bake at 325° for 55 minutes, then at 350° for 10 to 15 minutes, or until wooden pick inserted in center comes out clean. Cool in pan upside down until cool.

- While cake is cooling, prepare frosting. Combine butter, salt, powdered sugar, orange juice or milk, orange rind, and vanilla. Beat ingredients together, mixing well to form a good spreading consistency. Frost top, sides, and stack of cake.

Makes 16 servings.

When cooling a cake in a tube pan upside down, invert pan on the neck of a glass soft drink or beer bottle.

When frosting the sides
of a cake, place wax paper just
under the edges and remove
after frosting. The excess goes
with the wax paper and the
edge of the cake is neat and
ready for serving.

24 Karat Carrot Cake

The traditional cream cheese frosting is the perfect compliment to the not-so-traditional batter in this super-moist, super-delicious dessert.

Cake

3	sticks unsalted butter	½	cup pure apple juice
1	cup firmly packed light brown sugar	1½	cups grated peeled carrots (3 or 4 medium)
1	cup sugar	1	cup shredded peeled sweet potato (2 medium or 1 large)
2	teaspoons vanilla extract		
3	large eggs, at room temperature	1	large Granny Smith apple, peeled and chopped
2½	cups all-purpose flour	½	cup crushed pineapple, drained
1	teaspoon baking soda	1	cup coarsely chopped pecans, toasted
1	teaspoon baking powder		
1	teaspoon ground cinnamon	2	tablespoons heavy cream
¼	teaspoon salt		

Cream Cheese Frosting

16	ounces cream cheese, softened	1	tablespoon fresh lemon juice
1	stick unsalted butter, softened	2	(16-ounce) packages powdered sugar
2	teaspoons vanilla extract		

- **Butter and flour 3 (9-inch) cake pans. Set aside.**

- **In a large bowl, combine butter and sugars. Using medium speed of mixer, cream together until fluffy, about 4 or 5 minutes. (Be sure to scrape down the bowl throughout the mixing process.) Beat in vanilla. Add eggs, one at a time, beating for 20 seconds after each addition.**

- **In another bowl, whisk together flour, baking soda, baking powder, cinnamon, and salt. Add dry mixture in thirds to the butter mixture, alternating with apple juice. Beat for 45 seconds after each addition, and begin and end with the flour mixture. Stir in the carrots, sweet potato, apple, pineapple, and pecans; blend thoroughly. Divide the batter among the prepared pans, smoothing the tops.**

- **Bake on middle oven rack at 350° for 25 to 30 minutes, or until a wooden pick inserted in the center comes out clean. Remove the cake pans to wire racks to cool for 10 minutes, then turn them out onto the racks to cool completely. While the layers are still warm, brush each with 1 tablespoon heavy cream.**

- While cake is cooling, prepare frosting. Combine cream cheese and butter in a bowl and beat until smooth using medium speed of mixer. Add vanilla and lemon juice, beating until combined. Gradually beat in the sugar on low speed until well blended and smooth.

- Place a cake layer on a serving plate and spread the top with a thin layer of frosting. Place a second layer on top and spread with a thin layer of frosting. Place the remaining layer on top and frost the sides of the cake. Spread the remaining frosting over the top. Garnish the sides of the cake with the chopped pecans, pressing them gently on with hands. Refrigerate cake for 1 hour before serving.

Makes 16 servings.

Amaretto Pound Cake

3	cups sugar	2	teaspoons rum extract
1	cup margarine, softened	1	teaspoon orange extract
6	eggs	1	teaspoon almond extract
3	cups all-purpose flour	1	teaspoon lemon extract
¼	teaspoon baking soda	1	teaspoon vanilla extract
	Pinch of salt	1	cup amaretto
1	cup sour cream		

- Combine sugar and margarine; cream until light and fluffy. Add eggs, one at a time, mixing well after each addition.

- Combine flour, baking soda, and salt. Add to creamed mixture, alternately with sour cream, beating well after each addition. Stir in remaining ingredients and pour into greased and floured 10-inch tube pan.

- Bake at 325° for 1 hour and 20 minutes.

Makes 16 servings.

Aunt Ruth's Coconut Cake

**Make this moist, mouth-watering cake
3 days before serving. It is worth every bit of the effort.**

Frosting (Prepare the day before baking the cake.)

1   (12-ounce) container frozen
    nondairy whipped topping,
    thawed
1   cup sour cream

1   cup sifted powdered sugar
1   teaspoon vanilla extract
2   (12-ounce) packages frozen
    coconut, thawed

Cake Layers

4   eggs, at room temperature
2   cups sifted powdered sugar
1½   cups cooking oil
2½   cups sifted self-rising flour

1   cup buttermilk, at room
    temperature
1   teaspoon vinegar
1   teaspoon vanilla extract

Coconut Milk

1   (12-ounce) package frozen
    coconut

¾   cup sugar
1½   cups water

- To prepare frosting, combine whipped topping, sour cream,
  powdered sugar, vanilla, and coconut. Mix well, cover tightly and
  refrigerate overnight.

- To prepare cake layers, beat eggs, adding one at a time. Gradually
  add sugar, blending well after each addition. Very slowly, add the
  oil and blend; add half of the flour to the egg mixture; add
  buttermilk and vinegar; mix. Add vanilla and remaining flour,
  mixing well.

- Pour batter into 3 greased and floured cake pans.

- Bake at 325° for 25 to 35 minutes, or until wooden pick inserted
  in the center comes out clean. Let cool completely.

- While cake is baking, prepare coconut milk. Combine coconut,
  sugar, and water. Mix well, bring to a boil and simmer for
  2 minutes. Cover and remove from heat.

- Spoon coconut milk over cool cake layers. Spread frosting
  between layers and on top and sides of cake. Place cake in tightly
  covered container, and refrigerate for 3 days before serving.

Makes 16 servings.

Winter White Chocolate Cheesecake

**A beautiful dessert that can be served
with chocolate or raspberry sauce, if desired.**

Crust

¼	cup butter, melted	1	ounce white chocolate, grated
1¾-2	cups shortbread cookies, finely ground	¼	cup sugar

Filling

3	(8-ounce) packages cream cheese, softened	3	eggs
½	cup sugar	½	pound white chocolate, melted very slowly over low heat or in double boiler
½	teaspoon vanilla extract		

- Combine ingredients for crust and press evenly in bottom of 9-inch springform pan.

- Combine cream cheese, sugar, and vanilla, and beat at medium speed of mixer until well blended. Add eggs, one at a time, mixing well after each addition. Blend in melted chocolate. Pour over crust.

- Bake at 350° for 40 minutes. (Cake will be moist or "jiggle" slightly in center, and may even crack. This is okay.) Loosen cake from rim of pan; cool before removing pan rim. Refrigerate overnight.

Makes 12 to 16 servings.

Instead of flouring the cake pan and turning chocolate cake white on the outside, grease and "cocoa" the pan, using sifted unsweetened cocoa powder.

Chocolate Glaze

This multi-purpose icing is wonderful for any cake or brownie. You may even thin it with milk to make a yummy chocolate sauce for fruit or ice cream.

2 tablespoons butter

1 square unsweetened chocolate

2¼ cups powdered sugar

½ teaspoon vanilla

1½-2 tablespoons milk

• In double boiler, melt butter and chocolate over simmering water. Gradually add powdered sugar, stirring well. Remove from heat; add vanilla and milk, stirring until smooth and desired consistency is reached. Pour on cooled cake.

Cream Cheese Pound Cake

3	sticks butter	3	cups cake flour
2	cups sugar	½	teaspoon baking powder
1	(8-ounce) package cream cheese	2	teaspoons vanilla extract
6	eggs		

• Cream together butter, sugar and cream cheese. Add eggs, one at a time, mixing after each addition.

• Sift together flour and baking powder. Gradually add to creamed mixture and stir in vanilla. Pour batter into greased and floured tube or Bundt pan.

• Bake at 325° for 1½ hours.

Chocolate Cream Cheese Pound Cake: Replace ⅓ cup cake flour with ⅓ cup cocoa.

Coconut Cream Cheese Pound Cake: Replace 2 teaspoons vanilla with 1 teaspoon vanilla and 1 teaspoon coconut extract, and add 6 ounces shredded coconut to batter.

Frozen Peppermint Cheesecake

Deliciously cool!

1½	cups chocolate wafer crumbs	1	(14-ounce) can sweetened condensed milk
¼	cup sugar		
¼	cup butter or margarine, melted	1	cup crushed peppermint hard candy
1	(8-ounce) package cream cheese, softened	3	drops red food coloring
		3	cups whipping cream, whipped

• Combine first 3 ingredients; press firmly onto bottom and 1 inch up sides of a 9-inch springform pan. Chill.

• Beat cream cheese at high speed of electric mixer until fluffy. Add condensed milk, peppermint candy, and food coloring; beat well. Fold in whipped cream. Pour into prepared pan.

• Cover and freeze until firm. Garnish, if desired, with whipped cream and peppermint candy.

Makes 12 to 16 servings.

Angel Bliss Trifle

This a fun dessert to experiment with since you decide which fruits and flavors to use. We haven't discovered one yet that's not delicious!

½	gallon vanilla or fruit flavored ice cream or frozen yogurt, softened	2	tablespoons fruit liqueur or flavoring
1	angel food cake, cut into bite-size pieces	2	tablespoons rum or rum flavoring
2	tablespoons fruit preserves	½	cup fresh or frozen fruit

• **Mix all ingredients together and freeze.**

Makes 12 to 15 servings.

Chocolate-Kahlúa Variation: Use chocolate ice cream, replace fruit preserves with 2 chopped chocolate candy bars, omit fruit liqueur, and replace rum with 2 tablespoons Kahlúa.

New World Tiramisu

½	cup milk	3-4	tablespoons amaretto liqueur
1	tablespoon cocoa powder	5	egg yolks
⅓	cup sugar, divided	16	ounces mascarpone cheese
½	cup espresso or very strong coffee	30-36	lady fingers
			Garnish: cocoa powder

• Heat milk, cocoa powder and 1 tablespoon sugar over medium-high heat, stirring constantly, until boiling. Add espresso and amaretto.

• In a mixing bowl combine egg yolks and remaining sugar; mix well. Add mascarpone and mix until creamy.

• Place a layer of ladyfingers in the bottom of 8- x 10-inch baking dish. Pour half of the milk mixture over the ladyfingers and spread half of the mascarpone mixture. Repeat with second layer. Chill at least 8 and up to 48 hours before serving. Sprinkle with cocoa powder just before serving.

Makes 6 servings.

Milk Chocolate Candy Bar Frosting

Make sure it doesn't disappear before you ice your cake!

1 (8-ounce) package cream cheese, softened

1 cup powdered sugar

½ cup granulated sugar

10 milk chocolate candy bars with almonds, divided

1 (12-ounce) container frozen nondairy whipped topping, thawed

• Combine cream cheese and sugars. Beat with electric mixer on medium speed until creamy.

• Finely chop 8 candy bars. Fold cream cheese mixture and chopped candy bars into whipped topping.

• Spread frosting between layers, and on top and sides of desired cake.

• Chop remaining 2 candy bars. Sprinkle half on top of cake and press half around bottom edge of cake.

Makes enough frosting for 1 large layer cake or 2 sheet cakes.

Lemon Curd
Bread and Butter Pudding

**Add a scoop of vanilla ice cream or a dollop of
whipped cream for a dessert your guests will adore.**

Lemon Curd

½	cup butter	3	large lemons, grated into zest
1¼	cups sugar	3	eggs, beaten and sieved
6	ounces freshly squeezed lemon juice		

Bread Pudding

1	round brioche, Hawaiian bread, or other sweet bread	⅓	cup sugar
¼	cup butter, softened	1¼	cups milk
2	eggs plus 1 egg yolk, beaten	¾	cup whipping cream

- To prepare lemon curd, place all ingredients in the top of a double boiler over simmering water. Stir continuously until thick, about 20 minutes.

- Cut bread into 4 or 5 lengthwise slices. Spread with butter, then lemon curd.

- Butter a 2-quart ovenproof dish. Place bread slices in the dish, overlapping if necessary.

- Whisk together the eggs, sugar, milk, and cream. Strain over the slices. Let soak for 30 minutes.

- Place in a bain-marie (pan of water) and bake at 325° for 30 to 40 minutes. Allow to cool 5 minutes before serving.

Makes 4 to 6 servings.

Promptly refrigerate any lemon curd not used for bread pudding. Use it as a topping for vanilla ice cream or a spread on toasted pound cake or bread.

Blueberry Bread Pudding
with Maple Whiskey Sauce

An elegant combination reminiscent of days gone by.

Bread Pudding

2	cups whole milk	7	cups 1-inch cubes brioche, egg bread, or Hawaiian bread
½	cup plus 2 tablespoons sugar		
3	large eggs	1	(10-ounce) package frozen unsweetened blueberries, unthawed
2	large egg yolks		
1½	teaspoons vanilla extract		

Maple Whiskey Sauce

1	cup half-and-half	1	teaspoon cornstarch
3	egg yolks	¼	cup pure maple syrup
2	tablespoons sugar	2	tablespoons whiskey

• Place half of bread cubes in bottom of buttered 8-inch square glass baking dish.

• Whisk together milk, sugar, eggs, yolks, and vanilla in bowl.

• Top bread with half of blueberries. Pour half of custard over blueberries. Top with remaining bread, blueberries, and custard. Let stand 15 minutes, occasionally pressing on bread.

• Bake at 325° until pudding puffs and top begins to brown, about 1 hour 15 minutes.

• While bread pudding is baking, prepare sauce. Bring half-and-half to simmer in heavy medium saucepan.

• In medium bowl, whisk egg yolks, sugar, and cornstarch. Gradually whisk in hot half-and-half. Return mixture to same saucepan and stir over medium-low heat until custard thickens and leaves path on back of spoon when finger is drawn across, about 3 minutes (do not boil). Strain into bowl. Mix in maple syrup and whiskey. Serve sauce over warm pudding.

Makes 6 servings.

Southern etiquette dictates that white shoes should not be worn before Easter Sunday or after Labor Day.

Steamed Cranberry Pudding with Sauce

A nice change of pace from the usual holiday desserts.

Pudding

½	cup molasses	1	teaspoon baking powder
½	cup water	1½	cups all-purpose flour
2	teaspoons baking soda	1	cup fresh cranberries

Sauce

1	cup sugar	½	cup butter, melted
½	cup half-and-half	½	teaspoon vanilla extract

- Mix molasses, water, and baking soda in mixing bowl.

- Sift baking powder and flour together, and add to molasses mixture. Stir in cranberries. Steam for 2 hours in a greased double boiler.

- To prepare sauce, combine sugar, half-and-half, butter, and vanilla. Mix well and heat thoroughly over low heat. (Do not boil.) To serve, spoon pudding into dessert dishes and top with sauce.

Makes 8 servings.

Nouveau Napoleons

These are as much fun to eat as they are delicious!

1¼	cups orange juice		Nonstick cooking spray
¾	cup sugar	1	tablespoon cinnamon
2	tablespoons cornstarch	1	tablespoon sugar
2	whole eggs	½	pint strawberries, sliced in half lengthwise
2	egg yolks		
12	wonton wrappers	2	peaches, peeled and sliced

- In a medium saucepan, combine orange juice, ¾ cup sugar, cornstarch, whole eggs, and egg yolks. Bring to a boil, stirring over medium heat; cook 2 minutes or until thickened, stirring constantly. Cool completely.

- Place wonton wrappers in a single layer on a baking sheet. Spray wrappers with cooking spray and sprinkle with cinnamon and 1 tablespoon sugar. Bake at 325° for 6 to 8 minutes or until crisp. Cool completely.

- On each dessert plate, place one wrapper, then fruit, and then custard. Repeat layers two more times.

Makes 4 servings.

Notes

Merlot Sorbet

A perfect light dessert for a bridal luncheon.

2 cups water
1½ cups sugar
1½ cups Merlot wine
Garnish: mint leaves and stemmed Bing cherries

• In medium saucepan, combine water and sugar. Heat to boiling; reduce heat to low and cook covered for 5 minutes. Remove from heat.

• Add wine to heated mixture. Let cool and refrigerate until chilled. Transfer to freezer and freeze until serving, whisking occasionally. To serve, scoop into stemmed dessert glasses and garnish.

Makes 8 to 10 servings.

Peanut Butter Ice Cream

1	(12-ounce) jar chunky peanut butter	1	cup milk
1½	quarts half-and-half, divided	1	tablespoon vanilla extract
6	large eggs	2	cups sugar
1	(14-ounce) can sweetened condensed milk	3	tablespoons all-purpose flour

• Cook peanut butter, 2 cups half-and-half, and eggs in a Dutch oven over low heat, whisking constantly, 7 minutes or until a thermometer registers 160°. Whisk in remaining 4 cups half-and-half, condensed milk, milk, and vanilla.

• Combine sugar and flour; whisk into hot mixture until sugar dissolves. Pour into freezer container of a 5-quart hand-turned or electric freezer. Freeze according to manufacturer's instructions. Pack freezer with additional ice and rock salt, and let stand for 1 hour before serving.

Makes 1 gallon.

Banana Nut Ice Cream

Roasting the bananas adds a caramelized sweetness.

4	ripe bananas, unpeeled	2	cups sugar
3	cups whipping cream	8	egg yolks, lightly beaten
2	cups milk	1½	cups chopped pecans, toasted

• Place bananas on baking sheet. Bake at 350° for 30 minutes; cool and peel. Process in a food processor until smooth.

• Cook whipping cream and next 3 ingredients in a heavy saucepan over medium heat, whisking constantly, about 25 minutes or until mixture thickens and coats a spoon. (Do not boil.)

• Fold in bananas and pecans; cool slightly. Place plastic wrap directly on surface; chill until completely cooled. Pour mixture into freezer container of a 1-gallon hand-turned or electric freezer. Freeze according to manufacturer's instructions. Pack freezer with additional ice and rock salt, and let stand 1 hour before serving.

Makes 2 quarts.

Peaches & Cream Ice Cream

**Homemade peach ice cream is only a
roadside stand away during the summer peach season!**

1	cup sugar	1½	tablespoons vanilla extract
¼	cup all-purpose flour	3	cups peeled chopped peaches
¼	teaspoon salt	½	cup sugar
3	eggs, beaten	2	cups whipping cream
1	cup milk	2	cups half-and-half

• Combine 1 cup sugar, flour, and salt in a heavy saucepan; mix well. Stir in eggs and milk; cook over medium heat, whisking constantly, until mixture is thickened and bubbly. Remove pan from heat; stir in vanilla. Cool mixture completely.

• Combine peaches and ½ cup sugar; mix well, and let stand 5 minutes.

• Combine cooked mixture, peach mixture, whipping cream, and half-and-half; mix well. Pour into freezer container of a 1-gallon hand-turned or electric freezer. Freeze according to manufacturer's instructions. Pack freezer with additional ice and rock salt, and let stand 1 hour before serving.

Makes 2½ quarts.

Banana Split Ice Cream

4	eggs	2	cups half-and-half
1¼	cups sugar	1	tablespoon vanilla extract
6	cups milk	2	bananas, chopped
½	teaspoon salt	1	(10-ounce) jar maraschino cherries, drained and chopped
1	(14-ounce) can sweetened condensed milk	1	cup chocolate chips

• Beat eggs until frothy. Gradually add sugar, milk, and salt; mix thoroughly.

• Heat completely over low heat, stirring constantly. Remove pan from heat; Let cool.

• Stir in remaining ingredients. Pour into freezer container of a 5-quart hand-turned or electric freezer. Freeze according to manufacturer's instructions.

Makes 1 gallon.

Cinnamon Ice Cream
**Wonderful to serve
after a Mexican meal.**

6 large eggs
2 cups sugar
8 cups half-and-half
3 tablespoons ground cinnamon
2 tablespoons vanilla extract

• Beat eggs lightly in a large bowl. Add sugar, half-and-half, cinnamon, and vanilla; blend well. Pour into freezer container of a 1-gallon ice cream freezer and freeze, according to manufacturer's instructions. When completed, place ice cream in freezer to harden further.

Makes 2½ quarts.

Cherry Sauce

1 (10-ounce) can pitted
dark sweet cherries

2 tablespoons cornstarch

1 tablespoon prepared mustard

1 tablespoon molasses

3 tablespoons lemon juice

• Drain cherries, reserving
syrup. Add enough water to
cherries to make 2½ cups.

• In a small saucepan, blend
3 tablespoons of reserved syrup
into cornstarch until smooth; stir
in remaining syrup, mustard, and
molasses. Cook over low heat,
stirring constantly, until mixture
thicken and boils, about 3 minutes.
Stir in cherries and lemon juice;
heat slowly just until bubbly. Serve
warm over ice cream
or pound cake.

Makes about 3 cups.

Kahlúa Brownie
Ice Cream Sandwich

The ultimate splurge!

½	pound unsalted butter	1	cup chocolate chips
2½	cups sugar	2	cups chocolate-covered toffee bar pieces
4	eggs		
¾	cup cocoa powder	⅓	cup sour cream
	Pinch of salt	½	cup Kahlúa
½	teaspoon baking powder		Vanilla ice cream
1	cup all-purpose flour		Commercial chocolate sauce

• **In medium large saucepan melt butter. Add sugar and mix
thoroughly. Add eggs, one at a time, mixing well after each
addition; mix in cocoa. Add dry ingredients and mix until
combined. Stir in chocolate pieces, toffee bar pieces, sour cream,
and Kahlúa.**

• **Spread batter into well-greased jelly-roll pan. Bake at 350° for
20 to 25 minutes, or until set in the middle. Cool in pan.**

• **Cut cake into approximately 3½-inch squares. For each dessert
place one brownie on bottom. Layer vanilla ice cream and
another brownie on top. Drizzle with chocolate sauce.**

Makes 6 servings.

Strawberries in White Zinfandel

This mix of berries, orange juice,
and wine is a fabulous ice cream topper.

2	oranges	1	pint fresh strawberries, each hulled and cut into 6 wedges
6	cups water	1	pint vanilla ice cream
½	cup white Zinfandel wine		
¼	cup sugar		

- Remove only the colored peel from 1 orange. Cut peel into thin strips.

- Squeeze enough juice from oranges to equal ½ cup; set aside.

- Bring 2 cups water to boil in small saucepan. Add peel and return to boil. Drain. Repeat process two more times. Refrigerate drained peel.

- Bring juice, Zinfandel and sugar to a simmer in small saucepan. Cook 2 to 3 minutes, until sugar dissolves. Transfer to bowl; stir in berries. Refrigerate 1½ hours.

- Divide berries among four serving glasses. Top each with ice cream and sprinkle with peel.

Makes 4 servings.

Everyone's Favorite Caramel Sauce

There is no end to the
uses for this delicious treat!
So easy, too!

½ cup butter

*1 cup firmly
packed light brown sugar*

½ cup whipping cream

1 tablespoon vanilla extract

• Combine butter and sugar in heavy saucepan. Cook over medium heat, stirring frequently, until sugar melts. Stir in whipping cream; bring mixture to a full boil. Remove from heat and stir in vanilla. Serve warm over ice cream, cake, or fruit.

Makes about 1¼ cups.

Minted Raspberries with White Chocolate

A vibrant and interesting mix of flavors.

⅓ cup water

6 tablespoons sugar

2 tablespoons chopped fresh mint

6 cups fresh raspberries

1 ounce white chocolate, grated

• Bring water, sugar, and mint to boil over medium heat. Continue boiling for 3 minutes. Remove from heat and let stand for 30 minutes to cool. Strain; cover and refrigerate 2 hours.

• Spoon raspberries into bowls; drizzle with syrup and sprinkle with chocolate.

Serves 4.

Fresh Fruit and Vanilla Cream Sauce

Need a dessert in a hurry? This is it!

7	cups strawberries, peaches, pineapple or other fresh fruit	2	cups powdered sugar
1	(8-ounce) package cream cheese	1	cup whipping cream
		1	tablespoon vanilla extract
			Milk (to thin, as needed)

• Microwave cream cheese approximately 2 minutes on high, or until very soft.

• Combine cream cheese, powdered sugar, whipping cream and vanilla in a bowl and mix well. If necessary, thin with a small amount of milk. Pour over fruit and serve.

Makes 8 servings.

For variation, add ½ cup Grand Marnier or other orange liqueur.

Old-Fashioned Sweet Potato Custard Pie

A southern favorite.

3	cups mashed cooked sweet potatoes, at room temperature	3	tablespoons flour
½	cup (1 stick) butter	1	tablespoon baking powder
1	cup sugar	¼	teaspoon nutmeg
3	eggs	¼	teaspoon plus ⅛ teaspoon salt
		1½	teaspoons vanilla extract
		1	(9-inch) unbaked pie shell

• Combine butter and sugar in blender or food processor. Add sweet potatoes, eggs, and remaining ingredients, blending until smooth. Pour into pie shell.

• Bake at 375° for 15 minutes. Reduce oven temperature to 350°, and bake additional 30 minutes, until firm. (If edges start to brown too soon, cover with strips of aluminum foil.)

Makes 6 to 8 servings.

Almond Pear Pie
with White Caramel Sauce

Pie

1	(9-inch) unbaked pie shell	⅓	cup firm butter
5	Bosc pears, peeled, cored, and thickly sliced	1	cup sugar
		⅓	cup all-purpose flour
6	tablespoons ground almonds	¼	teaspoon cinnamon

White Caramel Sauce

¾	cup sugar	2	tablespoons vanilla extract
⅓	cup water	¾	cup butter or margarine
1⅓	cups whipping cream		

• Roll pastry into a 12-inch circle and fit into a pie pan. Set aside.

• In a medium mixing bowl mix sliced pears with ground almonds. Heap fruit into unbaked pie shell. Cut butter into small pieces and dot it over the fruit.

• In a small bowl mix sugar, flour, and cinnamon. Sprinkle over pie. Bake at 400° for 15 minutes. Reduce heat to 350° and bake for 1 hour more. (If the edges start to brown too soon, cover them with strips of foil.)

• While pie is baking, prepare sauce. In a heavy saucepan over medium heat, cook sugar and water, stirring often, about 15 minutes or until reduced to 6 tablespoons.

• Add whipping cream and vanilla. (Mixture will be lumpy.) Cook over medium heat, stirring often, 15 minutes or until reduced to 1 cup. Remove from heat and stir in butter. Spoon warm sauce over pie slices.

Makes 6 to 8 servings.

Sauce may be covered and refrigerated up to 3 days.

Cobbler

A distant cousin of the deep-dish pie, the cobbler originally got its name from its biscuit topping, which resembled cobblestones. (For a traditional cobbler, be sure the fruit filling is very hot when you drop the biscuit dough on it or the bottom of the topping might not cook properly!)

Sheets serve well as tablecloths. Look for flat sheets with great patterns at white sales or on the discontinued tables.

Back Porch Buttermilk Pie

Our tasters were fighting to get the last piece of this one!

3	tablespoons all-purpose flour	3	eggs
¼	teaspoon salt	1	cup buttermilk
½	cup (1 stick) of butter	1	(9-inch) unbaked pie shell
2	cups sugar		Garnish: whipped cream
2	teaspoons vanilla extract		(optional)

- Mix flour and salt in small bowl. Set aside.

- In mixing bowl beat butter until smooth and creamy. Add sugar, ½ cup at a time, beating until fluffy, about 2 minutes. Add vanilla and eggs, one at a time, beating well after each addition.

- Stir flour mixture into butter mixture. Stir in buttermilk. Pour filling into pie shell. Bake at 350° for 1½ hours or until set. (If crust browns too quickly, cover with strips of aluminum foil.) Cool on wire rack.

- Garnish with whipped cream, if desired.

Makes 8 servings.

For Buttermilk Pecan Pie variation, add ½ cup coarsely chopped pecans to pie filling. Garnish with whipped cream and pecans, if desired.

Margarita Pie

Refreshing and always a favorite!

1¼	cups finely crushed pretzels	⅓	cup fresh lime juice
10	tablespoons butter, melted	2-4	tablespoons tequila
½	cup sugar	2	tablespoons triple sec
1	(14-ounce) can sweetened condensed milk	8	ounces whipped topping

- Combine pretzel crumbs, butter and sugar. Press firmly on bottom and sides of a lightly buttered 9-inch pie plate. Set aside.

- Combine condensed milk, lime juice, tequila, and triple sec. Fold in half of the whipped topping. Pour into prepared crust and spread remaining whipped topping over pie. Freeze or chill until firm.

Makes 8 servings.

Toasted Coconut and Caramel Pie

¼ cup butter or margarine

1 (7-ounce) package flaked coconut

½ cup chopped pecans

1 (8-ounce) package cream cheese, softened

1 (14-ounce) can sweetened condensed milk

1 (16-ounce) container frozen whipped topping, thawed

2 (9-inch) pie shells, baked according to package directions

1 (12-ounce) jar caramel ice cream topping

Garnish: pecan halves

- Melt butter in large skillet. Add coconut and ½ cup pecans; cook until golden, stirring frequently. Set mixture aside and let cool slightly.

- Combine cream cheese and sweetened condensed milk; beat at medium speed of electric mixer until smooth. Fold in whipped topping.

- Layer ¼ of cream cheese mixture in each pastry shell. Drizzle ¼ of caramel topping over each pie. Sprinkle ¼ of coconut mixture evenly over each pie.

- Repeat layers with remaining cream cheese mixture, caramel topping, and coconut mixture. Cover and freeze pies at least 8 hours.

- Let frozen pies stand at room temperature 5 minutes before slicing. Garnish, if desired.

Makes 2 pies.

Fresh Blueberry Pie

½ cup sugar

2 tablespoons cornstarch

½ teaspoon allspice

½ cup water

2 teaspoons fresh lemon juice

2 pints (4 cups) fresh blueberries

1 (9-inch) pie shell, baked according
to package directions

Whipped cream

• Combine sugar, cornstarch,
allspice, and water in large
microwave-safe bowl. Microwave
on high 3 minutes, stirring halfway
through. (Mixture will be thick.)
Add blueberries and lemon juice.
Microwave on high 3 more
minutes, stirring halfway through.

• Spoon mixture into pie
shell and let set. Garnish pie slices
with whipped cream.

Serves 6 to 8.

Sour Cream Lemon Pie

This pie has a velvety lemon taste and melts in your mouth.

⅔	cup sugar	1	teaspoon grated fresh lemon peel
3	tablespoons cornstarch		
1	cup milk	¼	cup fresh lemon juice
3	egg yolks	1	(9-inch) pie shell, baked according to package directions
1	(8-ounce) container sour cream		
¼	cup butter or margarine		Sweetened whipped cream

• **In medium saucepan mix sugar and cornstarch. Whisk in milk. When smooth, whisk in egg yolks and blend well. Place over medium heat and cook until thick custard forms, 5 to 7 minutes. (Do not let mixture reach a full boil or it will burn and lump!) Stir in sour cream, butter, lemon peel, and lemon juice. Cool.**

• **Pour filling into baked pie shell. Cover loosely and refrigerate at least 6 hours or up to 2 days. To serve, top pie slice with dollop of whipped cream.**

Makes 6 to 8 servings.

Lemon-Blackberry Crisp

4	cups fresh blackberries	¼	cup all-purpose flour
¼	cup sugar	½	teaspoon ground cinnamon
2	tablespoons cornstarch	½	cup butter or margarine
3	tablespoons fresh lemon juice		Ice cream or sweetened whipped cream (optional)
25	vanilla wafers, crushed		
½	cup uncooked regular oats		

• **Place blackberries in a lightly greased 11 x 7-inch baking dish. Sprinkle with ¼ cup sugar. Stir together cornstarch and lemon juice; stir into berries.**

• **Combine vanilla wafer crumbs and next 4 ingredients. Stir in butter until crumbly. Sprinkle over berries.**

• **Bake at 400° for 30 minutes or until lightly browned. Serve with ice cream or whipped cream, if desired.**

Makes 6 to 8 servings.

Southern Christmas Fruitcake Pie

Even the harshest fruitcake critics will enjoy this pie!

Pastry

1¼	cups all-purpose flour	½	cup shortening
1	teaspoon salt	⅓	cup ice water

Filling

½	cup chopped pecans	½	cup light corn syrup
½	cup dates, chopped	¼	teaspoon ground ginger
½	cup candied cherries, chopped	¼	teaspoon ground nutmeg
¼	cup candied pineapple, chopped	¼	teaspoon ground cloves
6	tablespoons butter or margarine, softened		Pinch of salt
½	cup firmly packed brown sugar		Garnish: ¼ cup candied red and green cherry halves and ¼ cup pecan halves
3	eggs, slightly beaten		

- To prepare pastry, combine flour and salt; cut in shortening with pastry blender until mixture resembles coarse meal. Sprinkle ice water evenly over surface; stir with fork until dry ingredients are moistened. Shape into ball and wrap in plastic. Chill well. Roll chilled dough to fit a 10-inch pie plate. Line 10-inch pie plate with pastry; set aside.

- Combine chopped pecans, dates, and candied fruit; sprinkle over pastry shell.

- Cream butter and sugar until light and fluffy. Add eggs, corn syrup, spices, and salt. Beat at medium speed of electric mixer until well blended. Pour filling over fruit mixture in pastry shell and garnish with cherries and pecans.

- Bake at 350° for 45 to 50 minutes or until filling is set. Remove to wire rack and cool before serving.

Makes 6 to 8 servings.

"Bless her heart."
She made a sweet potato pie
and forgot the sugar!

Baked Blueberries and Peaches

Southern summer flavors at their best!

4 cups peeled and sliced fresh peaches

2 cups blueberries

⅓ cup shredded coconut

¼ cup sugar

1 tablespoon all-purpose flour

½ teaspoon ground cinnamon

¼ teaspoon ground nutmeg

• Coat a 9 x 2-inch round baking dish with nonstick cooking spray.

• Place peaches and blueberries in a large bowl; set aside.

• In a small bowl, stir together coconut, sugar, flour, cinnamon, and nutmeg. Add to fruit and stir until coated. Spoon into baking dish.

• Bake at 375° for 20 minutes. Stir; cover loosely with foil and bake an additional 15 to 20 minutes, until very bubbly. Cool slightly. Stir before serving. Serve warm.

Makes 8 servings.

Country Peach Dumplings

This old-fashioned treat for the taste buds is definitely worth the effort.

3	cups all-purpose flour	¼	teaspoon ground nutmeg
2	teaspoons baking powder	⅛	teaspoon ground cloves
½	teaspoon salt	6	medium-sized ripe peaches, peeled
1	cup butter or shortening		Milk
⅓	cup milk	2	tablespoons butter or margarine, melted
¼	cup sugar		Honey
¼	cup firmly packed brown sugar		
½	teaspoon ground cinnamon		
¼	teaspoon ground allspice		

• Combine flour, baking powder, and salt; cut in 1 cup butter with a pastry blender until mixture is crumbly. Sprinkle ⅓ cup milk, 1 tablespoon at a time, evenly over surface; stir with a fork until dry ingredients are moistened. Divide dough into 6 portions.

• Roll each portion of dough into a 7-inch square on a lightly floured surface. Trim edges of dough with a fluted pastry cutter, if desired.

• Combine sugar and next 5 ingredients. Reserve and set aside 2 tablespoons mixture. Coat each peach with remaining sugar mixture, and place in center of a pastry square. For each dumpling, moisten edges of dough with milk; pull corners of square over peach. Pinch dough together, sealing all seams. Freeze dumplings 30 minutes.

• Place dumplings in a lightly greased 13 x 9-inch baking dish. Drizzle each dumpling with 1 teaspoon melted butter and sprinkle with reserved sugar mixture. Bake at 425° for 35 minutes. Drizzle with honey before serving.

Makes 6 servings.

Caramel Cookie Bars

Easy to pack and carry, and always a favorite.

1   (14-ounce) bag of light caramels
⅔ cup evaporated milk,
       separated
1   (18½-ounce) package German
       chocolate cake mix
¾ cup butter or margarine, melted

1   teaspoon vanilla extract
1   cup chopped pecans
1   cup semi-sweet chocolate
       morsels
½ cup chopped pecans

- Melt caramels with ⅓ cup evaporated milk in microwave. Stir occasionally until melted.

- Combine cake mix, butter, ⅓ cup evaporated milk, vanilla and 1 cup pecans. Mix well.

- Spread half of batter into well-greased 13 x 9 x 2-inch pan. Reserve remaining batter for topping. Bake at 350° for 8 minutes.

- Sprinkle chocolate morsels over baked crust. Spread warm caramel mixture over chocolate morsels. Drop and carefully spread reserved batter over caramel mixture. Sprinkle with ½ cup chopped nuts. Bake additional 20 minutes. Cool in pan.

- Refrigerate approximately 1 hour to set caramel layer. Slice into bars.

Makes 48.

Coconut Key Lime Bars

A definite favorite among our tasters!

Crust

1	cup butter, softened	½	cup powdered sugar
¼	teaspoon salt	3	cups all-purpose flour

Topping

4	eggs, slightly beaten	¼	cup all-purpose flour
1	tablespoon grated lime peel	3	drops green food coloring
5	tablespoons key lime juice	1	cup shredded coconut
2	cups granulated sugar		

- Blend butter, salt, powdered sugar, and flour to make soft dough. Press evenly into ungreased 13 x 9-inch pan. Bake at 350° for 15 to 20 minutes until golden.

- While crust is baking, combine eggs, lime peel, lime juice, sugar, food coloring, and ¼ cup flour. Blend until smooth. Pour over baked crust. Sprinkle with coconut.

- Reduce heat to 325° and bake 25 minutes until firm. Cool and slice into bars.

Makes 2 dozen.

Peaches and Cream Bars

You will get rave reviews on these every time!

Crust

30	graham cracker squares (15 rectangles)	½	cup sliced almonds
⅓	cup sugar	6	tablespoons unsalted butter, melted

Filling

12	ounces cream cheese, at room temperature	2	eggs
½	cup sugar	1	teaspoon vanilla extract

Topping

2	tablespoons cold unsalted butter, cut into pieces	½	cup sliced almonds
¼	cup packed light brown sugar	2	tablespoons all-purpose flour
		1	(13-ounce) jar peach preserves

- Coat a 13 x 9 x 2-inch baking pan with nonstick cooking spray.

- Combine graham crackers, ⅓ cup sugar, and almonds in food processor or blender. Process until well combined. Pour in melted butter. Process until crumbs hold together. Press over bottom of pan. Bake at 350° for 10 minutes or until lightly colored.

- While crust is baking, beat together cream cheese and ½ cup sugar in large bowl with electric mixer until smooth. Add eggs, one at a time, beating well after each addition. Beat in vanilla.

- Remove crust from oven. Pour in cream cheese mixture and spread evenly over crust. Return to oven and bake for 15 minutes or until slightly puffed.

- To prepare topping, crumble together cold butter, brown sugar, sliced almonds, and flour in a bowl.

- Remove pan from oven. Stir preserves to break up clumps. Gently spread preserves over top of bar. Sprinkle with topping. Bake another 15 minutes or until hot and bubbly. Cool completely in pan on wire rack. For firmer bars, chill in refrigerator. Cut into bars.

Makes 2 dozen.

Many people often think of Georgia as the peach state, but South Carolina grows delicious peaches, too. There are many peach trees around Anderson and many people can't wait to taste the first ripe fuzzy peach of summer, and eat warm peach cobbler with "sweet" milk or ice cream with it.

Raspberry Walnut Bars

**Peach, apricot, or any other
flavor preserves may be used. Experiment!**

Crust

1½   cups all-purpose flour
¾   cup butter, softened
⅓   cup packed brown sugar

Topping

1   (12 to 15-ounce) jar raspberry
     preserves
¼   cup all-purpose flour
1   cup packed brown sugar
2   eggs, beaten
1   teaspoon salt
1   teaspoon baking powder
½   cup chopped walnuts
     Garnish: powdered sugar
     (optional)

• Mix together 1½ cups flour, butter, and ⅓ cup brown sugar on medium speed of electric mixer until well combined. Press mixture into bottom of ungreased 13 x 9 x 2-inch baking dish.

• Bake at 350° for 18 to 20 minutes. Remove from oven and spread preserves evenly over baked layer.

• Mix remaining ¼ cup flour, 1 cup brown sugar, eggs, salt, baking powder, and nuts. Spread over fruit.

• Return to oven and bake for 18 to 20 minutes or until done. Cool and dust with powdered sugar, if desired. When cool, cut into bars and serve.

Makes 2 dozen.

Praline~Iced Brownies

These rich fudge-like brownies are delicious at room temperature, refrigerated, or even frozen!

Brownies

1	cup (2 sticks) butter	2¼	cups sugar
4	(1-ounce) squares unsweetened chocolate	6	large eggs
		2	teaspoons vanilla extract
4	(1-ounce) squares semisweet chocolate	½	teaspoon salt
		1¼	cups all-purpose flour

Topping

5	tablespoons butter	2	cups powdered sugar
⅓	cup packed light brown sugar	½	cup pecans, coarsely chopped and lightly toasted
3	tablespoons bourbon		

- Line a 13 x 9-inch baking pan with foil; grease foil.

- In heavy 3-quart saucepan over low heat, melt butter and chocolates, stirring frequently. Remove saucepan from heat. With wire whisk, beat in sugar, and then eggs, until well blended. Stir in vanilla, salt, and flour just until blended. Spread batter evenly in pan.

- Bake at 350° for 35 minutes, or until wooden pick inserted in middle comes out clean. Cool brownies in pan on wire rack.

- To prepare topping, combine butter and brown sugar in a 2-quart saucepan over medium-low heat. Cook until mixture melts and bubbles, about 5 minutes, stirring frequently. Remove saucepan from heat. With wire whisk, beat in bourbon. Gradually beat in powdered sugar until mixture is smooth.

- With metal spatula, spread topping over room-temperature brownies; sprinkle with pecans. Cut brownies lengthwise into 8 strips, and crosswise into 8 brownies.

Makes 64.

If not using brownies within 1 day, cover with foil and refrigerate. Iced brownies may be frozen up to 2 weeks.

Don't try to be perfect when entertaining. People just like to be included in the fun.

Before radio, Morse code communicated play by play from the World Series around the world. Outside the offices of the "Daily Mail" in Anderson, this information was updated constantly on a huge board, which had figures to represent the players and a drawing of the diamond and bases.

Later, in Anderson, when the World Series was broadcast over the radio, we loved the game so much that it was announced through the radio over the PA systems in our local schools.

"Those" White Chocolate Brownies

Go ahead...Indulge!!

Brownies

1	cup butter	1	teaspoon vanilla extract
½	cup white chocolate pieces	3	cups walnuts, broken into pieces and toasted at 300° for 5 to 6 minutes
4	eggs, beaten		
2	cups sugar		
1½	cups flour, sifted		

Icing

½	cup butter	2	tablespoons half-and-half
⅓	cup white chocolate pieces	1	teaspoon vanilla extract
3	cups powdered sugar, sifted		

- To prepare brownies, melt butter and white chocolate in top of double boiler. Remove from heat and pour into large bowl. Mix in eggs and slowly add sugar. Add flour and vanilla. Fold in walnuts. Pour mixture into greased and floured 13 x 9-inch pan.

- Bake at 350° for 30 to 35 minutes. Allow to cool, and spread with icing.

- To prepare icing, melt butter and white chocolate in top of a double boiler. Remove from heat. Beat in powdered sugar, half-and-half, and vanilla. Spread over cooled brownies. Cut into small squares.

Makes 28

To make a pecan version, substitute 3 cups broken pecans for walnuts.

Almond Cross Cookies

½	cup (1 stick) butter, softened	1	cup ground almonds
¾	cup sugar	1	cup all-purpose flour
1	large egg white	¼	teaspoon baking soda
½	teaspoon almond extract	1	cup (96 pieces) almond slivers

- Combine butter and sugar, and beat on medium speed of electric mixer until light and fluffy. Beat in egg white and almond extract. Stir in ground almonds, flour, and baking soda. Shape dough into a ball, wrap in plastic wrap, and chill 2 hours.

- Spray 2 large baking sheets with nonstick cooking spray.

- Shape dough into ¾-inch balls. Place balls 2 inches apart on prepared baking sheets. Flatten slightly. Press 2 almond slivers crisscrossed into center of each cookie.

- Bake at 350° until just set, approximately 12 minutes. Transfer cookies to a wire rack to cool.

Makes 48.

Sunrise Cookies

The combination of the carrot and orange flavors is unusually delightful.

Cookies

1	cup cooked, mashed carrots	2	cups all-purpose flour
¼	cup shortening	½	teaspoon salt
¾	cup sugar	2	teaspoons baking powder
1	egg	1	teaspoon vanilla extract

Glaze

1	cup powdered sugar	Orange juice as needed for
	Grated rind from 1 orange	blending

- Combine all cookie ingredients and mix well. Drop by teaspoonful onto ungreased cookie sheet. Bake at 350° for 12 to 15 minutes. After 1 minute, remove to wire racks to cool.

- To prepare glaze, combine powdered sugar and orange rind. Mix in orange juice, a small amount at a time, until glaze reaches spreading consistency. Spread on cooled cookies.

Makes 4 dozen.

When a recipe calls for ground almonds make your own by grinding nuts in a food processor along with ¼ cup of sugar from the recipe. The sugar keeps the nuts from clumping together.

Oatmeal Toffee Cookies

1½ cups all-purpose flour

1 teaspoon baking soda

1 cup (2 sticks) unsalted butter, at room temperature

¾ cup granulated sugar

¾ cup light brown sugar

1 egg

1 teaspoon vanilla extract

1½ cups oats

1 cup dried cherries

1 cup (4½ ounces) bittersweet chocolate, coarsely chopped

1 cup toffee pieces

• Sift together flour and baking soda; set aside.

• In bowl of electric mixer, cream butter and sugars on medium-high speed until light and fluffy, about 2 to 3 minutes. Scrape down sides of bowl once or twice during mixing. Add egg and mix on high speed to combine. Mix in vanilla. Add the sifted flour a little at a time on low speed until well combined. Add oats, cherries, chocolate, and toffee pieces, mixing on low to combine.

• Divide the dough into 3 equal portions and roll into logs using plastic wrap, approximately 1½ inches in diameter.

• Cut logs into ¾-inch slices and place on parchment-lined baking sheets. Bake at 350° for 8 to 10 minutes, until golden brown. Remove from oven and transfer to a wire rack to cool.

Makes 2½ to 3 dozen.

Almond Cream Sandwich Cookies

This classy cookie is delicious with a cup of hot tea or coffee.

Cookies

6	tablespoons butter	2½	tablespoons whipping cream
1	cup sifted all-purpose flour		Sugar

Filling

¾	cup sifted powdered sugar	⅛	teaspoon almond extract
1	tablespoon softened butter	1	tablespoon whipping cream

• Cut butter into flour until mixture resembles small pebbles. Add 1 tablespoon whipping cream and mix gently. Repeat, using remainder of whipping cream. Divide dough in half and form into 2 balls; wrap each in plastic wrap, and refrigerate 1½ to 2 hours.

• Pour 2 cups sugar into medium-size shallow bowl; set aside.

• Lightly flour surface and roll dough out to about ⅛-inch thickness. Cut out cookies with 1½-inch cutter. Dip one side of each cookie in sugar. Place ½ inch apart, sugar side up, on ungreased baking sheet.

• Bake at 375° for about 8 minutes, until lightly browned. Cool.

• While cookies are cooling, prepare filling. Combine powdered sugar, butter, and almond extract. Stir until well mixed. Stir in whipping cream, a few drops at a time, until mixture reaches spreading consistency.

• Spread half of the cookies with filling mixture, and top with remaining cookies to make sandwiches (sugarcoated sides to the outside).

Makes 2½ dozen.

Lemon-Anise Biscotti

A surprising delight!

2	large eggs	1	teaspoon anise extract
¾	cup sugar	4	teaspoons anise seeds, crushed
½	cup vegetable oil	¼	teaspoon salt
1	tablespoon grated fresh lemon peel	2	cups all-purpose flour
1¼	teaspoons baking powder	1	cup chopped or slivered almonds

- Whisk eggs, sugar, oil, lemon peel, baking powder, anise extract, anise seeds, and salt in a large bowl until smooth. Stir in flour and almonds. Divide in half.

- Form each half into a 12 x 1½-inch log on greased baking sheet, leaving 4 inches between logs.

- Bake at 350° for 20 to 25 minutes until wooden pick inserted in center comes out clean. Cool 10 minutes.

- Transfer logs onto cutting board and cut ½-inch slices with a serrated knife. Lay slices flat on baking sheet, return to oven, and bake 10 to 15 minutes until golden. Cool on wire racks.

Makes 4 dozen.

Surprise Oatmeal Raisin Cookies

The surprise in this cookie is the raisins - they're chocolate-covered!

1¼	cups butter, softened	1½	cups all-purpose flour
¾	cup packed light brown sugar	1	teaspoon baking soda
½	cup sugar	3	cups oats
1	large egg	1	cup chocolate-covered raisins
1	teaspoon vanilla extract		

- In a mixing bowl, cream butter and sugars until light and fluffy. Beat in egg and vanilla. Add flour and baking soda, mixing well. Stir in oats and raisins. Drop by rounded tablespoonfuls onto ungreased cookie sheets.

- Bake at 375° for 8 to 9 minutes for a chewy texture, or 10 to 11 minutes for a crispy cookie. Cool on cookie sheets for 1 minute; remove to wire rack to cool completely. Store in an airtight container.

Makes 4 dozen.

Size is important. A few oversized platters or baskets on a buffet table look better than several small ones.

Carolina Crunch Cookies

This is one g-r-r-reat cookie!

1 cup butter, softened

1 cup sugar

*1 cup firmly packed
light brown sugar*

1 large egg

1 teaspoon vanilla extract

3½ cups all-purpose flour

1 teaspoon baking soda

1 teaspoon salt

1 cup vegetable oil

1 cup oats

1 cup crushed cornflakes cereal

½ cup flaked coconut

½ cup chopped pecans

• Cream butter, gradually adding sugars, until light and creamy. Beat in egg and vanilla.

• Combine flour, baking soda, and salt.

• Add flour mixture to butter mixture, alternating with oil. Stir in oats, cornflakes, coconut, and pecans. Drop by rounded teaspoonfuls onto ungreased cookie sheets. Dip fork in water and press down on each cookie.

• Bake at 350° for 10 to 12 minutes or until brown. Cool on cookie sheets for 1 minute; transfer to paper towels to drain. Store in airtight container at room temperature.

Makes about 7 dozen.

Tiger Tailgate Cookies

Wonderful for a crowd.

2	cups sifted flour		Grated rind of 1 orange
¾	teaspoon baking soda	½	cup granulated sugar
½	teaspoon baking powder	½	cup firmly packed brown sugar
¼	teaspoon salt		
½	cup peanut butter	1	egg, unbeaten
½	cup shortening	¼	cup orange juice

• Measure flour, baking soda, baking powder, and salt into sifter; sift 2 times onto waxed paper; return to sifter.

• Cream peanut butter, shortening, and orange rind in medium-size bowl; add granulated sugar and brown sugar gradually, creaming well after each addition. Beat in egg.

• Sift and add dry ingredients, alternating with orange juice; blend until smooth after each addition.

• Cover bowl and chill dough thoroughly.

• Shape chilled dough into balls about size of walnuts; place balls about 2 inches apart on greased cookie sheets; flatten balls into rounds with floured fork, forming crisscross pattern.

• Bake at 375° for 10 to 12 minutes, or until cookies are lightly browned. Run spatula under cookies to loosen from cookie sheets; remove to wire racks to cool.

Makes about 6 dozen.

The Best Ever
Peanut Butter Cookies

Do not attempt to eat without a big glass of cold milk!

1	cup butter	2	cups all-purpose flour, sifted
1¼	cups packed light brown sugar	¼	teaspoon salt
1	cup sugar	½	teaspoon baking powder
2	eggs	1	cup peanut butter chips
1	cup chunky peanut butter	1	cup dry roasted peanuts

- Combine butter and sugars in a mixing bowl. Beat at medium speed of electric mixer until thoroughly creamed.

- Using heavy-duty spoon, mix eggs into creamed mixture one at a time. Fold in peanut butter.

- Sift together flour, salt, and baking powder. Gradually stir into peanut butter mixture. Fold peanut butter chips and peanuts into batter.

- Drop by teaspoonfuls onto lightly greased cookie sheets, about 2 inches apart. Bake at 325° for 15 minutes or until the cookies are light brown around the edges.

Makes 4 dozen.

What to do when the electricity goes out?

Don't open the freezer and refrigerators any more than necessary. Don't leave electric ranges on during a power outage. This may prevent possible damage from a fire to your home in case you are away when the power is restored. Turn off heating and air conditioning systems and unplug sensitive electronic appliances. Be sure to wait 5 to 10 minutes before turning on appliances and heating systems when power is restored. Don't leave candles burning unattended, and keep them away from furniture and other flammable materials.

Ricotta Cheese Cookies

Different and very good!

Cookies

½	pound butter	1	teaspoon vanilla extract
2	cups sugar	4	cups all-purpose flour
3	eggs	1	teaspoon salt
1	pound ricotta cheese	1	teaspoon baking soda

Frosting

½	cup margarine	½	teaspoon vanilla extract
2	teaspoons vegetable shortening		Milk, for blending
1	(16-ounce) box powdered sugar		

- Cream butter and sugar together until smooth. Add eggs, one at a time, blending after each addition. Add ricotta cheese and vanilla, mixing to blend.

- Combine flour, salt and baking soda. Add to ricotta cheese mixture, mixing well.

- Drop by teaspoonful onto greased cookie sheet.

- Bake at 375° for 10 minutes. Allow to cool.

- To prepare frosting, cream margarine; add shortening and blend. Mix in sugar and vanilla. Add a few drops of milk to blend to spreading consistency. Frost cookies.

Makes 10 dozen.

On December 19, 1931, Double Springs Baptist Church "pounded" its pastor in appreciation of his service. In spite of the alarming name, the pastor received canned goods, "pounds" of staple food items, and other gifts for his pantry.

Double Delight Bourbon Balls

These decadent delights put a new twist on an old favorite. At first you are reminded of a cherry chocolate cordial - until you taste the bourbon!

1	(6-ounce) package semisweet chocolate morsels	1	cup chopped nuts
3	tablespoons corn syrup	½	cup powdered sugar
	Dash vanilla extract	⅓	cup chopped candied red cherries
½	cup bourbon		Sugar
1	(8-ounce) package chocolate wafers, crushed		

- Gently melt chocolate in a double boiler over low heat; remove from heat. Stir in corn syrup, vanilla, and bourbon; cool to room temperature.

- In a large bowl, mix wafers, nuts, powdered sugar, and cherries. Add the chocolate mixture and stir to blend. Let stand for 30 minutes.

- Shape into balls with fingers and roll in sugar. Store covered in refrigerator until ready for serving or packing as gifts.

Makes about 2½ dozen.

To give as gifts, place balls in small paper candy cups and arrange in box or basket lined with colored tissue paper.

Keep buffet fare simple; it shouldn't look like you labored in the kitchen all day. Start with no-fuss food stuffs, such as prepared cheeses, pre-sliced meats, and vegetables; then add finishing touches with fresh herbs and fruit garnishes.

To keep the party lively and traffic circulating, set up separate food and beverage stations, with seating close by to accommodate intimate chats.

Winnie's White Chocolate Drops

Wrap in decorative papers and place in a small tin for a special thank you or hostess gift.

4	(4-ounce) white chocolate bars, broken	1	cup unsalted dry-roasted peanuts
½	cup creamy peanut butter	½	cup semisweet chocolate morsels
1½	cups crisp rice cereal		
1½	cups miniature marshmallows		

- Cook white chocolate and peanut butter in a large heavy saucepan over low heat, stirring constantly, 5 to 6 minutes or until smooth; remove from heat. Stir in cereal, marshmallows, and peanuts.

- Drop mixture by rounded tablespoonfuls onto plastic wrap-lined baking sheet. Chill 10 minutes or until set.

- Place chocolate morsels in a small heavy-duty, zip-top plastic bag; seal. Submerge in hot water until chocolate melts. Snip a tiny hole in one corner of bag, and drizzle chocolate over candies. Chill 10 minutes or until set. Store in an airtight container.

Makes 2 dozen.

Buttermilk Pralines

2	cups sugar	1½	cups pecan halves
1	cup buttermilk	1	teaspoon vanilla extract
1	teaspoon baking soda	¼	cup butter
1	tablespoon white corn syrup		

- In heavy saucepan, using candy thermometer, combine sugar, buttermilk, baking soda, and corn syrup. Cook over medium heat to soft ball stage (120° to 125°). Remove from heat. Add pecans, vanilla, and butter, stirring until butter melts.

- Beat until mixture begins to thicken.

- Drop by teaspoonful onto waxed paper. Let stand until set. Store in airtight container.

Makes about 3 dozen.

Sugar & Spice Pecans

Sprinkle these on cheesecake, pound cake, or a baked sweet potato. Of course you can just eat them by the handful, too!

2	cups sugar	1	teaspoon grated fresh orange peel
½	teaspoon cloves	½	cup water
1	teaspoon nutmeg	4	cups (1-pound) pecan halves
2	teaspoons cinnamon		
	Dash of salt		

- Mix sugar, spices, orange peel, and water in large glass bowl; microwave on high for 8 minutes, stirring well after 4 minutes. Stir in pecans, and microwave on high for 4 additional minutes. Stir.

- Spread onto greased cookie sheets and break up clumps with fork. Let set. Store in airtight container.

Makes 4 cups.

Cashew Brittle

Be warned! This is addictive!

1	cup roasted salted cashew nuts	1	tablespoon margarine
1	cup sugar	1	teaspoon vanilla extract
½	cup light corn syrup	1	teaspoon baking soda
	Pinch of salt		

- Combine cashews, sugar, corn syrup, and salt in 8-cup microwave-safe dish. Microwave on high for 8 minutes, stirring well after 4 minutes. Stir in margarine and vanilla; microwave on high 1 minute longer. Add baking soda; stir gently until light and foamy.

- Pour on buttered baking sheet. Let stand until set. Break into pieces. Store in airtight container.

Makes 16 servings.

For variation, roasted and salted almonds or pecans may be substituted for cashews.

Food Safety in the Kitchen

Use a thermometer in the refrigerator and freezer. The refrigerator should be 30 to 40 degrees F and the freezer should be a 0 or below. Discard the following items if kept above 40 degrees for more than two hours: all meats, poultry, fish and eggs; milk, cream, yogurt and soft cheese; casseroles, stews or soups; lunchmeats and hot dogs; creamy-based salad dressings; custard, chiffon or cheese pies; cream-filled pastries; cookie dough; and mayonnaise, tarter sauce and horseradish sauce. Thawed foods that contain ice crystals may be refrozen.

Toffee Popcorn Crunch

Fill small plastic bags and tie with ribbon or raffia for guests or trick-or-treaters!

2	cups sugar		1	teaspoon vanilla extract
1	cup butter		½	teaspoon baking soda
½	cup light corn syrup		22	cups pre-popped popcorn
1	teaspoon salt		20	ounces deluxe mixed nuts

- In a large heavy saucepan, bring sugar, butter, corn syrup, and salt to a slow boil, stirring constantly to avoid burning. (Mixture should remain pale yellow in color. If it starts turning amber, reduce heat.) Once it begins bubbling, boil an additional 5 minutes without stirring.

- While mixture is boiling, combine popcorn and nuts in a very large heatproof bowl or stockpot, and set aside.

- Remove toffee mixture from heat. Stir in baking soda and vanilla. Immediately pour over popcorn and nuts, mixing until well coated. Pour into 2 (13 x 9-inch) pans.

- Bake at 250° for 1 to 1½ hours or until dry, stirring every 20 to 30 minutes. Remove from oven and cool. Store in airtight containers.

Makes 2 gallons.

When pouring popcorn mixture into pans, note that it tends to dry quicker in glass than in metal.

Contributors

Trina Alexander
Kimberly Anderson
Floy Anderson
Cathy Bagwell
Jennifer Bartless
Julie Bates
Lea Batson
Dale Baughman
Beth Bauknight
Michelle Bedenbaugh
Lauren Black
Diana Bolding
Elizabeth Bowen
Margaret Britt
Cindy Burriss
Amanda Byrd
Jeanie Campbell
Emily Chamblee
Anna Cheek
Joely Clary
Kelly Cleveland
Holly Corbett
Roberta Cothran
Kimberly Cox
Andrea Craft
Melissa Crowe
Loretta Davidson
Sandra Dickson
Misty Dillard
Cindy Dunn
Joy Finley
Lindi Foster
Portia Franklin
Shannon Freeman
Beth Gautsch
Kim Gennaro
Tina Gentry

Kim Glenn
Cindi Gosnell
Beth Gray
Mary Ann Groves
Karen Hagner
Andrea Harpe
Leslie Hayes
Brooke Helton
Dana Hill
Libby Holliday
Susan Hosea
Sandra Jamison
Dawn Jeffer
Beth Kersey
Dorian Kierce
Jean Kidd
JoVanna King
Lindsay King
Candice Kirven
Karen Kissell
Mary Beth Knobel
Laura Krulic
Julie Lester
Tamara Lindley
Mary Little
Mary Long
Linda Loparo
Teresa Lott
Martie Manning
Alicia Mansuetti
Kristi Martin
Anita May
Tracy McCowen
Stephanie McChesney
Cindy McDonald
Greer McDougald
Tricia McDougald

Patsy McGregor
Buffy McMann
Karla McWhorter
Fredda Meehan
Mary Ellen Middleton
Annaliza Moorhead
Meridith Moorhead
Sabra Nickas
Donna Oehmig
Melanie Oster
Debbie Otto-Sunderman
Adair Pederson
Melissa Pickens
Mary Platias
Barbara Preston
Angela Radford
Mykael Ramsey
Mary Galen Ratchford
Paula Reel
Mandy Reinert
Kristi Rice
Page Rice
Sherry Richardson
Sarah Ricketson
Teresa Rhoten
Sandra Rivers
Danielle Roberts
Kristin Roberts
Pam Roberts
Julie Roberts
Regina Roberts
April Robinson
Suzanne Rogers
Shae Rozakos
Carrie Rozakos
Debbie Salley
Amy Sanderson

Marie Schamens
Sharon Scruggs
Lottye Seawright
Tina Seawright
Donna Shannon
Kim Shuey
Kelly Shuler
Leslie Simmons
Dorothy Smith
Sibylle Smith
Alexandria Stathakis
Catherine Stathakis
Lynn Stoddard
Rette Stokes
Sandra Strickland
Clare Summers
Jackie Swizdaryk
Lee Tate
Lisa Taylor
Nancy Jo Thomason
Leslie Thrasher
Krissy Titus
Sandi Tolly
Kelly Turner
Lura Tysiac
Carrie Van Sickle
Jackie Walsh
Leah Watson
Paige Watson
Susan West
Courtney White
Tandy Wickiser
Cindy Wilson
Tammy Wilson
Elizabeth Yarbrough
Katey Yeats

Community Contributors

Catherine Bergstrom
Fred Whitten

Cookbook Equivalents

Liquid and Dry Measure Equivalents

This amount	*Equals*
⅛ teaspoon or less	a pinch
3 teaspoons	1 tablespoon
4 tablespoons.	¼ cup
5⅓ tablespoons	⅓ cup
8 tablespoons	½ cup
10⅔ tablespoons	⅔ cup
16 tablespoons	1 cup
2 cups	1 pint
4 cups	1 quart
2 pints	1 quart
4 quarts	1 gallon

Herb and Spice Guidelines

1 teaspoon dried equals 1 tablespoon fresh

Fresh herbs should be used immediately whenever possible. For short term storage, wrap fresh herbs in moist paper towels and then plastic wrap before placing in refrigerator. Dried herbs generally last 6 months to 1 year. To test for freshness crumble in your hand and sniff for aroma.

To soften butter leave out of the refrigerator for 1 hour.

Index

Please send me _____ copies of "Lights Over Carolina"   @ $22.95 each _____

Shipping and handling   @ $5.00 each _____

Additional copies to the same address   @ $2.00 each _____

                                                            Total _____

Name _____

Address _____

City _____ State _____ Zip _____

Make checks payable to *The Junior League of Anderson County* and send to:

The Junior League of Anderson County
PO Box 931
Anderson, SC 29622

- -

Please send me _____ copies of "Lights Over Carolina"   @ $22.95 each _____

Shipping and handling   @ $5.00 each _____

Additional copies to the same address   @ $2.00 each _____

                                                            Total _____

Name _____

Address _____

City _____ State _____ Zip _____

Make checks payable to *The Junior League of Anderson County* and send to:

The Junior League of Anderson County
PO Box 931
Anderson, SC 29622

- -

Please send me _____ copies of "Lights Over Carolina"   @ $22.95 each _____

Shipping and handling   @ $5.00 each _____

Additional copies to the same address   @ $2.00 each _____

                                                            Total _____

Name _____

Address _____

City _____ State _____ Zip _____

Make checks payable to *The Junior League of Anderson County* and send to:

The Junior League of Anderson County
PO Box 931
Anderson, SC 29622